HALLS OF DARTFORD
1785–1985

JOHN HALL (1764–1836)
Founder of the business in a small workshop in Dartford, Kent, in 1785

Harry Miller

HALLS OF DARTFORD

1785–1985

Founded in the Industrial Revolution, pioneer of refrigeration,
Halls of Dartford celebrate 200 years of progress.

HUTCHINSON BENHAM
London Melbourne Sydney Auckland Johannesburg

Hutchinson Benham Ltd

An imprint of the Hutchinson Publishing Group

17–21 Conway Street, London W1P 6JD

Hutchinson Publishing Group (Australia) Pty Ltd
PO Box 496, 16–22 Church Street, Hawthorne, Melbourne,
Victoria 3122

Hutchinson Group (NZ) Ltd
32–34 View Road, PO Box 40-086, Glenfield, Auckland 10

Hutchinson Group (SA) Pty Ltd
PO Box 337, Bergvlei 2012, South Africa

First published 1985
© Hall-Thermotank Limited 1985

Set in Monophoto Photina by Servis Filmsetting Ltd, Manchester

Printed and bound in Great Britain by
Anchor Brendon Ltd, Tiptree, Essex

British Library Cataloguing in Publication Data
Miller, Harry
Halls of Dartford 1785–1985.
1. A.P.V. Holdings—History.
I. Title
338.7′697′0009422312   HD9683.G74A2

ISBN 0 09 158490 6

Contents

CHAIRMAN of APV Holdings PLC, SIR RONALD McINTOSH

Foreword

by Sir Ronald McIntosh KCB
Chairman of APV Holdings PLC

A number of British engineering companies, which are active in business today, can trace their origins back to mid-Victorian times. Not many go back to earlier reigns and fewer still pre-date the French Revolution. This book tells the story of a company which was founded in 1785 and has continued in business, on virtually the same site, ever since.

During these 200 years, and through all the changes that have accompanied them, Halls of Dartford have stuck to their last. They are now, as in 1785, engineers. In the first 100 years the business was a general one; from the 1880s onwards the company has specialised in refrigeration in which its expertise is acknowledged throughout the world.

Halls of Dartford are now a division of APV with which (as Hall-Thermotank Ltd) they merged in 1976. They are thus an integral part of a wider engineering group dedicated to the same high standards of technical expertise and service to customers as have carried Halls successfully through the last two centuries.

Mr Miller's history traces all these developments and puts them, with rare skill, in the context of the changing environment in which the company has had to operate down the years. As chairman of APV Holdings I am grateful to him and to all those whose knowledge and recollections helped him to write this book.

Chapter 1

Introduction:
The Creative Revolution

There are no life tables for business, no inherent laws for expectation of life. Broadly, an enterprise may last as long as chance permits. But chance can be so hazardous that one always wonders, when confronted with swift extinction or lengthy survival, what caused the one to expire in twenty years and the other to last for two hundred years. The survivor has lived through murderous competition, economic disasters beyond its control, devastating wars, follies and miscalculations, take-over bids and perhaps the debilitating effect of a multiple assault by many adverse events simultaneously. Something more rational than a charmed life must have contributed. Since there is no formula for business longevity and forecasting is an exasperatingly short-term exercise, one must look for causes long after the event, hold an inquest on those that die young and make an appraisal of the centenarians. Both types of inquiry may be instructive, or at least interesting, especially the rare case of the ancient business that is not an antique or a museum piece, is still inventive and profitable and has a future.

The chapters that follow tell a business story of that kind. It is a record of progress and achievement, although growth has often been painful and the blessings mixed. Nothing so uncomplicated as consistent advancement is possible in a lifetime of two hundred years. There have been in this case triumphs and setbacks and at least one close escape from total extinction; mergers and all the consequent upheavals; internal conflicts, financial crisis, drastic administrative experiments, technical successes and some chastening failures, also marketing problems successfully overcome. Every enterprise is a continuing adventure in which risks are either deliberately taken or stumbled upon unawares. From the start it plunges into exploration, much of it in the dark and inadequately equipped – however knowledgeable, capable and careful the venturer may be. It is as well that at the outset he can neither guess the worst nor even imagine the best of what might be to come. The overriding aim is not wildly ambitious, but simply to make enough to live on. The business here described could not have been smaller or more insignificant in its beginnings, but it had a decisive advantage which only the distant future would make apparent: it could not have been launched at a more propitious time in industrial history. In those circumstances John Hall, just out of his teens, stumping the North Kent countryside for odd jobs and setting up a one-man workshop in a Dartford backwater, had little to lose but everything to gain.

The propitious time was the last quarter of the eighteenth century, the peak of what is popularly known as Britain's Industrial Revolution. If anyone had told John Hall that he was living in revolutionary times he would have been justified in dismissing the speaker as mad. Revolutions, he knew, were traditionally violent events on a massive scale, with yelling mobs, bloodshed and buildings set on fire. No doubt he remembered being told a few years previously – when he was still an apprentice – about the Gordon Riots in London, but these had nothing to do with industry; they were religious conflicts between Catholics and Protestants and did not impinge on the peaceful Hampshire countryside – at least a day's journey from the capital even when weather and road conditions were favourable – where John Hall had lived with his parents.

It was some late nineteenth-century economists who, examining the picture of eighteenth to nineteenth-century industrial changes through the foreshortening lens of history, saw in them the characteristics of a revolution. In recent times there has been a reaction against the revolutionary label as exaggerated and over-dramatic. A sequence of events covering about three-quarters of a century, it has been said, may be termed an evolutionary movement but hardly a revolution. As often happens, both points of view are valid with some reservations. Measured against the acceleration of discovery and development in the second half of the twentieth century, the industrial turbulence of the past looks less than revolutionary, at least in its immediate influence, but the long-term effect has been profound, changing fundamentally the direction of industrial progress. The period from around 1760 to 1830 constitutes a broad and deep cleavage in the technological, industrial and social structure of Britain. What preceded it was virtually a different world from what ensued. We must appreciate its real significance if we are able to place the humble little Dartford workman fairly in his niche among the inventive giants of his time, and to see the bicentenarian business he engendered as the child of one revoluton and a major contribution to at least one other.

One of the most remarkable features of the Industrial Revolution was the convergence within a comparatively short period of a number of great compatible innovations with potentially far-reaching utility. These were not sudden emanations from a cluster of Leonardo-like brains; they had undergone many years of trial and modification, often in stringent financial circumstances, before they were fit to be applied to industries facing grave productive problems. Prominent among those industries were cotton (and later wool) textiles spun and woven in thousands of homes on manually operated machines. Generally, wives spun the thread while husbands worked the larger weaving looms, and the children helped as soon as they were old enough to fetch and carry. All ate, slept and did the household chores on the business premises as it were. There were also larger establishments with one or two apprentices who lived with the family as in the time of the ancient guilds. The processes were effective, but too slow to keep up with a growing domestic and foreign demand. (It was wool rather than cotton which found good markets overseas for English kersey, a coarse woollen fabric which had been famous for centuries throughout the Mediterranean as far east as Turkey.) To this primitive industry came disruption and modernization from men with revolutionary ideas and designs for machines that no ordinary living room could accommodate. Every sixth-former knows the names of the inventors and their devices: James Hargreaves, whose spinning jenny was in fact small and simple enough to replace the traditional cottage machine, though it was many times more productive; Richard Arkwright, whose water frame was too big for muscle and had to be powered by water-wheel in the village stream; Samuel Crompton, whose spinning mule was so-called because it was a hybrid combining the qualities of the jenny and the water frame, and which enabled finer quality fabric to be manufactured; and in the weaving sector Edmond Cartwright's power loom which could be used with a variety of power sources, and John Kay's flying shuttle, which speeded up weaving and multiplied the productivity of the weaver. This mechanization of spinning and weaving forced textile production out of the cottage and into the factory. Within a couple of decades, by about 1785, cloth manufacture had become – in principle if not yet in scale and sophistication – a process that the modern industrialist would recognize as akin to his own. By comparison, the cottage industry of a quarter-century earlier was as remote as the Middle Ages.

Those whose ideas eventually transformed the cotton and wool industries formed a galaxy of such brilliance as few epochs in history can match and few other nations can boast. They lit the path to a source of prosperity which helped to make Britain the leading trading nation in the world. However, the changes did not occur suddenly or at headlong speed. Technical and social movements, however compelling, need time to spread and consolidate, otherwise the shock to a society can be destructive where it should be stimulating. So in the eighteenth and nineteenth centuries ancient and modern continued to exist for a time side by side, as they always do in an evolving situation. The pace at which the old retreats and the new takes over is the true measure of progress.

While the innovators in the textile industry were developing and patenting their designs, James Watt was struggling with the technical complications of applying a more effective form of power to production machinery than hand, foot and even the water-wheel could exert. Before the eighteenth century had ended Watt's steam-engine was in production at his Soho Foundry in Birmingham and in use to drive machinery in cotton mills and ironworks. The new industrialists had begun to recognize it as a power source with almost limitless possibilities for an economy on the move.

Watt's enterprise exemplifies in the clearest terms the interdependence of the major elements in the Industrial Revolution, and the fact that action results only when the linkage is complete. His steam-engine was necessary to set the spinning and weaving machinery in motion, to activate road and rail transport, to power the production and processing of iron ore and coal for the manufacture of more textile machines, more steam engines, more vehicles in a mechanized transport system. Industrial change was a vast chain reaction. But when Watt embarked on his enterprise he realized that the business itself needed to be powered by something very different from mechanical forces but equally important and no less potent. That power source was finance. Inventors are notoriously poor and Watt, earning a moderate living as a surveyor and consultant engineer, lacked the resources to build and supply his enormous engines on a commercial scale. It was not until Matthew Boulton joined him in partnership with an abundance of the missing ingredient that the famous firm of Boulton & Watt could set in motion the machinery of Britain's creative revolution.

Capital was available mainly from what was still – and would continue to be for some time – the nation's most lucrative occupation: agriculture. The controversial enclosures of what had been common land and improvements in methods of cultivation had provided surplus money which, together with the proceeds of home and overseas trade and developing industries such as building, engineering and mining, saw the new technology as rich virgin soil for investment. The money market (a grandiose term perhaps for those times, though an embryonic banking system was taking shape) was favourable to business adventures and money began to flow into promising new channels.

Profit was not the only motive, nor were the rich reckless in pursuing it. Compelling environmental factors were directing the financial current away from a sphere of acute raw material shortage to one of unlimited supply. The cottage spinning and weaving machines were made of wood; the factory plant was made of iron. There were many good reasons for the change: the size of the machines, the motive power employed, the unprecedented output, the necessity for smooth operation in a mechanized system, maintenance by metal workers instead of carpenters and the need to assemble the work force around the machines instead of collecting the product from small scattered production units. All these requirements were important, but there was one reason for the change to metal which outweighed all others: the crisis in the country's woodlands. Whatever regrets there might be at the passing of 'Old England' there was no escape from the fact that the approaching age of mass production would necessarily be an age of iron.

The claims upon the nation's resources of wood for domestic heating and for production of the small iron goods in common use – nails, horseshoes, spades, cutlery – had been depleting the woodlands for centuries. Ironworks had been sited in villages in order to be near the shrubs from which came the charcoal used to smelt the iron ore. Even forest trees had been sacrificed and suitable trunks now had to be imported to provide masts for British ships. A substitute for wood charcoal was urgently needed. Early in the eighteenth century Abraham Darby, at his ironworks at Coalbrookdale, Shropshire, had experimented successfully with coke derived from coal. Successive improvements of the process by his descendants had by mid-century established the new techniques as a means of saving the remaining forest lands and of increasing iron production to meet the demand for factory-sized production plant. Coal was plentiful: it had merely to be dug from the ground. Production from the mines increased enormously and in the second half of the eighteenth century it had almost trebled; by 1850 the figure for 1800 had more than quadrupled. Like the factories, the mines benefited from mechanization by the latest power plant and from other iron products made available thanks to coal; for instance, the use of iron pit-props made it unnecessary to leave columns of coal in place to hold up the roof. Coal became cheaper and so did iron. One of the most famous monuments to the genius of the Darby family is the iron bridge they built over the River Severn near their works: the place is called Ironbridge to this day. A less spectacular monument is coal gas, developed for street lighting by William Murdoch in 1802 and first used, appropriately, to light the Boulton & Watt works in Birmingham.

We must bear in mind constantly how many brains and hands and how much time and experiment went towards perfecting and establishing what can be so easily mistaken in the deceptive perspective of history for a flash of inspiration. A few names tend to dominate, but there were others before and after their monumental achievements without whose labours the developments would have been less effective or longer delayed. Some of these, Henry Cort for instance, are historic figures in their own right. The Darbys were fortunate in having a local coal supply with low sulphur content which enabled them to get good results with coke alone. Elsewhere smelting required an admixture of a proportion of charcoal. In the 1870s Henry Cort developed his rolling and puddling process which obviated the need for charcoal, rid the pig-iron of impurities and yielded wrought-iron, a comparatively tough alternative to the commonly used cast-iron which, because of its brittleness, was unsuitable and could be unsafe for some applications. We must bear in mind also the contribution of the iron-masters, especially the greatest of them all, John Wilkinson, who was inventor as well as business builder and a force in the industrial and financial growth of the nation.

The changes brought about by the need for more and cheaper iron and the incidental conservation of the woodlands were not welcomed everywhere. The charcoal burner's trade diminished, and householders in London and other centres of spreading population which were distant from adequate supplies of brushwood had to burn the hated 'seacoal' (so-called because it came by coastal vessels from the northern mines) in the domestic grate. In industry as elsewhere in human affairs every blessing brings its quota of discontent and distress. The removal of industry from the cosy family circle to the chilling factory environment was another cause of personal unhappiness. Population was sucked from the villages into towns growing rapidly in the vicinity of the coal-mines and ironworks. A vast social upheaval had started, a migration on a scale which this country had never before experienced. During the reign of George III, admittedly a very long one, the country's population had doubled from about 7 million to 14 million. Whole communities must have been on the move as a mainly rural was transformed into a mainly urban economy and the heavy industries found favourable conditions for expansion in the northern half of the country.

Expansion in coal and iron production and the development of new industrial complexes focused attention on the inadequacy of transport. Good roads were sparse and the rest – mostly mere tracks – were often impassable in bad weather except to pack-horses which were useless for carrying bulky material such as coal in quantity. Coal had to travel by river to the factory areas, hence more waterways were needed and canals seemed to offer the obvious solution. Canal construction became the rage – a 'mania', some commentators have said, comparable with the gold rush in other times and places, so eager were the rich to invest their money in what was known as 'internal navigation'. The labourers who built the canals were called navigators, popularly shortened to navvies. By the end of the eighteenth century thousands of miles of new waterways linked the Severn, the Thames, the Mersey and the Humber in a network covering the Midlands. Canal transport was slow, it was complicated by locks and the water tended to freeze in winter, but it served its purpose satisfactorily enough until the railways provided the ultimate solution in the nineteenth century.

The improvements in communications by internal waterways and by the work of Telford and McAdam, who gave the country the best roads since Roman times, had social and political consequences which were hardly less remarkable than those in the staple industries. They opened up the country, making it one nation in a geographical – as the technical developments were making it in an industrial – sense. Up to the middle of the eighteenth century places which good roads, fast coaches and later rail were subsequently to make easily accessible, were remote, self-contained and self-sustaining, small enclaves of villages grouped round a town to form a semi-independent trading and social unit. That medieval pattern was broken by the same revolutionary forces that transformed manufacturing industry by inventions and rationalized agriculture by the enclosures. Once-small provincial cities – Birmingham, Sheffield, Manchester, Liverpool – swelled to metropolitan size and nationwide influence. London in the south remained a special case. The 'Wen', as that fierce polemist William Cobbett insisted on calling it, retained and enhanced its importance as a centre of trade, authority and population. Within ten years of the end of the eighteenth century its population had exceeded a million, but it bore the marks, as did the industrial cities of the north, of hasty and selfish overgrowth. In some respects Cobbett's insult was an understatement.

There was a price to pay for progress, as many reformers demonstrated in word and deed. Exploitation of the lower ranks of workers continued for a time unopposed, and the crowding of the poor in squalid, insanitary alleys in the swelling cities added to the disease and deprivation their pitiful class had always suffered. The immediate effect of the highly productive machines was inevitably to displace labour and as always there was a painful time-lag before employment caught up with the boom.

One must, however, beware of exaggerating the early results of the Industrial Revolution. Agriculture continued to employ more people than cotton long after the new textile processes had taken root and begun to flourish. Far more women were still employed in domestic service than in the mines where, to the scandal of all those with a conscience, even before the expansion of coal production women and young children dragged trucks of coal underground like beasts of burden. Factory work was less inhuman, though the buildings were often grim and the environment depressingly impersonal. There was a parallel social revolution which helped to mitigate the harshness of industrial advancement and create a working nucleus out of which a new dispensation would eventually develop. The Industrial Revolution was not the golden age it might seem to some observers under the blurred light of history, but it was certainly not the disaster that others thought they saw through the jaundiced darkness of politics. It is some tribute to the overriding approval of the changes imposed that there was no general revulsion, no counter-revolution. At the same time we must recognize that all great historic revolutions, whether political or industrial, violent or bloodless, tend to attain an impetus which is irresistible. Whole nations are swept along by the current. Later arguments as to whether they were beneficial or otherwise are academic; they have been accepted and are irreversible.

There were national compensations for harm done. The size and stench of the slums and the vociferous campaigns of reformers provoked local authorities into improving the water supply and raising the standard of health and hygiene. Workers were in time better fed and clothed. Overseas trade expanded: increased imports of wool, corn and later meat improved earnings and living standards; exports of good quality finished products enhanced Britain's prestige as a trading nation. Indeed, the Industrial Revolution was itself a British export. Other countries learnt from us the new technologies and the processes of peaceful social change.

The workers who had most to gain in the early stages of the revolution were the engineers. An iron age must enlist the services of the metal craftsmen, from the designers of great machines and civil engineering projects to the blacksmiths and the nail-makers. Some of the engineering feats have more than historic interest and one of the most spectacular was that of Richard Brindley, builder of the famous Bridgewater Canal to carry coal to Manchester from the Duke of Bridgewater's mine at Worsley. The project involved carrying one waterway over another, and to this day viewers can goggle at the sight of vessels sailing high over other vessels in a two-tier water transport system.

At a humble level in the working hierarchy, but symptomatic of the new needs created by industrial developments, was increased esteem and employment for an expanding class of men: the mechanic, trained by apprenticeship in metal work, resourceful also in handling the minutiae of related crafts, educated and literate and a grade or two above the odd-jobs men who were often unskilled and unreliable. In that category was John Hall, a particle in the new industrial structure, but as will be seen in the following chapters an essential component in keeping the inventors' machines working satisfactorily. In every age, and no less today than in the eighteenth and nineteenth centuries, the industrialist needs the little man to supply the nuts and bolts for the big undertakings. Very few of the old inventors were businessmen or potential captains of industry, and even when a Boulton came along with the means to go into production the outside craftsman was called in to supply parts, effect repairs and even cooperate in constructing a prototype. Much of their work was manual; even screws were cut with remarkable accuracy before Henry Maudslay launched his screw-cutting lathe in 1797 to speed up and simplify the process.

The self-employed mechanics were both products of and contributors to the Industrial Revolution. What became of them is not difficult to guess in general terms. Most continued as freelances in a small way until they were too old to work and then the Poor Law saved them from starvation. Others found regular employment in the workshops of the more prosperous practitioners or with manufacturers. Some emigrated. A few established their own business and took their sons into partnership, becoming masters where originally they were servants. Most of these little businesses expired and left no record, but John Hall was a rare exception. The family name has lived on in a variety of combinations and so has the business, though changed out of all recognition.

The early pages of the story that follows cover the start, the rise and the fall of the family business after ninety years under the founder and his two sons. The fall was not fatal. The decrepit firm hung by a thread; but, lacking a third generation of Halls to take over, or anyone outside the ranks sufficiently able and bold to attempt a rescue, the situation seemed bleak indeed. As it happened, salvation came from within. An employee, Everard Hesketh, not much older than the founder was when he started his small practice, emerged as a business rebuilder with a mental and moral stature amounting almost to genius. He stiffened the tottering company with judicious management, combined discipline with compassionate human relations and set the tone and pattern for another century and more of prosperous and far-sighted innovation. He had the vision to recognize the possibilities of the ideas for refrigeration of foodstuffs and other products on an industrial and commercial scale which were then floating about in scientific circles worldwide, and in spite of the general business problems he had taken over with the miscellaneous activities of J. & E. Hall Ltd he hitched its future to that daring speculation. From that point onwards we can divide the story of the enterprise into 'pre-Hesketh' and 'post-Hesketh,' and the double century of the business into pre- and post- refrigeration. Nearly a decade before the bicentenary the refrigeration side of the operation had itself become a centenarian. The book thus celebrates a centenary within a bicentenary and closes the story with the business vigorous enough to embark on what could be – who knows? – a third century.

Refrigeration remains the leading theme. Impressive though survival for 200 years may be, it must yield in importance to the pioneering of a great new industry. Industrial refrigeration is worthy of comparison with the innovations of the great engineers of the Industrial Revolution. It has proved revolutionary in the social as well as the technical sphere and appropriately brings this story, in spirit at least, full circle to its beginnings in the eighteenth century. By the final chapter, where it halts at the 200th birthday in the mid-1980s, scientific and industrial revolutions have started to arrive so thick and fast, and the public have been made familiar with so much of the detail through their reading and television, that miracles tend to subside into routine. The sense of wonder, however, still finds expression. Electronics has been hailed as the second industrial revolution and its techniques, as these pages describe, have been incorporated in the latest applications of industrial refrigeration.

Here then is the story of Dartford Ironworks, J. & E. Hall Ltd, the Hall-Thermotank group of companies and the Hall-Thermotank division of APV Holdings PLC, variations on a theme of enterprise in the long history of a single progressive business.

CHAPTER 2

The Founding Father

On 1 April 1784, twenty-year-old John Hall travelled from his home in a Hampshire village to the Thames-side town of Dartford to seek, not the traditional story-book fortune, though that is what he achieved eventually, but modest jobs in the local mills. He had had such schooling as the times could offer an intelligent boy of good artisan family: that is, he was literate and had served a craft apprenticeship. Dartford was not alien territory. John's father, William, had worked there as a millwright thirty years before and was still remembered and respected in the town. He had left to join the Portal family's paper mill in Laverstoke, Hampshire and his position must have been a senior one in the business, for he was able to apprentice his four sons there to the millwright's trade. John was the second son and the most successful. William Hall in his last years joined his prosperous son in Dartford, and died there at the age of eighty-four.

Dartford and Laverstoke, so different in everything else, had one feature in common: both were centres of fine quality paper production. The Hampshire mills had been established in Whitchurch and its neighbour Laverstoke by Henri de Portal, one of thousands of Huguenots who had taken refuge in England from persecution in France. The Huguenots had been a Protestant minority in a Catholic country, and they had fought the French rulers in a succession of civil wars for over a century. Like so many refugees before and after their time, they enriched industry in the host country by introducing new crafts and many of them became leading citizens. In William Hall's period of service the Hampshire mills were supplying bank-note paper for the Bank of England, which had been founded half a century before in 1694 and had been granted the official right to issue paper money. Dartford mills had the privilege of serving the same customer.

It is possible that Kent preceded Hampshire in paper manufacture, for a paper mill established in Dartford in 1585 is believed to have started the industry in England. The founder was John Spielman, a goldsmith from Nuremburg who had become Queen Elizabeth's jeweller; he was knighted by her successor James I and anglicized his surname to Spelman. Before his time writing paper had been imported into England from the Continent, and all efforts to create a native industry had failed. Spelman had the advantage not only of being able to bring skilled workers and paper-forming moulds from his home town but also of being granted a monopoly to collect linen rags and other materials to make white paper. His enterprise and 'the benefit that paper bringeth' were celebrated in verse by a very minor poet of the period, Thomas Churchyard. It may not be too wild a fancy to wonder whether some of the original prompt copies of Shakespeare's plays could have been printed (or scribbled?) on Dartford paper.

Failing to find work in the town John Hall, wearing the leather apron and carrying the tool-bag that proclaimed the itinerant workman, walked a few miles south to the village of Hawley in the Darent valley. The little river rises in the North Downs near the southern rim of what is today the London region, and flows in a 20-mile curve to the Thames estuary at Dartford – the ford on the Darent. Its course is still dotted with mills as it was in John Hall's time. Paper manufacture, then as now, required an abundance of clean water, hence the choice of location on the banks of rivers such as the Test in Hampshire and the Darent among the market gardens of Kent. At Hawley a mill was being repaired and the owner, T.H. Saunders, offered John Hall a job. It lasted for a year. The mill-owner was impressed with the quality of the young man's work and promised to put jobs his way and recommend him to other local mill-owners if he would set up his own shop in Dartford. Incidentally, the Saunders mill survived until 1931, when it was bought by the Portal family who transferred its paper producton to their mill at Laverstoke. The whirligig of time has come full circle more than once in the Hall history.

John Hall was fortunate in having been apprenticed to his father and having learned his craft in a good-class mill. Apprentice training varied greatly in quality: many youths were used by unscrupulous bosses as a source of cheap unskilled labour and went out into the world with poor qualifications. In 1785, therefore, at the age of twenty-one, John Hall started as a self-employed smith in a shed in Lowfield Street, Dartford. That was the real beginning of the business which, as the Hall-Thermotank Division of APV Holdings PLC, is about to celebrate its 200th anniversary of continuous existence.

It was a time of opportunity for a young man of good background and proficiency in an expanding trade. Indeed for some, as Wordsworth was to say of the French Revolution a few years later, 'to be young was very heaven'. The accent was on youth even in politics. William Pitt, Prime Minister in 1783 at the age of twenty-four, though an exceptional man by any standards, seemed nevertheless to epitomise the spirit of the age. Great historic events were happening in the nation and the world, although the most momentous made comparatively little impression on the general public; for instance, only the military and the politicians were closely involved in the War of American Independence. National newspapers to headline and interpret events for the millions were still to come: but it is interesting to note that the year in which John Hall's small enterprise was launched also marked the birth of a modest little newspaper, the *Daily Universal Register*, which three years later was renamed *The Times*. Hearsay was a

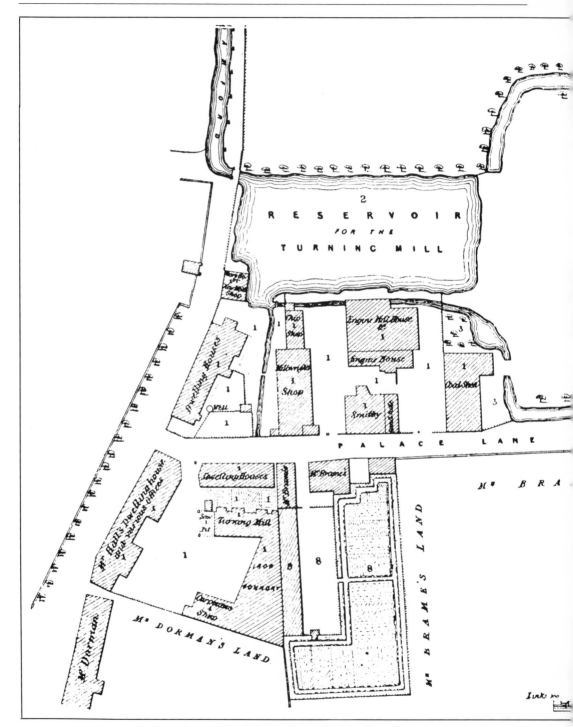

Plan of the estate in 1807, which had grown out of the 'messuage and tanyar

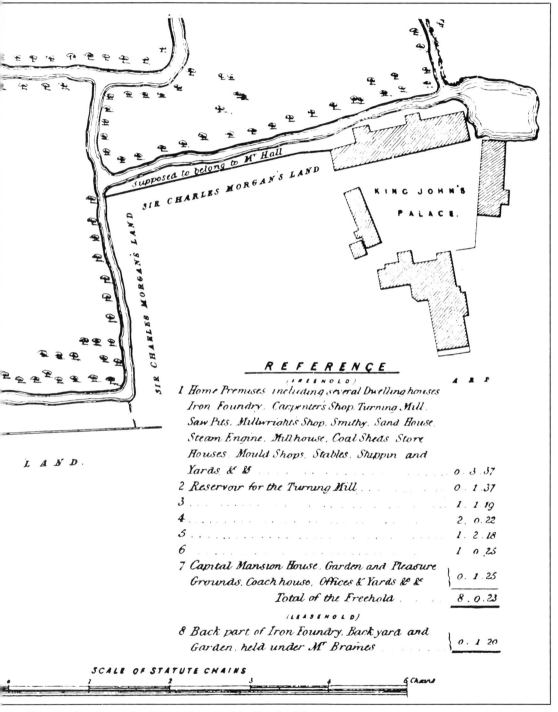

REFERENCE

(FREEHOLD)

1 Home Premises including several Dwelling houses
Iron Foundry, Carpenter's Shop, Turning Mill,
Saw Pits, Millwright's Shop, Smithy, Sand House,
Steam Engine, Millhouse, Coal Sheds, Store
Houses, Mould Shops, Stables, Shippin and
Yards &c .... 0 . 3 . 37
2 Reservoir for the Turning Mill .... 0 . 1 . 37
3 .... 1 . 1 . 19
4 .... 2 . 0 . 22
5 .... 1 . 2 . 18
6 .... 1 . 0 . 25
7 Capital Mansion House, Garden and Pleasure
Grounds, Coach house, Offices & Yards &c &c } 0 . 1 . 25

Total of the Freehold ...... 8 . 0 . 23

(LEASEHOLD)

8 Back part of Iron Foundry, Back yard and
Garden, held under Mr Brames } 0 . 1 . 20

SCALE OF STATUTE CHAINS

6 Chains

quired by the founder on land formerly owned by Dartford Priory useful though selective medium in the absence of mass circulations, and many more people must have known about the sensational feats being performed in the air than about events which broke or created nations. The Montgolfier brothers flew in a fire balloon in 1783, Vincent Lunardi made the first balloon ascent from London and a safe landing in Hertfordshire in 1784 and the Channel was first crossed by balloon in 1785. Young Hall, as a metal worker and millwright, would also no doubt have heard some details of James Watt's discovery and the trials of a more dependable and versatile source of mechanical power than wind and water.

Expansion came rapidly at the Lowfield Street workshop, for the corn, paper, oil and powder mills in and around the town had plenty of work to offer an honest and dependable mechanic. Simple though the mill mechanism might have been, there were frequent breakdowns and good repair and maintenance services were scarce. Manufacturers were not the only customers and the smith would undertake a large variety of small jobs: shoeing horses of course and supplying the metal parts of harness; providing meat-hooks, cooking utensils and garden tools; making and fitting window bars for houses; designing and erecting shop signs and decorative wrought-iron gates. At his best he was artist as well as tradesman.

Within five or six years John Hall needed larger premises and found them in a 'messuage and tanyard' in Waterside (now Hythe Street) on land which had once formed part of Dartford Priory. The site of the tanyard, and now much of the land around, is still occupied by Hall's main factories. Included eventually in the messuage was the historic Priory House, of which the firm made good use.

John Hall had bought his little property from a market gardener, Peter Brames, descendant of a Flemish merchant family. They became great friends and perhaps inevitably John married one of Peter Brames' pretty daughters. A descendant of one of the girls, Canon Nolloth, told Everard Hesketh in 1910 at the J. & E. Hall 125th anniversary celebration, that John Hall had been unable to choose which of the girls would make the most suitable partner. Calling early one morning at their parents' house, he found Sarah up and busy with the domestic chores while her three sisters still slept. The combination of beauty and industry proved irresistible to a keen businessman! He and Sarah married and had ten children.

The Brames family was Wesleyan and so were the Halls; since the Methodists were strongly represented in Dartford it was not surprising that they should come together. The sectarian link must have been a business asset as well as a source of family happiness. The contribution of the nonconformists, especially Quakers and Methodists, to the great upsurge of industry in the late eighteenth and early nineteenth century is a historic fact. These sober, industrious and enterprising people would have felt insulted to be bracketed with 'revolutionaries', if only in industrial terms: to them, revolution was the godless abomination that raged across the Channel. But the speed of change on the non-violent side of that waterway was creating, as we have already tried to convey, a hardly less extensive transformation.

The religious movement propelled by the zeal and energy of the free churches was closely interwoven with the secular features of the Industrial Revolution. There was strong prejudice against the dissenters – in his *Rural Rides* Cobbett fulminated against the Quakers in particular as parasitic non-workers – but they were on the whole an influence for good. It is remarkable how many of those whose brains contributed so brilliantly to the nation's economic progress ran counter to the establishment in their religious beliefs. For example, the Darbys were Quakers; Thomas Newcomen, inventor of the atmospheric steam-engine and a contemporary of Abraham Darby, was a Baptist; James Watt, whose decisive harnessing of steam power followed Newcomen's pioneering work, was a Presbyterian. But the most potent of the revivalists were the Wesley family. Religion was at a low ebb in the isolated villages and the bloated towns when John Wesley descended upon them with a compelling evangelism. He was the most persuasive preacher of his day and, despite the oddity of some of his beliefs and the fanaticism of some of his precepts, was a powerful moral influence not only in the business community but among the poorest and most ignorant workers, even the derelict and the vicious, in whom he strove to implant sobriety, self-discipline and a sense of duty. Many better educated middle-class people also drew strength from his teaching. The Brames and Hall families were admirable examples.

James Watt's steam engine, now in the Science Museum, London, embodied the revolutionary power principle that transformed manufacturing industry in the late eighteenth and early nineteenth centuries

John Hall had chosen better than he could have foreseen in landing on Brames property. He had gained good friends and a good wife, room for his business to grow, running water which could be harnessed for power despite periodical floods in adverse conditions of tide and weather, a market garden for present produce and as a future addition to the family business, and access to public transport when adjacent land was later bisected by the railway and a station built virtually on the firm's doorstep.

Indeed the town itself had been a happy choice, quite apart from family associations. It was a small market town of about 2000 inhabitants, a centre for the farmers and small tradesmen within pack-horse reach southwards. Its mills and forges did not pollute the air or the river, though some were noisy; for instance, the threshing mills and the mill – the first of its kind in England – built in Elizabethan times to split iron bars for making wire, and no doubt numbering John Hall among its customers. The powder mills were a hazard and the floods a nuisance; but the congested industrialized town, which Richard Church in our own day has defined rather unkindly as 'now a place to escape from as quickly as possible, though it has some points of interest', would have been unimaginable except to those who had seen the urban horrors that the Industrial Revolution was creating in the big cities.

There were, and in fact still remain, many points of interest in the historic town of Dartford. The High Street is part of the Roman Watling Street, the great highway which is still traceable from Dover to the City of London and beyond to the Welsh border.

Dartford *circa* 1830

Archaeologists have found evidence of Roman settlements in and around Dartford; a cemetery in the town and a military station and governor's villa in what is now the village of Darenth. The Darent river probably served as an additional line of communication and defence. The area remained vulnerable long after the Roman withdrawal. The Norman tower of Dartford's Holy Trinity Church, mentioned in Domesday Book, is believed by some to have been built mainly to guard the ford over the river. The town was often in the wars and was involved in violent political dissent many centuries before the peaceful incursion of religious dissenters in John Hall's time. In the fourteenth century Wat Tyler and his rabble swarmed into Dartford on their way to London, and that alarming event is commemorated in the Wat Tyler Inn, one of several venerable hostelries in the town. In 1553–54 Sir John Wyatt, rebelling against Queen Mary's proposed marriage to Philip of Spain, was cornered in Dartford and later beheaded in the Tower of London. In the Civil War Dartford must have been regarded as a strategic spot, since it housed a camp for Parliamentary forces. It was again in the line of fire during the Napoleonic Wars, when there were fears of invasion on the Kent and Sussex coasts. The town did experience happier historic occasions, however, some of them still marked by treasured monuments. The Dominican Priory, founded by Edward III, was an educational centre for young people from the county's most distinguished families before becoming a royal residence for Anne of Cleves under the Tudors. Dartford

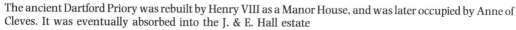

The ancient Dartford Priory was rebuilt by Henry VIII as a Manor House, and was later occupied by Anne of Cleves. It was eventually absorbed into the J. & E. Hall estate

had achieved fame also as the first stopping place out of London for Canterbury pilgrims, and had built many new inns to accommodate the influx of wayfarers. The boom ended when the pilgrimages ceased in the sixteenth century and shopkeepers selling images and other souvenirs were ruined.

To the medieval trader as to the wayfarer, Dartford was mainly an inland town. The two-mile gap between its northern edge and the Thames shore has always been an obstacle to water transport. Though no longer a no-man's land, it still means that Dartford is both a port and yet not quite a port, according to one's vantage point. It was a port to the shipbuilders who launched their wooden ships from many yards along the Thames between central London and Gravesend, and Samuel Pepys visited Dartford frequently, as well as Chatham and Rochester, in his capacity as Secretary to the Admiralty. To the Halls, in spite of the disadvantages, it offered via the winding creek a useful means of access to the great river highway: westwards into the heart of the world's largest, and most concentrated home market, and eastwards to the trading centres of Europe and the world. Barges might be frozen up in the creek and traffic congestion in the Thames (to say nothing of timber floated down to the mills) could be a problem, but from 1802 onwards, when the first London commercial dock was opened, Dartford participated in the easing of trade by the facilities for expansion. Much of the Thames congestion had been caused by the growth of overseas trade in the seventeenth and eighteenth centuries, and more berthing and warehouse space was urgently needed. It was the West Indian merchants who forced the pace of improvement and by the end of the nineteenth century most of the others had followed.

The Port of London has tended to move eastward since its heyday in the nineteenth and early twentieth centuries and the hub is now at Tilbury, virtually opposite Dartford on the other side of the river, but the changes have benefited Dartford as they have the entire ribbon of industrial development which now links the town almost continuously with central London 17 miles away. Halls, from their headquarters at Dartford, are associated directly and on a substantial scale with progress at Tilbury through the container terminal which is described in a later chapter. Streets in the centre of Dartford, widened in the mid-eighteenth century by demolition of the 'shambles' and market buildings, became too narrow for the 1980s traffic they had to carry, and a new bypass (the second in the twentieth century) had to be constructed to provide relief from what is one of the inevitable side-effects of prosperity. John Hall did indeed choose better than he realized, as his successors can confirm two centuries later.

John Hall prospered in spite of the worsening economic conditions in the country as a whole. The revolt of the American colonies, supported by France, Spain and Holland, had exhausted Britain. The Peace of Versailles, signed in 1783, left the Americans winners, the European powers losers and Britain both at once. Trade with the newly independent colonies declined and the armament and associated industries which had contributed to the victories in Europe slumped in the ensuing years of peace. The fall of the Bastille to French revolutionaries in 1789 had not yet involved other countries in a new round of wars stimulating a renewal of employment and an illusory boom. Two bad harvests added to the prevailing misery of poverty, and there were bread riots in England by 1795. The nation began to realize that it was no longer self-supporting in food. Few could perceive against this grim background the glow of another and not far distant industrial revolution.

BRYAN DONKIN (1768–1855)
Brother-in-law of John Hall senior and his associate in
pioneering developments in printing, papermaking and food
canning

There was unmistakable growth in some sectors of the economy and the paper mills were doing well. By 1791, when John Hall married Sarah Brames, his fame as an engineer and his experience of paper production had spread as far as Scotland, where he was supplying equipment to paper mills at Duns in Berwickshire and Penicuik near Edinburgh. This was routine work, but a more original contribution to paper production was to follow. The opportunity came through Bryan Donkin who, on the advice of John

Smeaton (veteran engineer and builder of the third Eddystone Lighthouse) had joined Hall as an apprentice in 1792 and incidentally became his brother-in-law by marriage to another of the Brames girls. Donkin wanted to specialize in service to the paper industry and would have liked to involve John Hall, but Hall preferred to remain a general engineer with as varied a clientele as chance and reputation could procure. He was content to let Bryan Donkin set up his own workshop in Dartford to make moulds and other accessories for the paper mills.

Paper making was still, at the turn of the century, a wholly manual process. The paper was made in single sheets, not yet in a continuous web to cope with rising newspaper circulations. The early issues of *The Times* were printed, as were all newspapers and periodicals, on single sheets; in the case of *The Times*, only 24 inches deep by 9 inches wide. Paper, a fibrous substance, was still made mainly from fabrics, especially clean white linen and cotton rags, but rarely such odd additions as leather and parchment fragments and old fishing-nets listed in Spelman's patent. The materials were crushed to a pulp in water in order to break up the long fibres. A workman then picked up some of the pulp on a tray containing a wire mould through which the water was drained away. The loose 'porridge' remaining was then subjected to heat and compression to make the fibres re-combine and form a smooth continuous sheet of paper. Hand-made paper in small quantities for special purposes is still produced in much the same way. The late eighteenth-century product was often of fine quality, but the process was slow and laborious and becoming inadequate for the needs of new progressive times.

In 1799 came the first hint of possible mechanization. A Frenchman, Louis Robert, patented a machine for making paper in a continuous web and sold the patent to his employers, Firmin Didot, famous typefounders and owners of a paper mill at Essonnes, south of Paris. Didot and his brother-in-law John Gamble brought a model of the machine to England and invited Fourdriniers, a large London firm of manufacturing stationers, to produce a prototype. Henry Fourdrinier enlisted the help of Bryan Donkin, who suggested asking his old employer John Hall to construct the machine. Hall

The Fourdrinier machine for making paper in a continuous web, redesigned and built by Hall and Donkin. (As drawn for students about the year 1855)

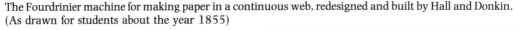

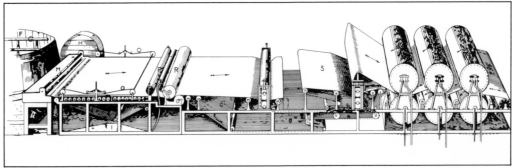

improved upon the original crude design, built an experimental machine and installed and tested it successfully in his iron-foundry. Since Hall was unwilling to be further involved, the Fourdrinier brothers built a factory to manufacture the machine at Bermondsey and put Bryan Donkin in charge. A small number of the machines were produced and sold in Hertfordshire and Kent, but unfortunately the enterprise was dogged by complications over royalties and after a number of years the promoters had to accept defeat. Henry Fourdrinier became bankrupt with losses of £60,000 and died in poverty.

The venture may have been a commercial failure but the machine was a technical success. After tests with an experimental model in Frogmore Mill, Hertfordshire, an improved model was installed in Two Waters Mill nearby. This version, the first practical continuous paper-making machine, proved to be ten times as productive as the current manual processes, and inevitably there were labour troubles. The workers, a decade ahead of the Luddites, feared that the machine would rob them of their jobs and threatened to destroy the mill. The manager, Marchant Warrell, foresaw that increased productivity would help the workers in the long run and, according to Everard Hesketh in his history of J. & E. Hall, quelled the rioters by persuasion and maintained production. Hall and Donkin lived to see other developers advance where they had shown the way and mechanization increase both output and employment in the paper industry.

Though John Hall was not prepared to specialize in paper-making plant, he did make other routine contributions to technical progress in the industry, and yet again provided a nursery for pioneers. He had two apprentices at the time of the Fourdrinier experiments, William and James Bertram who, after obtaining their indentures, left to start their own factory in Edinburgh and win fame for their innovations in paper-making technology. Among these were reeling and cutting equipment essential for continuous paper production, and here again John Hall helped with design and manufacture. Another Dartford man, John Marshall, a paper-makers' engineer and paper-mould manufacturer, invented the Dandy roll for watermarking the paper. He was appointed by the Bank of England to supply moulds for the manufacture of its bank-notes.

Donkin turned his talents into related channels and helped to design and produce the first rotary printing machine, one of which was bought by the Cambridge University Press. Like the paper machine it was ahead of its time, and similarly provided a base upon which others were to build fortunes. Another enterprise in which Donkin again partnered Hall and Gamble proved more immediately successful, and made these three far-sighted men the direct founders of a great industry. And here again, as with the paper machine, the honour of having discovered the principle belonged to a Frenchman of genius.

A year or two after the opening of the nineteenth century, vegetables preserved in glass jars were on sale in a Paris shop. The shop and the preserving process were the property of Nicolas Appert, a chemist who, after many years of experiment, had discovered how to keep foodstuffs fresh by heating them in sealed glass containers without causing the container to burst under heat or crack when cooling. In 1810 he published a book with the title *L'art de conserver, pendant plusieurs années, toutes les substances animales et végétales*. This was more than half a century before Louis Pasteur proved the bacterial cause of decay and the effect of heat in destroying the organisms.

John Gamble heard of Appert's patent while on a visit to Paris to discuss the paper-making machine with the Didots, and he and Donkin bought the English rights for £1000. They believed that tinplate cans would be as effective as glass jars for preserving food and of course had the advantage of not being breakable. In association with John Hall they set up the world's first food-canning factory in Bermondsey. Like Appert, they proclaimed their discoveries and boosted the products in a publication with the kind of lengthy all-embracing title common in their day: *Copies of the Official Reports and Letters relative to Donkin, Hall and Gamble's Preserved Provisions, which will keep perfectly fresh, retaining their original flavour and nutritional qualities for a considerable length of time and in any climate*. At the foot of the title page were the words: 'Printed with Mr Donkin's Patent Machine.' Bryan Donkin missed no business opportunities!

Appert had supplied his bottled goods to the French Navy; similarly the Royal Navy and Arctic explorers were among the early customers for Donkin, Hall and Gamble's canned meat and vegetables. The naval mutinies at Spithead and the Nore in 1799 were a protest against the abominable conditions under which the sailors lived and fought bravely for their country; the rotten meat and bread crawling with weevils were not the least of their miseries. Nelson campaigned for years against the neglect of his men and the experimenters in food canning did their best to supply some improvement in the diet. Explorers adventured into the new food techniques as well as into uncharted seas and Sir Edward Parry took canned provisions with him on successive voyages in search of the North-West Passage. On the third expedition in 1824 one of his ships was wrecked and her stores were abandoned; found some five years later by Sir John Ross and his crew after their ship had foundered, the food – fresh and palatable – sustained them on their long trek on foot across the ice.

That was a comparatively unspectacular test of Donkin, Hall and Gamble's products. The ultimate trial was to follow more than a century later when Parry brought back a few of the cans to England unopened; he gave one containing roast veal to the Royal United Services Institute at Greenwich and another containing carrots in gravy to the National Maritime Museum at Greenwich. Both cans were opened in the Bacterial Laboratory of the Food Manufacturers' Research Association 114 years after having been filled and sealed in the Bermondsey factory. The scientists tried the carrots and found them eatable. Though the meat smelt wholesome they lacked the courage to sample it themselves but, it is said, tried it on a cat who ate it eagerly and without ill effect!

Incidentally, these early canners added a word to the language. One of the products was labelled 'Soup and Bouilli', the latter a word in common use at the time meaning boiled or stewed beef. To servicemen, who are notorious for corrupting and at the same time enriching the language, this became 'bully beef' and in that form has lasted down the ages and through two world wars.

A century-old can of meat being opened for testing in 1958 at the British Food Manufacturing Industries Research Association laboratories in Leatherhead

Canning was just one activity among many for the resourceful John Hall. He undertook almost any assignment that was offered, and evidently gave satisfaction because the business grew along with his expertise. The local powder mills were among his customers: he supplied them with processing machinery. The mills had been a cause of much anxiety among the people of Dartford, on whose insistence a special road had been built in 1796 to avoid conveying gunpowder through the streets. John Hall, undeterred by the risks – physical or financial – went into ownership. When the government decided to close down its gunpowder factory in Faversham, Kent, he bought it and advertised the products in the following stately terms:

> This very superior Gun Powder is offered to Noblemen, Gentlemen and Sportsmen in general as manufactured on a system differing so materially from all others that it exceeds for cleanliness, quickness of firing and peculiar strength, any other Cylinder Gun Powder yet submitted to the Public; they are therefore invited to make trial of the same in the fullest confidence that it merits that decided preference it so justly deserves.

It gained that decided preference widely both at home and abroad and the manufacturer was known in the locality as 'Gunpowder Hall'.

Thames-side towns and marsh-lands were dotted with gunpowder mills and stores and explosions were too frequent for the residents' peace of mind. Halls were involved in

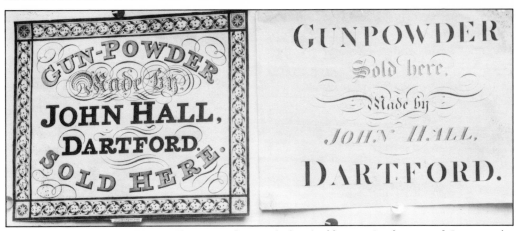

Trade cards advertising John Hall's gunpowder supplied to 'Noblemen, Gentlemen and Sportsmen'

the worst of these in 1864, when the founder's son Edward was head of the business; it was so serious that the military had to be called in from Woolwich to avert a vast disaster. Two magazines between Erith and Woolwich, one of them owned by Halls and holding 750 barrels of gunpowder, exploded with such force that the noise was heard all over London and some said up to 40 miles from the scene of the incident. The river wall was breached and barges and their occupants were blown to pieces. Two thousand troops and navvies worked day and night to rebuild the embankment and save a large area of low-lying ground from being flooded. The buildings were fortunately surrounded by 20 acres of open space, but even so nine men died and many were injured.

Though John Hall had not wished to embark on major technical developments in the paper industry with Bryan Donkin, he retained a financial interest in paper manufacture and bought a mill at Horton Kirkby. He continued to be interested in printing and supplied *The Times* with printing equipment. His business must have been one of the earliest conglomerates; he enlarged his collection by acquiring a flour mill at Chislehurst. When his father-in-law died he left his market gardening business to his eldest daughter, Mrs John Hall, and through her John Hall became a stallholder in Covent Garden.

It is not recorded why John Hall resisted the temptation to join Gamble, Donkin and other original minds whom he had helped to train and who set up their own specialized businesses to develop inventions. He was shrewd enough to realize that he was not of the fellowship of Watt and Arkwright and Donkin, but a technical contributor rather than a basic innovator. He was aware also that the paper-making and printing machines which he had helped others to design and improve had been only partly successful, and though technically sound had proved commercially disappointing. They obviously needed more effort and finance than he could reasonably spare and he was better at spreading the risk than at specialization, preferring to serve a variety of interests and customers as a general engineer rather than to court disaster in pursuit of a spectacular success. Besides, he had six sons to endow – the four daughters in those centuries of women's dependence would find themselves husbands – and the simplest way to achieve his aim would be to build up a miscellaneous group of separate businesses and share them out. He may also have had a presentiment that competition was mounting and the battle for orders would become harder. The Napoleonic Wars, like those of the previous century, had been followed by a slump in trade and employment which the workers, not without reason, attributed to mechanization. John Hall had decided, no doubt wisely, to remain a jobbing engineer.

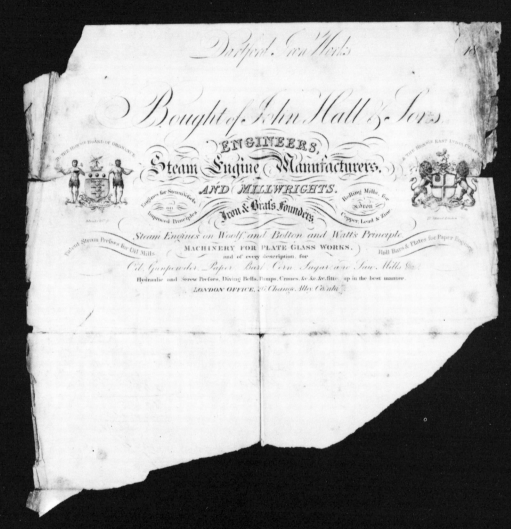

Fragment of a letter heading prior to 1836, listing the variety
of work handled at the Hall factory

CHAPTER 3

An End and a Beginning

The miscellaneous interests in John Hall's 'conglomerate' business were in effect sidelines, for he remained first and foremost an engineer. Born as he had been in the early years of the age of steam, the inventions of James Watt had formed part of his technical education; understandably, his main products as an entrepreneur were steam-engines. A fragment of a pre-1836 Dartford Ironworks letter heading, reproduced in the company's engineering apprenticeship booklet of 1950, describes John Hall & Sons as 'Engineers, Steam Engine Manufacturers and Millwrights, Iron and Brass Founders', and adds the following list of machining work undertaken: steam-engines on Woolff and Boulton & Watts principle; engines for steam vessels on improved principles; rolling mills for iron, copper, lead and zinc; patent steam presses for oil mills; roll bars and plates for paper engines; machinery for plate-glass works; oil, gunpowder, bark, corn, sugar and saw mills, hydraulic and screw presses, diving bells, pumps, cranes, etc. etc. 'fitted up in the best manner'. Steam-engines, as the order of priority shows, were dominant, and among these the firm's beam engines were justly famous and in wide demand.

Used to drive machinery in factories of all kinds, Halls' beam engines became a regular line, in production from John Hall senior's lifetime until well into the J. & E. Hall period under the two sons who inherited the works. In all 356 engines were built, the last one in 1879. They were remarkably tough and efficient and many had a phenomenal working record. A 40hp beam engine, supplied to the Royal Mint early in the nineteenth century, was sold about 1883 to J. & W. Nicholson & Company Ltd, and re-erected in their brewery at Bromley-by-Bow. It worked there continuously until 1947, when it was damaged by a fire in an adjacent building which housed the machinery that it drove, and was subsequently dismantled and broken up. A smaller (25hp) machine supplied to J. Davis & Bailey Ltd, agricultural machinery makers near Hemel Hempstead in Hertfordshire, worked there until the site was taken over for residential development in 1950. After a working life of over a hundred years, it was bought back by J. & E. Hall

An early beam engine, one of the most successful products of the Hall factory and erected in the foyer of their office building, where it was belt-driven by a small electric motor for the delight of visitors. In 1968 it was transferred on permanent loan to the Science Museum in South Kensington.

The firm's beam engines and boilers were exported to many European countries and as far afield as India and China. John Hall had apprenticed his sons John and Edward to the business and later took them into partnership. After Edward had served his time in the works, he was sent to Paris in 1817, at the age of eighteen, visited Spain, Belgium, Russia and other countries and remained the firm's overseas representative until called home when his father died in 1836. Edward was inventor as well as salesman. One of his inventions, according to Everard Hesketh in his history of J. & E. Hall, was a metallic packing for steam pistons to replace the gasket packing used at that time. One of his best selling lines was the firm's 'Elephant' boiler, a horizontal cylinder with three narrower cylinders parallel to and below it and connected to it by what Hesketh called 'necks'. Seeming as it did to stand on short thick legs, it resembled a docked and headless hippopotamus rather than an elephant. One of Halls' mechanics called Powell, who had been sent to France to install engines, started his own works in Rouen and manufactured so many Elephant boilers that they came to be known even in England as the French boiler. 'The Elephant Boiler', states one of Hall's advertising leaflets, 'is never afflicted with collapses.' Customers endorsed the claim and one of them, in a letter to *The Engineer* magazine in 1883, said, 'We have three which have been at work continually for 50, 40 and 41 years respectively, and the amount of repairs they have required has

Hall's famous and popular Elephant Boiler, 'never afflicted with collapses' as the firm's advertising claimed

been trifling. They are very sturdy steamers and we have never had any sort of accident with them. We have lately had them insured and the company's inspector has passed them – even the one that has been at work for over 50 years.'

Located as they were by the Thames, within a few miles of the new London docks constructed in the first decade of the nineteenth century, Halls would naturally find customers among the shipbuilders and owners, especially those who had ventured into steam. According to J. Dunkin's *History and Antiquities of Dartford* the first steamer to ply between Gravesend and London was the 70-ton *Margery* in 1815. Within twenty years steamships had ceased to be a novelty and by that time Halls were contributing to important developments in ship propulsion. One of these was the very first trunk engine, patented in 1835 by Francis Humphrys, of Humphrys & Tennant, manufacturers of

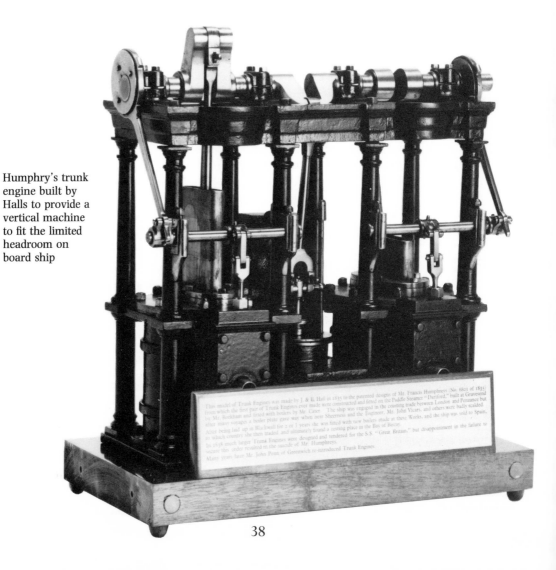

Humphry's trunk engine built by Halls to provide a vertical machine to fit the limited headroom on board ship

38

marine engines in Deptford. It was designed to fulfil the need for a vertical engine that would fit the very limited head-room on board ship. The engine was built by Hall and installed in the paddle steamer *Dartford*, engaged in coastal trade between London and Penzance. A few years later Humphrys and Hall designed much larger trunk engines to drive paddle wheels in Brunel's famous ship s.s. *Great Britain*, but the project proved abortive because Brunel changed his plans in favour of screw propulsion with a different kind of engine.

Humphrys brought to John Hall another of his inventions, a version of the beam engine for marine use. The beams were placed below instead of above the crankshaft and alongside the cylinders – again, as in the trunk engines, to save head-room, but with the added advantage that the heavy parts were low down in the ship. A pair of these engines with inverted beam were installed in 1836 in s.s. *Wilberforce*, built at Blackwall for the Humber Union Steamship Company of Hull, and others in s.s. *Batavia* built for the Steam Navigation Company.

Halls' marine business grew and diversified. Among the products were powerful punching and shearing machines supplied to the dockyard at Northfleet, where s.s. *Dartford* was built, for use in four ships being built for the West India Mail Service. There were also customers in more distant shipyards and these created an increasing problem. The goods were heavy – an engine and its boiler might weigh as much as 60 tons – and hauling them by road was laborious and enormously expensive. The logical way would be to transport them by water down the Thames estuary and round the coast, but to do this it would be necessary to bring ships to Dartford. The town was connected to the river by a winding creek $3\frac{1}{2}$ miles long, which was the northern portion of the Darent where it flows into the Thames. The creek was navigable for barges, but adverse winds and tides could hold up small vessels for days. John Hall realized that it could be deepened and straightened by a canal which would reduce its length to no more than two miles. Canal construction in England, as we have noted, was the rage in the late eighteenth and early nineteenth centuries and John Hall's project presented no great financial or technical problems.

The Dartford & Crayford Ship Canal Company was formed in 1835 and plans, surveys and estimates were prepared. It was estimated that an entrance lock at the Thames, together with the necessary wharves, docks, bridges and weirs would cost no more than £65,000. Dartford people on the whole welcomed the scheme, realizing that it would bring trade to the town, but when the sponsors applied for parliamentary consent certain vested interests intervened to oppose legislation and kill the scheme. According to Everard Hesketh the main opposition came from the railway company, which had planned a line from London to Dover via Dartford. A less ambitious plan to straighten part of the creek was authorized by Act of Parliament in 1840 and the work was then carried out. Meanwhile, however, Edward Hall had attempted a partial straightening, but this time nature had intervened when a very high tide broke over the creek wall, washed away the earthworks and flooded a large stretch of the marshes. Floods were frequent in and around Dartford, caused by high tides in the Thames estuary and by rapid melting of snow in the upper reaches of the Darent river which flows through the town. Streets were often under water and at times John Hall's workshops were awash.

The frustrations suffered by John Hall senior and his heirs were part of the growing pains of the enterprise, but growth – aided by increasing sophistication – was continuous and impressive. For the first sixteen years of its existence the factory was powered by a windmill; then in 1801 John Hall obtained an order from the justices to harness the stream of water that flowed along Waterside in order to turn a water-wheel in his works. J. Dunkin in his history of Dartford describes it more quaintly than Hesketh; he says that John Hall 'constructed an ingenious piece of mechanism, first turned by the wind and afterwards by the waters of the Cranpit, thereby enabling him to execute certain portions of his mill work with accuracy and facility. The machine was ultimately superseded by a steam engine.' A plan dated 1807 shows the reservoir fed by the stream for the turning mill, and also indicates how the premises had grown in twenty-two years. They included, in addition to the iron-foundry, a carpenters' shop, saw-pits, millwrights' shop, smithy, sand house, mill house, coal-sheds, storehouses, mould shops, stables, shippon yards, garden, offices, the family dwelling and other houses. (Shippon or shippen was and still is a dialect name for a cowhouse.)

The factory had its share of mishaps in addition to the occasional flood. A printed notice dated 26 March 1821 and headed 'Fire at the Foundry,' expresses the owner's gratitude to friends and neighbours for their help in extinguishing the fire. 'Nothing but a momentary interposition of Providence,' it says, 'averted the destruction which at one time threatened the whole Manufactory, and most likely would have been equally calamitous to the Property of surrounding individuals.'

By the 1830s Dartford Ironworks was a substantial business with very much more than a local reputation and clientele. It had an office in the City of London at 26 Old Change Alley, Cornhill and another at 9 Rue d'Enghein, Paris. Its engines were installed in factories throughout England and Scotland and, thanks to Edward Hall's salesmanship, in France and other parts of Europe. Amid much jobbing work of high quality the Halls had helped to give operational life to ideas which might have had no more than curiosity value without the interpretive mind and mechanical skill of the manufacturer. The glamour of the inventor tends to obscure the vital contribution of the commercial partner, but the Industrial Revolution owed its success as much to craftsmanship as to creative genius. The Halls had proved the point in work on the Didot and Appert patents.

Much the most famous person to join John Hall and enlist his services in giving practical form to revolutionary concepts was Richard Trevithick, a fellow Methodist who joined the firm in 1831. Trevithick was one of the most fertile brains of the Industrial Revolution in England, an outstanding figure even among the giants of the great engineering century from 1750 to 1850. He was born in 1771, son of a mine manager in Cornwall, and himself became engineer in charge of one of the most important Cornish mines in his twenties. At that time he invented an improved mine pump and a water-power engine. In 1800 he built the first high-pressure expansion steam-engine for raising ore from deep mines: it was later taken up by John Hall and others, and remained with little variation the standard type of beam engine for nearly a century. High-pressure steam was a startling – and, leading engineers thought, a foolhardy – notion; no known material, they believed, could stand the strain. The pioneers of steam – Newcomen, Watt and others – had played for safety and used low pressure for power purposes. James Watt said that Trevithick ought to be hanged for his irresponsibility and when an explosion (due to the negligence of the boy in charge) caused several deaths, he petitioned Parliament for legislation to suppress this dangerous innovation. His opposition was understandable bearing in mind the deficiencies of materials and manufacture in his day, but history vindicated Trevithick for it was his high-pressure engines that made the steam locomotive possible. The earlier low-pressure cylinders and boilers, requiring a large amount of water for condensing, were considered at that time too bulky and heavy to mount on wheels.

In 1801 Trevithick had a locomotive built to his design by a small smithy in Camborne, Cornwall, whose plant consisted of one foot-lathe and two blacksmiths' fires. ' She was going faster than I could walk,' said an awed passenger at the first successful trials. In a later trial the model caught fire and was destroyed, but the possibilities had been demonstrated convincingly enough for Trevithick to be granted a patent in the following year. By 1808, despite lack of funds, he had built and exhibited in Euston Square the historic locomotive weighing ten tons and running on a circular track at twelve miles an hour. In the intervening years he had produced a high-pressure engine for boring brass cannon, a steam dredger (the first of its kind), a steam winch and a steam-driven digger for bringing new ground into cultivation. A plan for a tunnel under the Thames proved abortive because the directors of the company concerned failed to agree on the expense, but when Brunel built the first Thames tunnel a generation later he acknowledged his debt to Trevithick's designs.

By 1813 Trevithick's reputation spread and brought him contracts which relieved the acute shortage of money. He claimed that he was giving work to thirty foundries and that he had thirty-six engines in operation and sixteen under construction; these included machines for stone crushing and rock boring, grinding, sawing and ploughing. In 1812 and 1815 he took out patents for one of his most famous and widely applied inventions, the screw propeller for ship propulsion. His fame soon spread overseas. Some of the richest silver mines in Peru had become waterlogged and unworkable, and an influential official came to England in search of pumping machinery. He approached Boulton & Watt but their low-pressure steam-engines were too bulky, even when taken apart, to be transported by mule to the mines 20,000 feet up in the Andes. He found the answer to the problem in one of Trevithick's machines working with high-pressure steam and without vacuum or need for condensing water. After satisfactory trials he placed an order for six engines with pumps and, moreover, persuaded Trevithick to go to Peru to supervise the work.

The inventor was treated like royalty in Peru and according to Dunkin, he was received by the Viceroy and escorted to the mines by a guard of honour. He stayed in Peru for ten years and was said to have earned as much as £100,000 a year, which figure may be legendary but the ultimate catastrophe was not. The Spanish colonies in South America were in a ferment, the people had risen against their European overlords and an army led by Simon Bolivar, supported by British naval forces under Lord Cochrane, was bringing independence to Peru. Unfortunately, the populace turned against all foreigners indiscriminately, smashing Trevithick's machines and throwing them down the mines. In his flight he lost all his possessions and, after five years of adventure and hardships in other parts of the continent, eventually arrived in England penniless in 1827.

Trevithick's brain was still working even if the funds needed to fuel further creations were missing. He was one of those innocent geniuses who can work miracles but cannot make or keep money like lesser people. When he came to John Hall in 1831 he was poor and ageing, but certainly not a broken man. He developed – and Halls manufactured and supplied to several customers – steam boilers up to a pressure incredible in those times of 150 pounds per square inch. Only an engineer with John Hall's vision would have had the courage – some would have said the temerity – to provide the practical backing, but he evidently had more confidence than most engineers in the strength of the available materials. Giving evidence in 1817 before a select committee of the House of Commons on steam boats, he expressed the opinion that cast-iron was a safer material than wrought-iron for steam boilers. Pressures of 150 pounds per square inch did not become generally accepted until fifty years after Trevithick and Hall had first taken the risk.

Some ideas are too far ahead of their time because the current technical resources are insufficiently advanced to enable them to be carried out. Trevithick's contemporary Charles Babbage, for example, designed his calculating machine nearly a century before engineering science was sophisticated enough to bring it to life. Sir Henry Bessemer, as prolific an inventor as Trevithick, failed to develop a ship's stabilizer for the same reason. With John Hall's help Richard Trevithick actually achieved a prototype of one of his most imaginative concepts, a vertical reciprocating engine with pump for the propulsion of vessels by water-jet. It was installed in a ship and put through a long series of experiments, but it was beyond their capacity or indeed anyone else's at that time to develop the necessary power.*

Another interesting Trevithick design was a steam turbine, or 'whirling engine' as he called it; this is described with technical clarity but appalling spelling in a long letter accompanied by detailed technical sketches addressed in 1832 to Davies Gilbert, a lifelong friend who later became president of the Royal Society.

*Now, 150 years later, by using gas turbines rather than reciprocating engines as the power source, water-jets successfully propel the large modern passenger-carrying hydrofoil ship.

One further idea, dropped almost casually from that richly endowed brain, has special interest in view of the industrial refrigeration achievement described in this book. It is contained in a letter written by Richard Trevithick, in his characteristically grotesque spelling, to a friend in 1820:

> A few days since I was in company where a person who was saying that as much as one hundred thousands per year was paid in this place for the use of ice, the greatest part of which was brought by ships sent to the greenland seas for that express purpose. A thought struck me at the moment that artificial cold might be made very cheap by the power of steam engines by compressing air into a condencer surrounded by water, and also an injection in to the same, so as to instantly cool down the verry high compress air to the tempture of the surrounding air, and then admitting it to escape into liquid. This would reduce the tempture to any rate of cold required.

This prophetic suggestion, quoted by Everard Hesketh in his history of J. & E. Hall Ltd, anticipated by exactly half a century Hesketh's historic introduction of just such a cold-air machine into the business that he built out of the remnant of the old Dartford Ironworks.

Trevithick did not proceed further with the idea: he was busy on dozens of other inventive projects. It would be interesting to speculate on the possible consequences for the business and for the development of refrigeration and other technologies if Trevithick could have met John Hall when both were in their prime instead of near the end of their lives. A Hall and Trevithick partnership might have been as successful and famous as Boulton & Watt of steam-engine fame. Trevithick died at the age of sixty-two, and his coffin was carried to the churchyard by fellow workers. There is a macabre comment on the times in the fact that the coffin had to be strongly reinforced and sealed as a safeguard against body-snatchers. Trevithick is commemorated by a bronze tablet erected by Everard Hesketh and others in Dartford parish church and a stained-glass window in Westminster Abbey.

John Hall senior died in 1836 aged seventy-one and was buried in the parish church at Dartford, where a commemorative plaque pays tribute to his 'vigorous mind and habit of untiring application'. He had built up a substantial business employing about three hundred people and had been a humane employer; in 1825 he had built in Waterside a long row of cottages called Hall Place for his employees. He was a respected and public-spirited citizen and as a deeply religious man he had remembered throughout his life a valedictory exhortation he had received from a local preacher in his youth: 'Now you will prosper in the world. I charge you in the name of that God whose I am, and whom I serve, when you have the means to build a Methodist chapel.' The fulfilment came in 1794 when he founded Dartford's first Wesleyan chapel and Sunday school in two converted cottages on his land, his fellow trustees being Bryan Donkin and another prominent Methodist, John Edwards. Within four years the attendance had outgrown the accommodation and a new building was provided, but in 1819 this too had to be enlarged. John Hall was active also in promoting local public services and his

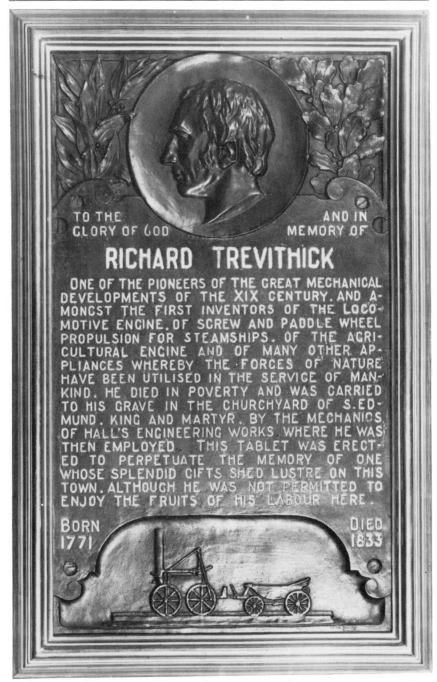

Memorial tablet in Dartford Parish Church to Richard Trevithick (1771–1833),
one of the great inventive brains of the Industrial Revolution, who worked with
John Hall senior on many engineering innovations

own craft. In association with Donkin, Simpson, Penn and other leading engineers he helped to found a Society of Master Millwrights in 1805. When the Dartford Gas Company was established in 1826, he became a member of the Board.

In his will John Hall left the engineering business to his sons John and Edward, together with four additional acres of land; his gunpowder factories at Faversham and Davington, with factories which he had bought at Erith and Tredegar, went to his sons William and Peter; and his paper mill at Horton Kirby to his son Henry. Edward returned from his long spell abroad to join his brother John in control of the main business, Dartford Ironworks, under its new name J. & E. Hall.

The two sons of John Hall who inherited his Dartford Ironworks. *Right*, John Hall junior (1792–1850), and Edward Hall (1799–1875). Edward survived to within a decade of the firm's first century

The firm had shed its powder mills, but it continued to supply gunpowder production plant to other manufacturers. Among its customers were the British, Indian, Chinese and Argentine governments, as well as private powder mills. The firm also produced heavy war material for home and overseas customers. The wars against France and the American colonies were over, but Britain remained the world's greatest military power and armaments were needed to sustain her dominance. J. & E. Hall acquired fresh fame as gunsmiths and built a special gun foundry in 1844 to fulfil a large order for 20-pounder bronze guns from the Mexican government. Many of these guns were captured by the American Army in the Mexican War of 1846–48 and are still exhibited at Trophy Point, West Point Military Academy. The guns were cast with elaborate decorative designs, unlike military material today which is severely utilitarian. The Victorians were artists in ironwork and their fire-backs and coal-hole covers are now collectors' pieces. Halls also made ornamental gun carriages for the Royal Arsenal; one of these, with an alligator emblem on the body and very ornate wheels, was used to mount a bronze cannon made in 1524 by Murad, son of Abdullah, chief gunner to the Turkish Army, and captured by the British in Egypt in 1801. It found a peaceful retirement in Horse Guards Parade, Whitehall, where it stands to this day.

Mixed engineering remained the primary function of the firm under the two brothers as under the founder. They supplied machinery to a Dartford oil and mustard mill which worked day and night to meet demands for its products at the time of the Crimean War in 1855–56. The slump in the mill-owner's products when the war ended put him out of business, but the neighbouring householders who had suffered from the noise of the stamper mills caught up on their sleep. Halls built a sawmill for a customer at Crayford Creek, who re-erected the plant in London in order to cut blocks for the first wood paving in Oxford Street. A list in Everard Hesketh's book itemizing work carried out between

Ornamental gun carriages were among the varied products of the old ironworks. This one, still standing in Horse Guards Parade, London, supports an ancient Turkish cannon captured by the British in 1801

1835 and 1885 includes a zinc-plate rolling-mill, nail-making and wire-drawing machinery, engines and rolling-mills for the Royal Mint, calico-printing machinery, sawmill plant for the East India Company, machines for making porcelain and plate glass for France, a waterworks at Cadiz, printing machines for *The Times*, the *Illustrated London News* and the *Melbourne Argus*, continuous passenger lifts (an interesting line which developed after the end of the Hall family era), and machinery for making Portland cement.

Halls built complete works for the manufacture of Portland cement at Faversham and other places, this product providing yet another example of the firm's association with pioneers of important modern industries. Portland cement was patented in 1824 by a Leeds bricklayer Joseph Aspdin, but was believed to have been produced by chance many years before either by the patentee – as his son seemed to think – or, as Everard Hesketh has suggested, by another Aspdin, owner of lime kilns at Northfleet in Kent which had been equipped with boilers and other machinery by John Hall senior. This Aspdin, said Hesketh, had levelled some very rough roads near his works and tried in the interests of economy to make lime by calcining the mixture of chalk and clay removed. As it did not slake well and could not be sold, he used it in building a wall at his works; when the wall was demolished some years later the bricks were found to have been powerfully bonded by what was, in fact, Portland cement in all but name.

Like their father, John and Edward Hall had close connections with the local community and like him they helped to fight its battles. One of these conflicts concerned a Parliamentary bill of 1846 to bring the railway to Dartford. The railway directors had drawn up plans showing the line running through J. & E. Hall's works, but Edward Hall won a concession that the line should not come nearer than a specified number of yards north of his existing buildings. It has been said that in order to get the most out of the concession he extended his territory by deliberately – and hurriedly – putting up a new 'existing' building. The story may be apocryphal, but the fact remains that when the railway was built in 1849 it ran much further north than was originally proposed.

John Hall junior died in 1850 aged fifty-eight and Edward remained in sole control for another twenty-five years. The loss of the elder brother must have been a serious blow to the firm, for he had been the business brain and Edward the production man. It is possible that the old family business had already passed its peak, for decline is rarely sudden but in retrospect may appear so because it has been imperceptible for many years. The Hall business had been born out of a revolution. Revolutions can change course for good or ill; they can also go soft. In the much larger historic sphere during J. & E. Hall's existence, one can see how the fierce dynamism of the French Revolution and the Napoleonic era crumbled into the pathetic fiasco of the Franco-Prussian War. So the impulse which had carried the founder of the Hall enterprise to wealth and influence had spent its force. The business had been in existence for sixty-five years at the time of the second John Hall's death and was being overtaken by political, social and industrial change.

This jumble of belting and apparent confusion of chains and engines in the

chine shop produced machines which gave up to a century of continuous service

The founder had not been the only bright young entrepreneur in the early years of the business, and competition had built up alongside him. For decades he was one of the leaders in his field, but leadership – unlike assets – cannot be passed on to the next generation. Orders were harder to get and customers harder to please in the last twenty years of Edward Hall's life. This was as true of foreign trade as of the domestic market, for the American Civil War had built a nation and the USA had become a power. At home a social revolution was in progress. By mid-century the example of Robert Owen's experiments in industrial relations at New Lanark and the influence of the Chartist agitation, coinciding with a great increase in trade-union membership, had made workers more aware of their value and therefore more assertive. Through the repeal of the Combination Laws they had won the legal right to make collective demands for shorter hours and better pay.

Manufacturing industry was growing up and among the multiplicity of small workshops there was now a sprinkling of large factories. Developments in the machine-tool industry were encouraging mass production and the technical movements had left J. & E. Hall behind. Towards the end of Edward's life the firm was in very poor condition, still doing competent work but with hopelessly out-of-date equipment. 'No new tools had been introduced for many years,' wrote Everard Hesketh. 'There were no travelling cranes, in fact hardly a building with parallel walls which could contain them. The foundry, in which castings of over six tons were made, was served by an old timber jib crane, the winch being worked by eight men, the top of the crane post being carried by the roof timbers of the building.'

Poor health in Edward Hall's later years may have contributed to the neglect of the business. Canon Nolloth remembered him being in a bath-chair, but said that the old gentleman was ingenious to the last and invented a pedometer, which he fixed to one of the wheels to tell him how far he had travelled. He had in fact travelled – and taken the business with him – to the edge of extinction. The management had aged beyond repair and like the tooling had not been replaced. Now young blood was needed in the top ranks to plan and execute a reorientation, for the old formula of general engineering was no longer good enough to save the business from extinction.

Edward Hall died in 1875 aged seventy-six. As he had no male heir the Hall dynasty had come to an end and it seemed inevitable that the business would die with him. Instead of sudden collapse, however, the firm was dying by inches and those inches left room for an attempt at revival. In the event the death of Edward marked an end and a beginning. A distinguished enterprise had ended in senile decay, but fortunately a senile business can be rejuvenated and to J. & E. Hall salvation came about almost by chance. Young and energetic management, new ideas and technical achievements were to provide the business with a second founder after ninety years.

Meanwhile, what was left of the business marked time for a few years. Edward Hall's executors sold the firm to E.L. Beckwith and F.E. Burke, who kept its out-of-date plant at work, trading on the reputation the Hall name had built in the old days. It was in this

EVERARD HESKETH (1858–1942)
The 'second founder' of Halls of Dartford. He restored the firm
from dereliction to prosperity, and in more than forty years as
Chairman (1880–1921) made it the world's leader in marine
refrigeration.

languishing business that twenty-year-old Everard Hesketh took a job in 1878. His father was Robert Hesketh, a successful City of London architect and surveyor to the Goldsmiths' Company. Everard had been educated at Marlborough College, took a degree in engineering at King's College of London University and was awarded the Easton Prize which procured him a three-year apprenticeship at the engineering works of Easton & Anderson in Erith, Kent. He stayed with the firm for a year after his articles had expired. His father, who knew Beckwith but apparently knew nothing about engineering nor the condition of Beckwith's business, advised him to seek further experience at J. & E. Hall.

So Everard Hesketh entered the drawing office at Dartford Ironworks. There were, he said, one and a half draughtsmen in the department besides himself! The one was James Snowden, who had joined the firm in 1837, risen to be chief draughtsman and was for a time young Hesketh's boss and mentor; by the time he retired in 1880, their relative status had been reversed. The 'half' draughtsman was Burdett, competent in his job despite having only one arm. Hesketh was depressed by the dinginess of the town but even more so, after the smartness of Easton & Anderson, by the derelict state of the business he had joined. It seemed, he said many years later, 'in a rotten condition and ripe for winding up'. He decided to stay for a year and then move on to more promising employment.

Circumstances decided otherwise. Within eighteen months Burke pulled out and offered Hesketh his shares and his partnership in the business. A year later Beckwith became seriously ill and had to retire. His share too devolved on Hesketh, who was now left in sole charge. All his money was now tied up in its crumbling buildings, a decrepit plant and a shrunken work force of just over two hundred people. There was no escape.

Years of hardship followed and there were times when he did not know where the week's wages were coming from. He was, he said, 'estimating clerk, designer, progress department, buyer, seller and traveller, and had to keep the bank manager in a sweet temper when overdrafts were very frequent'. He worked prodigious hours: one morning when he arrived at five minutes past the usual starting time of six o'clock, he wrote in his diary 'Late'. The works were still engaged mainly in the manufacture of engines, boilers and gunpowder machinery, and continued to serve the cement and paper mills against increasing competition. For some years the catalogue of miscellaneous engineering items – wheels, pulleys, forgings and castings – remained unchanged. The factory continued locally to be called 'The Foundry' until well into the twentieth century. Specialization was a long way off, the immediate preoccupation being to restore the buildings and put profits and borrowings into more up-to-date machines.

Some remnant of originality had still clung to the firm even in the last years of Edward Hall. A product of more than ordinary interest had been added to the list and continued to be marketed with some success under Hesketh. This was the 'Cyclic Elevator', a continuously moving passenger lift. It consisted of a number of cars without doors hung on a continuous chain, not stopping at any floor but travelling slowly enough for people to step safely on and off. The principle was like that of buckets on an endless chain used in the early years of mechanization for drainage, except that the Cyclic Elevator did not spill its contents at the downward point of the cycle. The circuit was planned so that the cars remained upright all the way.

Two of these lifts were still in use in an old building off Cheapside in the City of London until 1940, when the building was destroyed by bombs in the Second World War. Among other customers for these lifts were several blocks of flats in the City of London and the West End and in the head office of the *Glasgow Herald* in Glasgow. The newspaper's general manager said that the device was superior for simplicity and safety to anything he had seen in the USA. *The Engineer* magazine reported in its issue for 26 January 1883 that: 'Ladies and elderly gentleman avail themselves of it without hesitation.' Some still do. A continuous lift – a much later and more advanced type but constructed on the same principle – is still functioning in the reception area of the office block in Dartford and is used by the more agile employees in a hurry. Most elderly gentlemen prefer to wait for the orthodox lift!

William Bernard Godfrey shared the burden with Hesketh as partner and director from 1881 to 1910

The burden of one-man management was eased for Everard Hesketh when he was joined as partner in 1881 by his friend Bernard Godfrey, an electrical engineer and son of a former P. & O. director. His special function in the business was to look after finance,

53

but he was also responsible for the London office which had moved to 23 St Swithin's Lane. Godfrey remained a director of the company until 1910; 'a faithful comrade, always optimistic even through all the dark days,' said Hesketh, reporting Godfrey's death at the Annual General Meeting in 1922:

> He came down to Dartford to join me in the very uphill task of re-creating a business which certainly had the distinction of being old established, but was also old in every other respect. Very old buildings which were almost impossible to carry on work in, and machinery and equipment which were quite out of date. Well, we had a very difficult task, and we were bold enough, perhaps I should say rash enough, then, to undertake a new industry in taking up refrigeration machinery.

As the business approached its first century, youth and optimism were again at the helm.

The Dartford Works of J & E Hall
circa 1885
The works were established a hundred years previously by John Hall in 1785

CHAPTER 4

In Pursuit of Freezing

Hesketh realized that the decision to commit his business to an entirely new industry based on a commercially untried technology would be deemed either foolhardy or masterly according to the outcome. In fact, the outcome showed his judgement to have been decisive in restoring the flagging fortunes of J. & E. Hall, but it achieved much more than that: it gave the firm a coherence and a direction which it had lacked and made it a world leader in a development of immense social and industrial worth. It is doubtful whether the business could have flourished for upwards of another century, even re-launched by Hesketh's capable hands, with nothing more potent than general engineering flanked by comparatively short-term specialities. Though an engineer and businessman and not a scientist, he was aware that the advanced scientific ideas he had adopted represented the realization of an age-old dream – to give mankind a dependable and controllable method of cooling which would be independent of variables such as climate, seasons and weather. The time was ripe not only for his own modest business purposes, but also for world needs.

Before the nineteenth century, cold – unlike heat – was a climatic phenomenon only. Man had been able to acquire warmth by artificial means as far back as the Stone Age, but nature alone could create cold. Indeed, the absence of cold might often cause more serious problems than its presence. People could contrive to keep warm even in Arctic conditions, but summer heat had to be endured or else enjoyed according to circumstances. Even in temperate Britain this brought disadvantages as well as comfort and the chief adverse effect of high temperature was on perishable foods.

Country people, if they were not too poor to afford meat, could have it fresh and dwellers in the fishing ports enjoyed freshly-caught fish; but for the towns dependent upon horse-drawn transport for their supplies, meat and fish had to be preserved by smoking or by pickling with salt. In Tudor and Stuart times the taste was improved by lavish use of spices and even meat that had deteriorated was similarly masked though sometimes imperfectly. Samuel Pepys complained in his *Diary* about 'bad meat of which

I made but an ill dinner,' and again, 'At the Office all the morning, then home to dinner where a stinking leg of mutton, the weather being very wet and hot to keep meat in.'

Spices were understandably a leading item of import trade – and of plunder – for centuries. Rivalry between the English, the Dutch and the Portuguese for control of the Spice Islands blazed repeatedly into fights at sea. The urgency for food seasoning and preservation, as well as the desire for precious stones and metals, were motives for exploration in the Far East. Columbus, seeking a new route to those sources of wealth, believed that he had reached the Indies and the general name of his landfalls in the Caribbean islands perpetuates the error to this day.

The taste and the stomach for highly spiced foods diminished in the eighteenth century, but the need for food preservation became even more acute in succeeding generations. The Industrial Revolution, by transforming Britain from a mainly agricultural to a mainly manufacturing nation, accentuated the problem. Urban growth at the expense of the traditional rural economy made it increasingly difficult to feed the nation from the produce of its land. The Americas and Australia had surpluses of meat for export, but it was not until after the middle of the nineteenth century that a way was found to keep the cargoes fresh on the long haul to Europe.

The preservative property of ice was common knowledge. Rich families in Europe had harnessed it for centuries and most large estates had an ice house, an underground store in which blocks of ice could be kept for the summer. Some communities filled wells with snow for summer use. According to Fernand Braudel, in his great work, *The Mediterranean and the Mediterranean World in the Reign of Philip II*, it was not only the rich who could afford the luxury. Ice and 'snow water' were brought down from mountains only a few miles from sub-tropical coastal areas and sold to the common people for quite small sums.

In Turkey in the sixteenth century pashas made fortunes from trading in snow, and relays of fast horses carried snow from Syria to Egypt. Of course a mild or dry winter caused problems for the summer that followed; nature still called the tune. As nations advanced economically they envisaged more important uses for cold than the enjoyment of ice-cream and cold drinks. It was not surprising therefore that among the leading engineers and chemists of the nineteenth century some should turn their minds to ways of producing cold independently of winter. In experiments spread across many decades and half a dozen nations they formulated the principles of refrigeration and built the first crude but workable pieces of equipment.

Refrigeration was not the most spectacular product of the Industrial Revolution. For instance, it could not compare for public appeal with Richard Trevithick's steam locomotive roaring round Euston Square on its circular track and driving pedestrians to cover with its terrifying shower of sparks. But refrigeration was no less revolutionary in its impact on society. It enabled a winter environment to be created anywhere at any time, delayed the processes of decay in foodstuffs for long periods, controlled the ripening of fruit in transit and in store and brought to British tables produce which existed only in travellers' tales. Moreover the food industries reflect only a part, though an important part, of refrigeration's contribution to human betterment.

Hesketh, and Halls, were neither the inventors of the technology nor even the first to make it the basis of a new industry. Hesketh had, as he said, 'taken up' refrigeration. A method of cooling had been known and applied in remote centuries by primitive peoples who had no need to understand the principle or possess any other equipment than a porous water pot; it had to be porous so that some of the water could seep to the outside surface. All that was needed to keep the contents cool was to expose the vessel to the hot wind, for the hotter the wind and the harder it blew, the more effective would be the cooling.

Cooling by natural evaporation and the collection and storage of snow and ice were useful makeshifts for domestic purposes, but of little use commercially and industrially. What scientists sought in more sophisticated times was a mechanical technique for creating cold at will; but the principles were not easy to deduce from traditional practice, to say nothing of the designing of the necessary machinery. From the early years of the nineteenth century onwards, scientists built up a progressive body of thought upon which engineers could construct their working models later in the century.

Modern research began, understandably, with examination of primitive man's expedient. The earliest investigators in the second half of the eighteenth century had to accept the fact that engineering skill was not sufficiently advanced to provide the hardware they needed. In the first quarter of the nineteenth century the artificial production of cold had been demonstrated experimentally. The breakthrough cannot be attributed to any individual; it was in a sense a collaboration stretching across at least fifty years. Robert Salmon took out a patent in 1819 for his artificial cooling of liquids, and this may be said to have started the scientific refrigeration movement. The vapour compression refrigeration machine produced by James Perkins in 1834 was another landmark. Michael Faraday had already succeeded in liquefying chlorine, sulphur dioxide, nitrous oxide and other gases and pointed the way for liquefaction and the eventual solidifying of oxygen and hydrogen by Sir James Dewar and the founding of a science of low temperatures. Physicists, and the industrialists who later channelled their findings into business empires and the development of social utilities, have acknowledged their debt especially to Carnot, Clausius, Joule and Kelvin, who founded the science of thermodynamics and formulated its laws. James Prescott Joule and William Thomson (later Lord Kelvin) can be regarded as the true progenitors of mechanical cooling. The famous Joule-Thomson effect, described in 1853, showing how a fall in temperature is produced by the expansion of a gas in a vacuum, establishes the basic principle underlying the artificial creation of cold and marks the starting point of a system of industrial refrigeration.

After all that the scientists had contributed in terms of theory, a great deal of work remained to be done in planning and constructing a workable refrigeration machine. Some of the pioneers impoverished themselves and ruined their health in the effort, leaving imperfect models upon which others were to build. The path of discovery in many scientific disciplines, and in refrigeration more than most, has been paved with despair. No individual was supreme either in theory or application. Many experienced the all-too-familiar difficulty in gaining recognition for new ideas, however firmly based on experiment and deduction. Joule suffered the frustration of being rejected by leading scientists and the learned institutions, partly because of the conservatism which large brains share with small ones, but also because he was a brewer and not an academic and was therefore regarded as an amateur. It was only when the much younger but more influential Thomson gave support that respect from the scientific establishment followed. By the time that Halls entered the field there were several primitive types of machine in existence and a few development engineers who had put one or other of them to work. Halls remained among the smaller operators for some years. Luck and vision had procured them an entrée; technical skill, judgement and keen marketing were to put them in the lead.

The Prince of Wales, later Edward VII, inspecting the British Section at the opening of the Paris Exhibition, 1878

Hesketh must have known something of these developments before he joined J. & E. Hall. He had been with them only a few months when he took time off to visit the great International Exhibition in Paris, opened in 1878 to display the achievements of French scientists and industrialists before the world. There he saw a machine invented and patented in 1873 by Paul Giffard, which produced a cooling effect artificially by the compression and expansion of air. Hesketh was immediately interested and wanted to test this cold-air machine in his works. The opportunity came through one of the great pioneers of trade unionism, Robert Applegarth, a forceful man respected by Hesketh but hated – because feared – by less enlightened industrialists. Hesketh implies in his history of J. & E. Hall that Applegarth brought one of Giffard's machines to England on the advice of Sir E.J. Reed, a celebrated naval architect. Like Hesketh, Applegarth sensed the industrial and social possibilities of refrigeration and sent the machine to Halls with a view to its manufacture and sale in Britain.

Since Giffard had to create the conditions for cooling, his cold-air machine could not be a scientific refinement upon the porous pot technique. It had to work on quite a different principle: the cooling effect obtained when air or any other gas is compressed and then allowed to fall rapidly from a high to a low pressure.

In a paper presented at the Naval and Submarine Engineering Exhibition in April 1882, Everard Hesketh explained the theory of the cold-air machine as:

Paul Giffard's cold air machine, the starting point of Hall refrigeration

based upon the well-known fact that heat and work are convertible terms; any substance therefore which is made to perform work without deriving heat from any extraneous source must convert some of its own internal heat into work, and thus become sensibly colder. Thus, in the case of air, if a given volume can be made to do work by expanding against any resistance without the addition of any heat, the expanded air, having converted some of the heat into work, must be at a lower temperature than it was before expansion, and the number of units of heat lost must be proportional to the work done.

Hesketh's 'well known fact' is of course the mechanical equivalent of heat as propounded by Joule a generation earlier; and implicit in this statement is the working out in commercial practice of the Joule-Thomson effect by Halls' cold-air refrigeration machines installed in cargo ships around the world.

In describing the machine Hesketh emphasized that, in addition to the compression cylinder which one would expect to find associated with any power-driven pumping engine, there was also an expansion cylinder. Thus air, drawn in and compressed to high pressure in the first cylinder, is allowed to expand and do work in the second cylinder after some of the heat of compression has been removed. Since steam was almost universally used as the power source, it was usual to manufacture the basic cold-air machine as a three-cylinder assembly using a connecting crankshaft. While the steam cylinder provided the main power, part of the driving force was provided by the expansion of the compressed air against resistance in the expansion cylinder, prior to discharge at low temperature and at atmospheric pressure into the cold store.

The unwanted heat in the compressed air could be removed either by injecting water into the compression cylinder or by enclosing the cylinder in a water jacket. The former method was rejected because of the difficulty of ensuring a sufficient degree of purity even in fresh water, and because salt water – which would be used at sea – would have corroded the metal parts. Water jacketing avoided these disadvantages.

There was a more obstinate disadvantage due to the moisture in the air which, on cooling, was precipitated as snow. If not cleared from time to time the snow would either accumulate in the expansion cylinder and stop the machine, or be carried into and choke the air trunks in the cylinder. The Giffard patent incorporated a 'cut snow' valve which was supposed to prevent the clogging of the outlet, but Halls found that the valve was not entirely dependable. They compensated for its deficiencies by devising a snow-box to intercept the snow, pass it automatically over the pipes carrying the compressed air from the coolers to the expansion cylinder, and so enable it to melt and flow away.

However, these were later refinements upon Giffard's machine and the original was put through many weeks of testing in J. & E. Hall's works. On the premises were the parts of a small beam engine which had been made for stock many years before. When assembled the engine was used to provide belt-drive for the cold-air machine and ran for long periods without need for attention. Realizing that the potential customers would be mainly shippers of perishable foods, Everard Hesketh invited several prominent shipowners to see a demonstration. The machine had been running for thirty consecutive hours before the visit and all seemed well, but as soon as the visitors arrived the machine stopped and resisted all efforts to start it again. That J. & E. Hall were not eliminated from the international refrigeration contest but survived to lead the field must have been due to very persuasive salesmanship by Hesketh and Godfrey.

J. & E. Hall were not the first to put a cold-air machine on board a ship. There had in fact been brave but abortive attempts to transport frozen meat many years before a workable refrigeration machine had been produced. Several British patents for machines using ammonia as the refrigerant had been taken out in the 1860s jointly by Thomas Sutcliffe Mort, an English-born wool broker and financier who had settled in Australia, and Eugene Dominique Nicolle, a French engineer employed in a Sydney firm. In 1861 Mort built the world's first meat-freezing works, and demonstrated the success of his techniques some years later by feeding 300 visitors to his factory on beef and mutton which had been kept frozen in store for eighteen months. But he had greater ambitions – to ship surplus meat from Australia so that, as he said, 'the half-starved nations of the earth should be fed'. He spent over £$\frac{1}{4}$m on the project. In July 1877 he and Nicolle equipped the P. & O. steamer *Northam* with their newly patented nitrate of ammonia machine for the purpose of transporting frozen meat to England. The plant unfortunately failed at the last moment; someone had accidentally opened a cock, causing pipes to explode, and the *Northam* sailed without its cargo. It was later reported that the machine had been repaired and restored to working condition during the voyage, but the damage to Mort's spirit and fortune was irreparable and he died the following year.

It is significant that Britain and Australia should have been most assiduous in early efforts to achieve refrigerated transport for meat. Both had an acute problem: Britain a shortage and Australia an excess of meat, plus an unbridged geographical and technological gap between them. Refrigeration was the catalyst that would achieve a multiple miracle – provide a new source of revenue for Australia, New Zealand, Argentina and the shipping lines, protect meat against decay for weeks or months on voyages through tropical seas and deliver it to British tables in as fresh a condition as when it left the slaughterhouse.

Where Mort had nearly succeeded, a British firm triumphed and made refrigeration history. H. & J. Bell, meat importers of Glasgow, had sought Lord Kelvin's advice on fitting refrigeration in ships, and he had recommended them to consult Joseph James Coleman, a research chemist employed by a firm of mineral oil manufacturers. The Bell brothers and Coleman jointly took out a patent on a cold-air machine and formed the Bell-Coleman Mechanical Refrigeration Company to exploit it. A promising experimental voyage to North America in the Anchor liner *Circassian*, fitted with the firm's first machine, was followed by a more ambitious trial with their second cold-air machine installed in s.s. *Strathleven*, chartered by McIlwraith, McEachern & Co for a return voyage from England to Australia. The ship left Sydney on 29 November and Melbourne on 6 December 1879 with about 40 tons of beef and mutton, and arrived in London on 2 February 1880 with its cargo in good condition.

Cargoes of meat had been transported by sea for many years in comparatively small quantities, packed round with blocks of ice. But the source of cold in the *Strathleven* was a machine enveloping the cargo in a continuous stream of cold air which, with careful maintenance and control, would last throughout a voyage of any length under any climatic conditions. The event was a triumph for the cold-air principle. There had been successful efforts a year or two earlier by French pioneers. *Le Frigorifique*, equipped with a vapour compression machine patented by Charles Tellier and using methyl ether, had transported frozen meat from Buenos Aires to Rouen in 1877; and the steamer *Paraguay*, equipped with an ammonia refrigeration machine based on a design by Ferdinand Carré, brought 5500 carcases of mutton from Argentina to Le Havre in 1878; but the *Strathleven* had demonstrated the first completely successful carriage of a refrigerated cargo on a three-month voyage half way round the world.

Bell & Coleman had passed the post eighteen months ahead of their nearest British rival. The runner-up was Alfred Seale Haslam of Derby, who had been working on cold-air machines since 1878. In 1881 s.s. *Orient*, fitted with a Haslam machine, brought a cargo of meat from Australia, and in 1882 the sailing barque *Mataura* arrived in London with a cargo of meat from New Zealand after a voyage of 103 days.

Behind these calm voyages legal storms were brewing and J. & E. Hall were soon to be involved. In 1884 Bell & Coleman brought an action against Haslam for infringement of a patent in which they had an interest, but Haslam invalidated their opponent's case by buying up the patent. Haslam then took action against J. & E. Hall who, they maintained, had infringed this same patent for abstracting moisture from the air before expansion in order to reduce the formation of snow. Though it was proved in court that neither the deposition of water nor its removal by a drain cock was a new idea in itself, the judge ruled that the combination of the two did constitute a patent which had been infringed. Legal complications followed, in which Halls obtained a favourable verdict on a secondary point, but in the process frustrated their right to appeal against the decision on the main point at issue. Everard Hesketh found a way out, making an arrangement with Haslam to amend the original patent and averting further conflict by inventing a very effective method of removing by centrifugal action the moisture held in suspension in the air.

Improvements patented by J. & E. Hall produced cold-air machines which differed almost out of all recognition from Giffard's primitive original. They designed horizontal and vertical types to conform to the varying requirements of ship design and for ten years they successfully supplied refrigeration plant to owners of ships on the Australian and South American runs. They were not yet leaders in that field, but they did participate in some unusual projects. One of these was the shipping of 30,000 frozen carcases of mutton (a record at the time for a single cargo) from the Falkland Islands in the 3040-ton s.s. *Selembria*. There were no suitable materials or labour in the islands to

FROZEN MUTTON FROM THE FALKLAND ISLANDS,

Per S.S. "Selembria," fitted with

J. & E. HALL'S COLD AIR MACHINES.

S.S. "SELEMBRIA"—3041 TONS REGISTER.

Extract from "THE TIMES" of the 16th July, 1886.

FROZEN MEAT.—The importation of frozen meat to this country continues to increase, and the recent arrival in the East India Docks of a cargo of over 30,000 frozen carcasses of mutton in excellent condition is the latest and as yet the most extensive contribution that has been made in the form of a single cargo to the meat supply of this country. This has been brought by the steamer Selembria from the Falkland Islands, and when one considers that East Falkland was only colonized by British subjects in 1853, and West Falkland in 1861, and that there are now nearly 600,000 sheep in the islands, it seems indeed, little short of marvellous. Those brought over are described as being of prime Canterbury type, well fleshed, and with no superfluous wasteful fat, and they average from 60lb. to 70lb. each. Sales have been effected of portions of the cargo at over 5d. per pound. The steamship Selembria, chartered by the Falkland Islands Meat Company, who have entered into agreements with the owners of sheep for the supply of 60,000 per annum, is a steamer of 3,041 tons register, and was fitted out completely by Messrs. J. and E. Hall, of Dartford and London, for this trade. She left England in December last, and would in the ordinary course have returned in April but for the preparations that it was necessary to make in the first instance before the meat could be shipped, as no labour or materials were to be found on the other side. Thus it was necessary to take out a staff of butchers to deal with the meat in the first instance, stevedores to stow away the carcasses in the lower hold as soon as these were frozen, this latter operation being carried out in the 'tween decks, and mechanics to erect the necessary buildings, tramways, and derricks at the three principal ports where the meat is obtained, all this plant being taken out in the ship. The colonists have hitherto contented themselves with what they could realize with the wool, skins, and tallow, to be obtained from their sheep, but now, in consequence of this most recent development in refrigerating machinery by means of cold dry air, they will be able to send their mutton to the English market, not only to their own advantage, but also to that of the consumers over here; and there appears to be every reason to expect that the enterprise which has been entered into in so practical a manner will result in a complete success.

8B, RUMFORD PLACE,
LIVERPOOL.
28th August, 1886.

MESSRS. J. & E. HALL,
London.

DEAR SIRS,—The Cold Air Machines fitted by you in the S.S. "Selembria," froze very satisfactorily 30,000 carcases of mutton on the voyage at and from the Falkland Islands, the whole cargo arriving here in perfect condition.

Yours faithfully,

CROW, RUDOLF & CO.

SS *Selembria* which in 1886 brought 30,000 frozen carcases of mutton from the Falkland Islands to England in perfect condition prepare the cargo for shipment, and these had to be supplied from Britain. *The Times* of 16 June 1886 reported the event:

> It was necessary to take out a staff of butchers to deal with the meat in the first instance, stevedores to stow away the carcases in the lower hold as soon as they were frozen, this latter operation being carried out in the 'tween decks, and mechanics to erect the necessary buildings, tramways and derricks at the three principal ports where the meat is obtained, all this plant being taken out in the ship. The colonists have hitherto contented themselves with what they could realise with the wool, skins and tallow to be obtained from their sheep, but now, in consequence of this most recent development in refrigerating machinery by means of cold dry air, they will be able to send their mutton to the English market, not only to their own advantage, but also to that of the consumers over here; and there appears to be every reason to expect that the enterprise which has been entered into in so practical a manner will result in a complete success.

This example gives due prominence to the other side of the twofold benefit which nations have derived from refrigeration. It not only helps to feed vast populations in the affluent customer countries, but also to develop and bring prosperity to comparatively new and struggling populations in remote parts of the world. The same issue of *The Times* put the point eloquently: 'When one considers that East Falkland was only colonized by British subjects in 1853 and West Falkland in 1861, and that there are now nearly 600,000 sheep in the islands, it seems indeed little short of marvellous.'

Remarkable in a less dramatic way was the eventual outcome of New Zealand's first shipment of frozen sheep carcases and butter to Britain in s.s. *Dunedin* in 1881. Before that date there had been no direct service between the two countries; by the end of the decade direct and frequent traffic had been established and trade in other commodities had been added to enormously increased shipments of frozen food.

The full extent of the benefit brought by mechanical refrigeration to the stock raisers in South America and Australasia will be better understood when we realize that they had become reconciled to the fact that meat was largely a waste product. Lacking a sufficiently large market for meat in their own underpopulated territory, and unable to tap the potential markets in the populous developed countries of Europe, the producers bred their beasts for wool and hides and scrapped the carcases. When refrigeration arrived the farmers found that any price they could get for their meat was pure gain, instead of the former dead loss. The people of Britain should have leapt at the opportunity to get cheap meat, but for a time conservatism proved stronger than appetite. The general public were suspicious of the low prices and prejudiced against refrigeration, imagining that the thawed meat lacked flavour. Contrary to the general opinion even in the trade, butter was found to suffer no deterioration in quality or flavour when brought over frozen from Australia in ships fitted with J. & E. Hall's cold-air machines. S.s. *Strathleven* had carried two tons of butter and delivered it in excellent condition, but it took time for people to appreciate their good fortune.

The benefits were not only dietary and economic but also hygienic. When one realizes how recklessly food was exposed to flies and dirt, and handled in unhygienic conditions, one is surprised that food poisoning and epidemics did not wipe out whole populations. Attempts were made from the mid-nineteenth century onwards to clean up the environment by public health legislation. Apart from health hazards, diet was generally poor in quantity and variety in Victorian Britain, and not only among the labouring classes. The rich over-ate (chops for breakfast were not a myth) and many of the poor starved, but even the fairly comfortable middle classes ate little meat and fresh vegetables. Import of live animals was officially restricted for fear of spreading cattle diseases, and meat was scarce and comparatively expensive. Yet *Strathleven*'s first cargo of frozen meat had to be sold at half the prevailing retail prices and made a loss. It took three or four years for consumers to overcome their suspicion and benefit from reduced prices, and for the optimism of the importers of frozen meat to be vindicated in profitable sales.

By the time Hesketh delivered his paper on the economics of refrigerated food the market was on the way to recovery. He explained the benefits with figures which have only a period interest today, but which reveal his detailed knowledge of what his products brought to the user.

SS *Elderslie* built at Jarrow in 1884; the first ship built specifically to bring refrigerated meat from New Zealand. (*Courtesy of the National Maritime Museum, Greenwich*)

Mutton can be obtained in Australia at . . .	1¼d to 2d per lb
Cost of freezing and carriage to the coast . . .	0¾d ,, ,,
Cost of freight by the Orient Line . . .	2½d ,, ,,
Charges in London including storage at docks, carriage and all dues . . .	0½d ,, ,,
Total cost per lb . . .	5¾d

A cargo of 6,000 sheep lately sold in London at 6½d per lb, showing a profit of ¾d per lb, but of course the price at which it will sell depends upon the condition of the market. One advantage of this system is that it can be kept at the docks in chambers which are provided for the purpose, until such time as the market price is good. At the Victoria Docks, the London and St Catherine's Dock Company have fitted up 11 chambers which are capable of containing in all nearly 8,000 carcases of sheep. There are two cold-air machines connected with them, which are capable of reducing the temperature to the required degree of coolness to maintain the meat in a frozen condition. It is evident from the figures above that even when the market is at its lowest a very good margin of profit is left.

Hesketh anticipated other uses for refrigeration which are now commonplace. One of these was for the preservation of ships' provisions – dairy produce and vegetables as well as meat. 'It is hardly too much to expect,' he said, 'that before many years have passed all first-class passenger steamers will be provided with cold-air machines, not only on account of the greater inducements which ships so provided will be able to hold out to passengers over any not so provided, but on account of the saving effected in the actual cost over the practice of carrying livestock.' He explained how his machines could be used to blow cool air into cabins for the comfort of passengers and crews voyaging in tropical seas, and thus foresaw the eventual relationship between refrigeration and air-conditioning. Fishing vessels equipped with his smaller cold-air machines could stay out longer and take advantage of favourable conditions instead of having to hurry back to port only partly laden in order to deliver the catch in marketable condition. He recommended that marine users of refrigeration should install two machines so that if one broke down a valuable cargo would not be lost. A further advantage was that if both machines were of equal capacity both could be used in tropical conditions, while one alone might be adequate in temperate waters.

For ten years following Everard Hesketh's momentous visit to the Paris Exhibition J. & E. Hall developed and produced machines based on Giffard's principles. They were supplied almost exclusively to importers of perishable foods and to the dock companies for installation in the cold stores into which the cargoes were transferred. Halls issued full instructions on the operation and maintenance of the refrigeration plant, and on how to identify and deal with possible causes of trouble. They explained how to stow meat, poultry and fish in the refrigerated chambers, how to deal with milk and vegetables and how to produce ice. Some of the instructions read rather quaintly today;

The meat chamber should, during the voyage, be entered not oftener than once a day, and the door should be closed while the man is in. The vegetable chamber can be entered oftener, but only as often as is actually necessary. (Men entering the cold chambers should take the precaution of breathing only through the nose and not through the mouth.)

J. & E. Hall won high praise for their cold-air machines, gaining the highest award at the Cork Industrial Exhibition in 1883 for preserving dairy produce, and the gold medal in the same year at the International Fisheries Exhibition. In 1884 they won one gold medal (the highest award) for conserving, storing, conveying and distributing fresh foods of all kinds, and another for preparation of articles of food. Further honours came from Paris, Vienna and New Zealand. Despite the acclaim, however, the cold-air period was not highly profitable for the firm. 'In those ten years,' said Hesketh, 'I don't think that we made five per cent on our capital.'

What he did make, of course, was much bigger than immediate profit. Marine refrigeration, permitting the successful transport of beef, mutton and lamb from distant countries, was probably the biggest advance in industry since 1851, the year of the Great Exhibition which had displayed Britain's inventive talent and enterprise to the world. It had influenced beneficially the eating habits and nourishment of the people and had incidentally laid the foundation of a profitable future for the company. Not everyone welcomed the innovations. The domestic stock raisers grumbled that the meat imports had clipped their prices and diminished their industry, which was true enough, but there are losers as well as winners even in the most beneficent revolutions.

Cold-air refrigeration was not the only system on the market. It had advantages for J. & E. Hall and their customers because it provided direct cooling of the air where the produce was stored, without the complexity of ammonia and other refrigerating systems with their associated pipelines and indirect cooling arrangements. Cold-air refrigeration was a simple system with comparatively few components and its complete lack of toxicity made it particularly suitable for marine requirements. In the improved designs developed by Hesketh, Halls' cold-air machine launched the company well and truly into the international market for refrigeration, but cold air was not in general the most efficient medium. By the end of the nineteenth century, systems based on different principles were to take over and provide the foundation for modern refrigeration practice.

One of these principles was partly implicit in the primitive methods briefly referred to earlier, of evaporating water from a porous vessel. Since heat is required to evaporate a liquid, most of the heat needed to evaporate the water in the vessel is taken from that water, which is cooled in consequence. The necessary heat for this evaporation is known as 'latent' heat: it may be defined as the amount of heat absorbed by a substance in the process of changing from a solid to a liquid and from a liquid to a vapour. Similarly, latent heat is released when those two processes are reversed. For instance, when ice is melting no increase in the amount of heat will change the temperature of the substance

J. & E. HALL'S
COLD DRY AIR MACHINES (PATENT.)

   "Z" SIZE.

BRONZE MEDAL, 1883.

London Offices: 23, ST. SWITHIN'S LANE.
Telephone No. 1846.

GOLD MEDAL. 1883.

Works: DARTFORD, KENT, ENGLAND.

PRICE £125.
Approximate size of Cold Chamber 1,000 cubic feet.

Engineers, Millwrights,

Founders and Boilermakers.

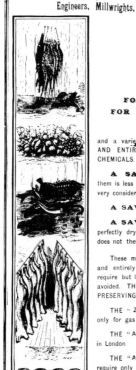

FOR PRESERVING

MEAT	BUTTER
FISH	EGGS
POULTRY	FRUIT
MILK	VEGETABLES

FOR MAKING ICE, FOR BACON CURING,
FOR COOLING LIQUIDS, CHOCOLATE, BEER, &c.
FOR REFINING OIL,

and a variety of other purposes by means of **COLD DRY AIR ONLY** AND ENTIRELY WITHOUT THE AID OF DANGEROUS GASES OR EXPENSIVE CHEMICALS. These Machines effect

A SAVING IN WORKING EXPENSES. The cost of working them is less than that of using ice. In hot weather the difference will be found to be very considerable.

A SAVING OF SPACE. The space occupied by the ice is entirely saved.

A SAVING OF MEAT, &c. The air from the Machine being delivered perfectly dry no moisture is deposited on the meat as when ice is used—the meat does not therefore require to be trimmed, and a considerable saving is effected.

These machines can be applied to existing Refrigerating Rooms or Meat Safes. and entirely take the place of ice. They can be set to work at any time, and require but little attention. All trouble and expense in obtaining and carting the ice is avoided. THEY ARE ALSO BEING MOST SUCCESSFULLY EMPLOYED FOR COOLING AND PRESERVING MILK, BUTTER, &c., &c.

THE "Z" SIZE MACHINE driven by a 2-horse Gas Engine costs 3d. per hour only for gas in London, or it can be worked from any existing motive power.

THE "A" MACHINE driven by a Gas Engine costs only 7d. per hour for gas in London.

THE "AA" MACHINE and all larger sizes have a steam cylinder combined, and require only a boiler for supplying them with steam.

Prices and Particulars of Boilers sent on application.

For larger sizes for preserving Meat Cargoes and Stores and for Preserving Food on Passenger Ships. apply for Complete Catalogue.

ESTABLISHED 1785.

"A" SIZE.

PRICE £225.
Approximate Size of Cold Chamber 2,650 cubic feet.

"AA" SIZE.
(With Steam Cylinder.)

PRICE £250.
Approximate size of Cold Chamber 2,650 cubic feet.

"B" SIZE.

PRICE £450.
Approximate size of Cold Chamber 9,000 cubic feet.

Poster to advertise Hall's Cold Dry Air Machines, which were shown in operation at the International Health Exhibition, 1884, where the firm was awarded a Gold Medal for conservation, storage and distribution of fresh food.

until it is all converted into water; and when water is boiling no amount of heat will increase its temperature until it is all converted into water vapour. In short, any change in the state of a substance from liquid to gas or vice versa and from liquid to solid and vice versa, results in the transference of heat without a change in temperature.

It is also well-known that the boiling point of water is lower on a mountain top where air pressure is lower than at sea level, and higher in a deep mine where the air pressure is higher. This relationship between boiling temperature and pressure was recognized by Michael Faraday in 1823, and he made a significant contribution to the art of refrigeration as we know it today by proving that, if the vapour of a volatile liquid is compressed, the increased pressure results in the condensation process occurring at a higher temperature. This change of boiling temperature with change in pressure is the fundamental principle of mechanical compression refrigeration. A fluid, which is known as the primary refrigerant, is evaporated at the appropriate pressure and the latent heat absorbed gives the cooling effect. The vapour formed is then compressed to a higher pressure, so that the condensation temperature is above that of some readily available cooling medium such as air or water, the latent heat of condensation being rejected. The liquid refrigerant formed as a result is then passed through a flow control device and is returned to the evaporator.

This system was originally demonstrated as being viable by Jacob Perkins in 1834 when he first made ice using ether as the primary refrigerant and employing a hand-operated compressor. Carl von Linde, a German engineer, patented a refrigeration machine working on this principle at much the same time as Giffard, but he used ammonia as the primary refrigerant. Ferdinand Carré, a French inventor, had patented a system of refrigeration by absorption of liquefied gases or condensed vapour as early as 1860, and designed an ammonia machine which preceded by only a year or two those put to limited but successful land use by Mort, Nicolle and others. But Linde was the great pioneer of this development in refrigeration technology. He put his first ammonia compression machine to work in a Munich brewery, formed companies to exploit his invention in many countries including Britain, established a Refrigeration Research Institute in Munich and engaged in low-temperature research. J. & E. Hall with their cold-air machine were small fry by comparison and their day was still to come; indeed, it came a generation before Linde's death in 1934 at the age of ninety-two.

Linde was ahead of his time in using ammonia. Its dangers were known and many potential users felt, with some justice, that technology at that time was not adequate to prevent dangerous leakage. Ammonia is toxic and can prove fatal if inhaled; high concentrations can lead to an explosion hazard. J. & E. Hall were aware of the limitations of cold air as a refrigerant and appreciated the superiority of systems based on the compression and expansion of more volatile gases. They were wary of ammonia because they realized that the possibility of leakage and the risk of contaminating food made it more suitable for use on land than in the confined space of a ship's hold. Though they did make some slight use of ammonia refrigeration machines on land before the end of the

Cold air machine for use on
land, designed and built by
J. & E. Hall.

Hall's No.6 Cold Air
Machine, built in 1886

century, it was not until 1910 that they introduced ammonia refrigerating plant into
their product range. In 1887, sensing that cold air would before long be outclassed by
more sophisticated techniques, they decided – wisely as it turned out – to switch to a
safer gas than ammonia, called at the time carbonic anhydride (or dissolved in water,
carbonic acid) but familiar to us as carbon dioxide, CO_2. This was an inspired decision
and a momentous one in the history of the business which put Halls ahead of the
competition particularly in the marine sphere and largely determined the course of the
business throughout more than a century of refrigeration practice.

CHAPTER 5
CO₂ *Takes Over*

As with cold air, so with its successor a decade later Hesketh played for safety. Air might have seemed a timid choice when for more than half a century pioneers of refrigeration had been experimenting with potentially explosive or poisonous gases, as well as with the mild ubiquitous medium in which we all live and breathe. There had been plenty of evidence besides the work of Giffard to show the possibilities of cold air, as there was also in 1887 for the chemically inoffensive CO_2. In 1835 a French physicist named Thilorier had solidified carbonic acid and used it as dry ice to solidify mercury. In the same year a Scottish chemist, Kenneth Kemp, solidified carbonic acid for the first time in Britain. In 1867 an American inventor Thaddeus Lowe had described how carbonic acid or other gas could be used for refrigeration by compressing it into a liquid state and then relieving the pressure so that it reverted to the gaseous state. He had used CO_2 to freeze meat for coastal transport in the USA. Hesketh decided that the most practical and up-to-date system based on CO_2 was that of Franz Windhausen of Brunswick. Windhausen was known in Britain for his experiments with a variety of refrigerating agents; he had worked on cold-air machines at about the same time as Giffard and taken out patents in 1869, 1873 and 1876. He had also patented sulphuric acid machines in 1878 and 1880, and one of them was used by the Aylesbury Dairy Company. In 1886 he patented a compressing pump for a carbonic acid compression machine. The following year Hesketh acquired for J. & E. Hall the right to manufacture on a royalty basis their first range of CO_2 machines, based on one of Franz Windhausen's patents.

In 1887 also, Everard Hesketh was joined by a brilliant engineer, Alexander Marcet, and it was to Marcet that he gave the main credit for the firm's successful development of the CO_2 machine. Marcet was, like Hesketh, educated at Marlborough College and London University. He was articled to George Forrester & Company of Liverpool, manufacturers of large marine engines. In 1883 he joined the East Ferry engineering works and was put in charge of the erection of hydraulic machinery at Millwall Docks. He was twenty-eight years old when he became a partner in J. & E. Hall and started the

71

long series of experiments that gave CO_2 and Halls the lead in the refrigeration industry in Britain.

Hesketh's description of these experiments has commercial as well as technical interest, because it shows how much remains to be done in the workshop before theories can be converted into practice and prototypes remodelled into effective working machines.

Alexander Marcet, third member of the restoration team, as
Hesketh's partner and director of the business till
his death in 1903

The first CO_2 machine made by J. & E. Hall was a two-stage compressor, in which the first stage of compression was effected in the orthodox way by the action of a piston in a horizontal cylinder, and the second stage completed in a vertical cylinder containing a column of glycerine. An unsatisfactory feature of this second stage was that some of the glycerine was carried over with the CO_2. However, a machine of this type was installed on 16 August 1889 in a frozen meat store in Smithfield and set to work. At 2 a.m. the pipe conveying the gas from the first to the second stage compressor burst because of a mechanical fault. 'The pipe was literally blown to ribbons,' said Everard Hesketh, 'and had it not been for the sides of the water tank surrounding the compressor (afterwards discarded as unnecessary) my head, which was only a yard away, would have been the target for some of the pieces.'

The pipe had been tested to a pressure of 3000 pounds per square inch, but it was believed that the pressure when it burst had been between 7000 and 8000 pounds. To prevent such accidents in future, Halls invented a safety-valve which relieved the excess pressure and was at the same time completely gas-tight. The use of glycerine was discontinued and a simple double-acting compressor replaced the two-stage type. Leakage of CO$_2$ had occurred through the perishing of the leather used at the hot joints of the machine. Lead was tried as an alternative, but was not sufficiently elastic to compensate for contraction due to the cooling of the joint. Eventually, a joint ring made out of solid drawn copper pipe was fitted and proved so successful that it was also adopted by other makers of CO$_2$ compressors. An even more tricky problem, to make the piston rod gland tight, was solved by a device which procured a valuable patent for the firm. It involved the precision grinding of high carbon steel – difficult to achieve on the machine tools used at that time. There were other problems with materials; the smaller compressors were made of gunmetal which tended to be porous, but the deficiency was overcome by more precise methods of mixing, moulding and casting.

These were just a few of the embryonic difficulties which had to be eliminated before the CO$_2$ system was fit to be installed in a ship. The first vessel to be fitted with Halls CO$_2$ refrigeration was the *Highland Chief* in 1890. Even at that stage the complications had not been completely mastered and Hesketh and Marcet stayed on board for three weeks until they were satisfied that no weak link remained. The shipment was a brilliant success and the cargo, consisting of 39,000 carcases of mutton and 2000 quarters of beef, was landed in excellent condition. 'We have not had or heard of any cargo this size', wrote the shipowners James Nelson & Sons, 'having been heretofore landed without a single pound of meat (as in this case) being destroyed or damaged.' Within five or six years Halls had supplied eight more large machines to this firm.

As in refrigeration systems to this day the basic plant consisted of four parts: a compressor, a condenser, an evaporator and an expansion device. CO$_2$ gas, drawn from the evaporator into the compressor, was compressed to a point at which it could be liquefied and became warm in the process. The warm gas then passed into coils of pipes in the condenser, where the surrounding cooling water caused the gas to liquefy. Finally, the liquid CO$_2$ passed through an expansion device into coils of pipe in the evaporator. In these pipes, surrounded by the medium to be cooled, the liquid vaporized at the desired temperature. This process of compression, condensation, expansion and evaporation was then repeated in a continuous cycle, using the single original charge of CO$_2$ with very slight loss requiring only an occasional replacement. An interesting fact about Halls' CO$_2$ system was that the compressor formed only one part (though, of course, the basic part) of a combined unit, which comprised also a built-in condenser and evaporator, a steam-engine serving as the prime mover in the larger plants together with, in some cases, a steam condenser. Obviously, packaged units are a much older concept than is generally realized.

It was the cyclic character of the machine's operation that distinguished it most radically from the cold-air machine. The latter blew cold air directly into the refrigerated chamber, but the volume of air was small and resulted in an uneven temperature around the cargo. This defect was partly overcome by the use of fans, which caught up the cold air and distributed it more evenly throughout the space. The cooling effect of the gas compression machine, however, could not be applied directly to the cold chambers because the refrigerant was contained in a closed cycle. The cold generated by the machine had to be conveyed to the cargo space by lengths of piping containing brine fixed to the walls of the hold. It was those brine pipes, used on a scale never before attempted, which gave Hesketh and Marcet so much trouble during their last-minute day and night work on the ship. The source of the trouble was the method of connecting the lengths of piping into a continuous channel for the brine. The connection was a cast-iron U-bend secured by a nut on the end of a rod passing through the pipe. The bends were sealed with rubber jointing rings, and it was a long and arduous task to ensure that the joints were leak-proof.

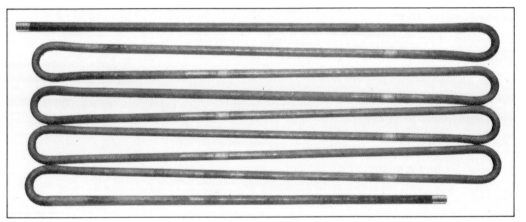

Welded brine grid

Lessons learnt on this job led to an important innovation. J. & E. Hall were already using electric welding to make firm joints in the coils of tubing enclosed in the condenser and the evaporator of a refrigeration machine. They had probably been the first engineering works in the country to apply this technique, and believed that it could be used with equal success for the much heavier piping of the brine grid. With a pipe-bending machine of their own design and their electric welding expertise, they were able to produce jointless piping in prefabricated sections which could be erected on site with minimal jointing work to form a continuous system up to 200 feet and more in length. This method eventually became standard practice among manufacturers of refrigeration plant. The brine grids were tested after erection by air pressure instead of by water, and this method too was adopted as standard by all makers. The *Highland Chief* was the first ship to be fitted with brine pipes, and much of its success in delivering a record cargo of meat without loss was attributed to the innovation.

In Europe it was Halls' CO_2 machines and Linde's ammonia machines, rather than the cold-air technique, which established the principle of refrigeration as we know it today. In both cases the use of a rather mysterious gas instead of the familiar air caused misgivings among customers. The toxicity of ammonia was known, but even CO$_2$ was for a time suspect. The Board of Trade had ruled that machines using ammonia and other poisonous gases should be housed away from the engine room and passenger quarters in ships, in a well-ventilated space with easily accessible exit for the attendant. Makers of ammonia machines, disturbed over the competitive success of CO$_2$, petitioned for the same ruling to be applied to CO$_2$ machines and Halls were obliged to defend the harmlessness of their refrigerant:

> Instead of arguing the point, [wrote Everard Hesketh] the firm asked the Board to send a surveyor to a ship lying in London fitted with a large duplex CO$_2$ machine located in the engine room. Mr Marcet met him and (the surveyor having got up to a safe place on an upper platform) proceeded to blow out the complete charge of CO$_2$, first from one side of the machine, then from the other, while workmen were working in the engine room. The Board was presumably satisfied, as no new regulation was issued.

The safety of CO$_2$ should have been widely understood, since it was already being used to aerate mineral waters and bottled beers. It had no smell or taste, was non-corrosive and non-inflammable and could not contaminate food or drink. It was of course a by-product of fermentation in brewing. Halls not only sold refrigerating machines to brewers for cooling purposes, but as early as 1890 had supplied Arthur Guinness & Sons in Dublin with plant to liquefy and collect the gas; its capacity was 200 pounds of liquid CO$_2$ an hour. This branch of the firm's service grew along with other land applications of refrigeration.

A cloth-bound illustrated catalogue and handbook published by the firm in 1896 shows how far the business had progressed. It explains the CO$_2$ system and its applications, lists land and marine users, illustrates and describes the range of machines, gives instructions for operating and maintaining them, quotes letters from satisfied users in all parts of the world and reprints a description of Dartford Ironworks from the 1 May 1895 issue of *Shipping*. Among the customers were the British War Department, the governments of Russia, Niger Coast Protectorate, Nepal and Australia, all the leading shipping lines, cold stores, brewers, ice factories, bacon curers, dairies, and 'gentlemen's private mansions'. By 1896 Halls had manufactured 400 CO$_2$ machines and were producing 150 more a year. The machines were remarkably dependable. The risk of meat being delivered in bad condition was so slight, said Hesketh in 1935, that insurance rates against all risks in the Argentine trade had fallen to less than one quarter of what they had been in the 'cold air' days of 1886. The machines were also foolproof in use. Thanks to the small amount of CO$_2$ used and the patent safety valve, states the old catalogue, 'even the neglect of the attendant is provided for and nothing in the nature of an explosion can possibly occur'.

There was no abrupt change from cold air to CO$_2$. Cold-air machines continued to be used in naval craft for some time after the introduction of Halls' carbonic anhydride machines. According to figures published in 1893, cold-air machines were installed in about 120 steamships other than naval vessels and in more than seventy land-based establishments. Many users of the cold-air machines, however, switched to CO_2 and reported savings of four-fifths of the coal consumption. The versatility of the new machines was a further source of economy. Chilled as well as frozen meat was now being imported into Britain; s.s. *Gothic* brought the first cargo of chilled beef from New Zealand in 1895. Some ships from the River Plate brought both chilled and frozen beef in different chambers, requiring different temperatures. To save the customer the expense of installing separate refrigeration machines, Halls introduced the 'warm brine' tank from which brine was circulated to the higher temperature holds; these brine circuits were cooled by controlled injection of cold brine from the main system serving the colder compartments.

The freezing capacity of the CO_2 system has yielded a piece of mythology such as most major industrial developments seem to generate. The story goes that one of Hall's erecting engineers, having completed a large installation in a ship for the frozen meat trade, put it through a thirty-hour trial, bringing all the holds to 35°F. below freezing point. He and the owner's superintendent engineer, satisfied that all was well, left the ship at 5 p.m., forgetting that they had omitted to switch off the refrigeration. Since nobody else had the authority to interfere, the plant was left running all night and next morning the ship was found to be frozen hard to the dock wall!

Special machines and ancillary equipment were designed for land use and one of Halls' patents was the brine wall. This consisted of parallel steel plates fitted together to form hollow panels in which the brine circulated. The panels were suspended at intervals in the cold store and the meat was hung on hooks in the spaces between. The cold brine walls absorbed the heat radiated from the meat, reducing it quickly to the desired temperature. The brine in the walls remained cold long after the machine had been stopped, which was very convenient for butchers and fishmongers who could keep unsold goods in store overnight or at the weekend without the further cost of running the machine.

Brine walls were also used for cooling fruit, creating a constant circulation of air at an even temperature in conditions dry enough to prevent mildew but not so dry as to shrivel the fruit. Fruit imports, mainly from South Africa, Australasia, Canada and the Caribbean increased substantially in the 1890s. Soft fruit such as peaches, tomatoes and grapes as well as apples and pears responded well to refrigeration. Unlike meat and fish, however, fruit is a living organism which would be destroyed by freezing; therefore it is kept at a temperature just cold enough to arrest ripening in order to ensure that it is as fresh on arrival as when despatched. Bananas were a special case and carried in special ships, as they still are. J. & E. Hall played an important part in the development of what was, before the beginning of the present century, virtually a new trade.

Up to 1897 bananas were imported into Britain almost exclusively from the Canary Islands. The trade was fairly small, but other sources were too distant for the fruit to survive the voyage in the absence of temperature control. The bunches of bananas were packed in crates and usually carried on deck, but taken below in cold weather. A larger

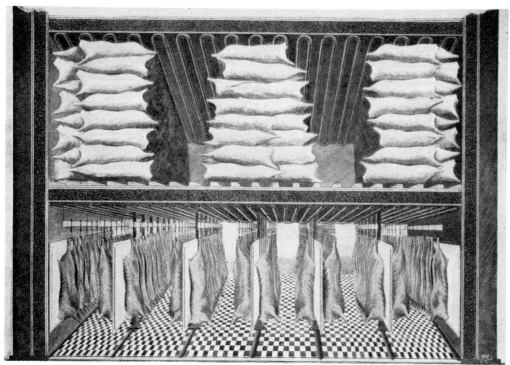

J. & E. Hall's patent brine wall system of meat freezing and chilling by radiation

variety of banana was grown in Jamaica in abundance, but shippers did not know how to handle bananas on a long voyage and a Jamaican company had chartered Australian meat ships to bring bananas to London with disastrous results.

Jamaica's sugar industry was in decline and the British Colonial Secretary Joseph Chamberlain was anxious to help the island to develop a banana trade with Britain. He approached A.L. (later Sir Alfred) Jones, chairman of Elder, Dempster & Co. of Liverpool, with regard to establishing a subsidized line of special banana boats. After some difficulty over the size of the subsidy and an abortive attempt by the Colonial Office to launch the project through another source, Jones agreed to take over and to enlarge two ships, the *Port Morant* and the *Port Maria*, and run them through a new organization, the Imperial Direct West India Mail Service. Meanwhile Arthur H. Stockley, manager of Elder, Dempster's Canary fruit department, inquired into methods of mechanical cooling of fruit cargoes which might be adapted successfully for bananas. He knew that apples were coming regularly from Australia in White Star Line ships equipped by J. & E. Hall with a system of cooled air circulated by steam-driven fans, and Alexander Marcet confirmed that the same method would be suitable for bananas. The banana boats were therefore fitted with Hall duplex CO_2 machines, air coolers and fans, and the bananas, instead of being crated at great expense, were stacked loose in bins in the refrigerated chamber in such a way that cold air could circulate between the bunches and the individual bananas.

Associated with Stockley and Marcet in this pioneer scheme was H.J. Ward, at that time (1900) in charge of Elder, Dempster's construction department. He was soon to join Hesketh on the Board of J. & E. Hall, and eventually succeed him as chairman of the company.

The original ships were soon joined by two larger vessels, *Port Royal* and *Port Antonio*, and a few years later by a much larger and more up-to-date ship *Port Kingston*. This was very different from the ordinary conception of a 'banana boat'. It was of 7000 tons burden and carried second-class passengers in accommodation equal to that of Atlantic liners, in addition to 40,000 bunches of bananas or the equivalent in other fruit. For the benefit of passengers and crew the ship was fitted with one of Hall's combined plants to supply refrigeration to the wine cooler, meat room, fish room, general fruit and vegetable room, an ice-making plant and water coolers in various parts of the ship. As the trade prospered a separate company, Elders & Fyffes Ltd, was formed to handle it by a merger of Elder, Dempster's fruit department and a long established Canary firm Fyffe, Hudson & Company.

More ships were added to the banana fleet, all equipped with cooling plant by J. & E. Hall. The association proved long and rewarding for all concerned, not least for Jamaica. The British public also gained by the addition of bananas – cheaply and in quantity – to their diet. As demand increased in Britain and on the Continent, Elders & Fyffes joined forces with the American United Fruit Company to ensure a continuous supply through their Caribbean and Central American interests. This brought orders to J. & E. Hall for refrigeration plant in United Fruit Company ships serving the USA market. Further orders came to Halls when Italy and France developed banana imports from their respective African colonies of Somaliland and the Cameroons.

Food and drink producers and suppliers were and have remained the biggest users of refrigeration both at sea and on land. Ice manufacture was largely accessory to food processing and preservation and was one of the early results of attempts by inventors to produce a commercially viable system of refrigeration. Americans have claimed that honour for John Gorrie and the Australians for James Harrison. When Gorrie patented his ice machine in 1850 he was condemned in some quarters as a crank who believed he could make ice as good as God Almighty.

In the 1890s and until well into the twentieth century, ice was invariably made in large oblong blocks for delivery by lorry mainly to fishmongers and caterers. These blocks were produced in galvanized steel or tinned copper moulds immersed in a brine tank refrigerated by a CO_2 plant, and were released from the mould by thawing. Ordinarily the ice would be opaque owing to the presence of microscopic air bubbles, but crystal-clear ice for use in bars and restaurants was produced by a process of water agitation to drive out the air. Hall machines for ice-making were supplied to the Middle East, India, Burma and Australia.

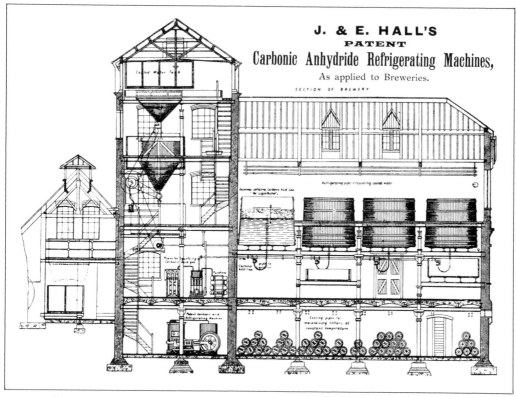

J. & E. Hall's patent carbonic anhydride refrigerating machines as applied to breweries

Additional to Hall's refrigeration service was the supply of liquid CO_2 in sealed cylinders, mainly for aerating mineral waters. Marcet claimed, in a paper read before the Institute of Brewing in 1894, that it saved three-quarters of the power, labour and cost of conventional aeration methods. Used in bottling beer, liquid CO_2 reduced the maturing process from three weeks to three days. The liquid was also used for a variety of other purposes, from aerating bread to hardening armour plates.

Industrial (i.e. non-food) applications of refrigeration on land were not very far advanced prior to the twentieth century. Apart from brewing, which is not strictly 'non-food', refrigeration was used on land for such purposes as cooling oil and for rubber, gunpowder and chemicals manufacture. An exceptional marine user outside food transport and processing was the Royal Navy. In 1897 H.M.S. *Sans Pareil*, a battleship, replaced its cold-air machine with a Hall CO_2 plant for magazine cooling, and other fighting ships – and navies – followed.

An obvious non-food use of refrigeration was for making ice rinks. Halls were not the first refrigeration specialists to prepare skating surfaces, but their contribution helped to improve comfort and safety. Earlier rinks had been formed by circulating brine (a solution of calcium chloride in water, with a low freezing point) through a system of pipes immersed in shallow water; but the water froze unevenly, leaving a bumpy surface which had to be levelled by scraping. Moreover, in those days before the development of pipe welding on site leaks sometimes occurred at the pipe joints, causing discolouration and local melting of the ice. In order to avoid these disadvantages Halls, in cooperation with the firm of Tyler & Ellis, designed a new type of patented floor, the first of which was installed successfully in 1896 for the National Skating Rink (formerly Hengler's Circus) at Argyle Street in London's West End. The floor consisted of a shallow water-filled tray of thin steel in which a continuous stream of cooled brine flowed to produce a two-inch-thick ice surface. According to a Hall catalogue of that date, 'the brine, being also under a small pressure, acts as an elastic cushion, and although forming an absolutely reliable support, it has sufficient elasticity to prevent a serious concussion. The effect produced is an exact reproduction of the natural ice when first formed on the surface of a lake.' Time has yielded a wry comment on Hall's boasted claim to the superiority of their method, since modern rinks have reverted to the use of pipes for freezing, though plastic piping is now often preferred to steel.

Up to the end of the century J. & E. Hall continued to supply the miscellaneous items of a general engineering workshop, but the CO_2 machine had become their major speciality. It had restored the firm's profitability and put them at the head of the refrigeration league table with a considerable lead over their nearest rival. The machines gained top awards year after year at international exhibitions. In 1895 Hesketh reported that Halls had seventy-three CO_2 machines permanently working in the tropics or on board ships constantly passing through the area with cargoes of frozen or chilled meat and fruit. The completely innocuous character of CO_2 had won the confidence of the food industries and the meticulous construction, operation and economy of the machines were creating what would prove to be long and happy business connections. In 1891, after repeated efforts to gain a footing in Harland & Wolff's Belfast yard, Everard Hesketh obtained contracts worth £70,000 for refrigeration plant to be installed in two big White Star Line ships. 'Since that time,' he said in 1928, 'we have never had to approach the Belfast yards again.'

To cope with the increasing business the factory buildings were modernized and the latest machine tools were installed. The old foundry was demolished and a larger building 130 by 30 feet erected which had a capacity of a hundred tons of castings a week. Another building 200 by 90 feet housed the engine shop, the boiler shop and the tube-bending and electric-welding plant. The ramshackle business that Hesketh had taken over less than twenty years before was now one of the leading employers in Dartford and had a world-wide sale for its products. The good name of J. & E. Hall had survived the years of decline and the meticulous quality of Hall refrigeration under the Hesketh command had reaffirmed the reputation established by the founding family.

Testing of components and finished products at Dartford Ironworks was severe and pipes and joints were subjected to three times the pressure they would have to withstand in practice: Lloyds and the Board of Trade required tests only twice the working pressure for boilers and engines. First came a hydraulic test up to 3300 pounds per square inch; next, a compressed air test at 1400 pounds per square inch under water to reveal not only weakness in a joint but any porosity in the metal; and finally the assembled machine was made to cool a measured quantity of water to a definite temperature before it was allowed to leave the works. All this was apart from tests *in situ* conducted by the company's erecting engineers. No chances were taken with the quality of materials; since CO_2 was non-corrosive the parts were made of wrought steel. 'Cast-iron is entirely avoided on account of its treacherous properties,' declared the publicity material. If a present-day engineer could be transported back to the nineties to see the factory at work, he might be amused by the jungle of belting overhead and shocked perhaps by the clutter on the floor, but he would admire the professionalism of the products and recognize the testing as comparable in quality with the exacting requirements of the industry three-quarters of a century on.

The old manually operated timber jib crane in the foundry, typical of the out-of-date condition of all the shops in 1878 when Hesketh joined the firm

Halls were noteworthy for being among the earliest industrial users of what was perhaps the most spectacular scientific discovery of the last quarter of the nineteenth century. As far back as 1882 Hesketh's partner Godfrey, who was experienced in electrical work, had installed electric lighting in the factory buildings. That was only two years after Edison's – and Swan's – independent invention of the carbon incandescent lamp. Apart from a few progressive manufacturers such as J. & E. Hall and experimental installations in public places (Paddington Station was one of the earliest), the use of electric lighting spread slowly for some years after it first became practicable. There was no national source of electricity supply until the electrical companies began to appear late in the eighties; meanwhile the user had to have his own generating plant. Electric light was thus at first too expensive and its operation too noisy for office and domestic use. Gradually it was introduced into the main shopping areas in London and other big cities, and with the production by Edison and Swan in partnership of the electric light bulb as we know it today, opulent householders led the way in the domestic sphere. Ship-owners were less inhibited by cost and operational snags. In a skirmish off Alexandria in 1881 the vessels of the Royal Navy turned searchlights (the word had not yet been coined) upon the shore gunners, who fled in panic from what they thought was a new and deadly weapon. By 1889 electric traction had begun to challenge the horse and the steam-engine and at Northfleet, only a few miles from Dartford, an experimental electric tramway offered pedestrians a foretaste of amenities soon to come.

The reasons for the success of the reborn J. & E. Hall are to be found partly, but not mainly, in the circumstances of the time. The euphoria of the Industrial Revolution had evaporated long since, national economic and social problems had multiplied in the 1870s and the firm achieved its victories in the eighties against a background of depression, labour disaffection and unemployment. There were, as we have seen, a few hopeful signs in human and production needs which could be satisfied with ingenuity and enterprise. The maturing of refrigeration and the world-wide need for a reliable aid to food preservation in transit and in store were a godsend to a capable engineering business; but the choice of CO_2 instead of ammonia to follow cold air as the basic ingredient was due to judgement, not chance. The firm might have been an also-ran or even a drop-out instead of the leader; the catalyst as in every great enterprise was management. Everard Hesketh has paid generous and deserved tribute to Alexander Marcet and other helpers, but it was his own exceptional qualities that gave the company a direction and a character which persisted long after age had forced him to hand over to others.

Hesketh's energy was prodigious. He worked a twelve-hour day like his employees, but still made time to found and preside over local institutions, lecture to learned societies on progress in refrigeration and maintain a paternal interest in the welfare of his employees which eased the rigours of work in those harsh times and inspired an uncommon loyalty. In 1897, when some of his employees were caught up in a strike, Hesketh in association with the vicar of Dartford took steps 'to see that my strikers have a Christmas dinner'. This was no naïve or sentimental gesture. Strikes were far too frequent for employers to be misled and hardly any major industry escaped disruption from that cause in the eighties and nineties. In 1888 alone there were more than 500 strikes, though more than half of these were resolved by arbitration. The trade unions were not popular with businessmen and it must be admitted that few of their leaders were as statesmanlike as Applegarth. But in Hesketh's values a man on strike still had the right to be treated with humanity and his family to have their Christmas dinner.

Nevertheless, Hesketh was a wise enough leader to combine paternalism with discipline. He drafted and had printed in pamphlet form an eloquent homily for distribution to his employees, also inviting their comment and question. This explained the folly of restrictive practices; the fallacy of the belief that opposing piecework, reducing working hours, going slow and insisting on 'one man, one machine' even though the machines were automatic and labour-saving, would enable the company to take on more employees. He explained how such practices would raise costs, reduce orders and inhibit growth, and quoted examples from several trades of how mechanization and increased productivity benefit a business and all engaged in it:

> Take an example from our own works. Some years ago, the cheapest refrigeration machine we turned out cost about £250. The price was too high for butchers, dairies etc. who require such a machine, and the number of orders for them was few. Within the last few years, by improved designs and improved machinery and methods, we have been able to put on the market a machine of equal power costing £150. The effect has been that we get at least twelve orders to one we got before or, in other words, £1,800 instead of £250.

The lesson is as true today and certainly no less needed.

A few years earlier Everard Hesketh had come into conflict with the local gas company which decided to extinguish the street lamps before 6 a.m. in winter, with the result that his men had to walk to work in the dark. The gas company had done this ostensibly in the interests of economy, but Hesketh believed that the motive was to make excessive profits. He had placed a big contract for a gas supply to his works and thought of switching to oil when it came up for renewal. Wimbledon, Winchester and other municipalities used oil lighting and he visited those places and wandered about the streets between midnight and 3 a.m. in order to test the efficiency of the lighting. In the end he did not need to make a change: at the threat of competition the Dartford Gas Company reverted to its former street-lighting practice and reduced its prices to customers.

By the standards of their day J. & E. Hall in the last quarter of the nineteenth century were exceptionally good employers. In 1882 a social club, the Dartford Ironworks Institute, was started under the railway arches. It had a reading room and a library stocked by Mrs Hesketh which formed the nucleus of a public library for the town. Refreshments were available and this facility developed into the firm's canteen. Entertainments were organized for the winter months, which the Heskeths attended. Educational classes, started under the arches, were the forerunners of Everard Hesketh's subsequent distinguished contributions to education and welfare in Dartford.

In spite of his hard work and dedication to the job, involving much travel abroad (he visited the USA, the West Indies, Argentina, Egypt, South Africa and most European countries), he found time to participate constructively in local affairs. He was the first county councillor for Dartford on the formation of Kent County Council in 1889; founder of Dartford Working Men's Club and its president for fifty-four years; he also contributed time and money to technical education in Dartford and to local health service. He rescued a piece of ground from the developers and presented it to the municipality as a public park bearing his name, subsequently adding a sports ground. In 1936, when retirement had brought him the necessary leisure – and despite advanced age and poor health – he published his history of J. & E. Hall; a contribution to an important sector of Britain's industrial history from 1785 onwards, and now a collector's piece.

Up to 1888, J. & E. Hall was a partnership. On 2 May in that year the firm was registered as a private limited company, with a capital of £50,000 in 5000 shares of £10 each. The directors were Everard Hesketh, Bernard Godfrey and Alexander Marcet. J. & E. Hall were among hundreds of businesses to take advantage of the new limited liability legislation embodied in a succession of Acts of Parliament since the early 1850s. Small businessmen complained that this facility favoured the larger companies – and Halls were already in that fortunate category – but the nation's business was ripe for a measure that would hasten the release of accumulated capital by encouragement of enterprise.

By the end of the century the company's commitments in refrigeration and the prospect of rapid growth made a public issue of shares desirable. Accordingly a new public company was formed in November 1900 to take over the business and the name of the former J. & E. Hall Ltd, with a capital of £250,000 divided into 30,000 Cumulative Preference Shares of £5 each at six per cent per annum and £100,000 Ordinary Shares of £1 each. The Board of Directors was increased to four with the election of Frederick William Wright, the general manager of the company. The objects of the company as set out in its Articles of Association included, in addition to the multifarious products and activities of a general engineering business and the exploitation of existing and future patents:

> . . . to establish, conduct and carry on ice works, ice stores, meat freezing and chiller establishments, . . . to carry on business as ice manufacturers, ice merchants, refrigerators and factors . . . and to purchase, lease or otherwise acquire or to construct lands, houses, buildings, water privileges, engines, machinery, apparatus, appliances, ships, craft, materials and things . . .

That final, all-encompassing word was an inspiration. Evidently there was no telling, as from 1900, into what realms of enterprise refrigeration might lead!

CHAPTER 6

Supreme on the Seas

For many reasons the year 1900 marked an important dividing line in the history of J. & E. Hall Ltd. The business had not only grown substantially, but had grown up and as a public company could now look to the outside shareholder for development finance in addition to what it could plough back out of profits. The market would impose new responsibilities and disciplines and provide a measure of management competence and business progress. At the same time the company could feel satisfied with the implied acknowledgement of its success and the confidence of the business world and manufacturing industry in the future of its speciality.

That confidence was a compliment also to the directors of the business and especially to the leader of the team, Everard Hesketh. The turn of the century had bisected the Hesketh reign at a significant point. He had become chairman in 1880 and was to hand over the command in 1921, though remaining on the Board for many more years. He had taken over a defeated business, restored its profitability, steered it into the new and still unexplored stream of refrigeration, chosen wisely among several possible refrigerants and beaten the competition to make his company supreme in the most important sector – refrigeration of perishable cargoes on the seas. Now, in the second phase of his commanding half century, Everard Hesketh had to maintain the impetus in a particularly trying period of industrial instability and social upheaval.

The first quarter of the twentieth century was shaken by wars, labour unrest and economic troubles. The wars in the first half of the period – the Boer War of 1899–1902, the Russo-Japanese War of 1904 and the Balkan Wars in the second decade – were fateful in ways that were not immediately apparent to either the winners or the losers. Britain's costly miscalculations in the prolonged war against the despised South African farmers were the first signs that her vast Empire had begun to crumble at the corners. Russia had in effect already been undermined by an internal revolutionary movement by the time the Japanese delivered their crushing naval defeat; and the power of Japan had been unsuspected until it was proved against the tottering Russian colossus. In

85

eastern and south-eastern Europe the small squabbling countries were the fragments of two disintegrating empires and constituted a zone of weakness which the free world's enemies were to exploit successfully in two world wars.

Parallel with all those geographically remote conflicts were civil troubles in Britain whose consequences were equally difficult to predict. Frequent strikes by railway workers, coal-miners, dockers and seamen, culminating in the General Strike of 1926, injured the national economy and hit J. & E. Hall where they were most vulnerable – in the shipping and shipbuilding industries. The effect was reflected in the company's fluctuating profits for the years prior to the First World War. There had been a spate of naval building in the 1890s and some less sustained activity in the shipyards in the first decade of the twentieth century to match the build-up of German armaments: the First World War had cast an ominous shadow twenty years before the event. That war, as will be seen, left Halls in a comparatively strong position. This was followed by a brief period of loss replacement in shipping circles, but then came the shipping slump of the mid-twenties which led steeply into the grim economic depression of the 1930s.

J. & E. Hall survived and in spite of some setbacks flourished, because they had chosen their main activity judiciously long before those disasters and handled it with great managerial skill. The brilliance of that initial decision cannot be overstated. Any one of at least a dozen of Halls' miscellaneous engineering lines might have been expanded into a reasonably successful business, but refrigeration was potentially of a much wider dimension, a whole new industry and a creator of industries. Having chosen refrigeration as their growth point they had to decide upon the operative medium; they settled on CO_2 because it gave them a hold on the biggest sphere of application, the merchant marine, especially that vital sector bringing meat for the nation's millions. Britain was the biggest importer of food in the world and those who helped to maintain the supply would weather natural and man-made calamities with least damage.

Making the choice was a function of management, and Halls were fortunate in having a succession of able managers. The initiative for finding and appointing executive talent devolved of course on the Chairman, Everard Hesketh, whose choice of top men as of technology was shrewd. Two early recruits to the Board after the formation of the public company were Jules de Saugy and Herbert John Ward. De Saugy, a Swiss with experience in refrigeration engineering, was a director for ten years; he retired from the Board in 1912 to become the company's continental manager and died in harness in 1924. Ward's training as marine engineer and naval architect, plus his previous service with Elder, Dempster brought to J. & E. Hall first-hand acquaintance with the shipboard environment in which their refrigeration plant had to play a highly responsible part. He had great charm and is remembered with affection by retired members who were new recruits in his day. He succeeded Godfrey as managing director in 1910 and followed Hesketh as Chairman in 1921. It fell to him to steer the company safely through the Depression years, and the strain told severely on his frail constitution.

Another of Hesketh's brilliant recruits was Lord Dudley Gordon, second son of the

Marquis of Aberdeen. He had opted for an industrial apprenticeship instead of going up to Cambridge after leaving Harrow, and had spent three years in an Aberdeen shipyard and eighteen months in an engineering workshop before joining J. & E. Hall in 1907 at the age of twenty-four. After a period on the firm's 'outwork' staff – that is, on installation work at the ports – he joined the executive staff at Dartford and was made a director in charge of land refrigeration in 1910. In J. & E. Hall's vocabulary, 'land' meant 'non-marine', although brewery work subsequently became extensive enough to warrant a separate department. Like Ward, it was obvious from his pupil days that Gordon was top management material; he followed Ward as Chairman of the company in 1936, but preferred to dispense with the title in the works where he was 'Colonel Gordon' to the employees.

Dr Frank Ainsworth Willcox was another leading member of the powerful team around Everard Hesketh – an example, more common in those days than in our own age of sharply defined specialization, of multiple expertise in simultaneous practice. Trained as a chemist, he became in 1911 financial and scientific director at J. & E. Hall. He had had a varied and valuable early training, working in a shipyard, studying at night school, gaining a D.Sc. at Durham University and teaching science for a time before joining the family firm of consulting engineers. The firm lent him to Halls, with whom they had done some business, to carry out trials on Halls' first ammonia refrigeration machines. During his long service with J. & E. Hall he became a member of the Institute of Chemical Engineers and President of the Institute of Refrigeration. His son Arthur, a heart specialist at Middlesex Hospital, was adopted as unofficial medical consultant to Halls, whose executives used to go to him for a check-up before business trips abroad.

Though mature men with specialized experience were recruited to the Board from outside, the company also sought potential directors from among the boys who came as pupils or apprentices. These included William Charles Lempriere, who joined the firm in 1895, became a director in 1912 and was in charge of the marine department when he retired from the Board twenty years later; Gordon Guthrie, a young recruit in 1908, who succeeded Dudley Gordon as head of the land refrigeration department and joined the Board in 1945; William Ball, a pupil in 1914 who, after service in the First World War, helped to build up the brewery refrigeration department and became director in charge in 1948; Charles R. Croucher, an apprentice in 1927, who became works director in 1958 in succession to Victor Patterson, and at the time of retirement was managing director of the group's subsidiary, Axstane Properties Ltd.

Every member of the Board was an executive director responsible for a department or a branch of the activity; but serving as they did a comparatively small company, they had to be able to turn their hands to a variety of jobs. There were no 'demarcation' conflicts, no 'guinea pigs' or figure-heads. 'We have never had a director,' said Everard Hesketh, 'who was not a whole time man.' Nor was there any nepotism in the worst sense of the term, though there were enough family connections to give Halls something

LT-COL LORD DUDLEY G. GORDON

Second son of the Marquis of Aberdeen and successor to the title late in life. Fifty-three years with Halls, 1936–1960 as Chairman. He served with the Gordon Highlanders in the First World War and was awarded the DSO in 1917

of the flavour of a family business. H.J. Ward's wife was a stepsister of Gordon Guthrie; Victor Patterson – who joined the firm in 1911, became a director in 1925 and was Deputy Chairman and Managing Director from 1949 to his death in 1957 – was Ward's brother-in-law; Hugh Pasteur, who joined the firm in 1919 and became a director in 1947, was related to Marcet through his grandmother. For a time there were two Willcoxes on the Board: Dr Frank Willcox and his nephew Philip. None of these appointments, however, was primarily a matter of 'jobs for the boys'. The boy had to be worth the job.

Halls was a family business to many people well below Board level and it was quite common, in the compact Dartford community, for three generations to be employed there at the same time. The employees were glad to avail themselves of the paternalism which was a feature of good management in the first quarter of the century. Paternalism has become discredited since the State became the universal though impersonal substitute for a father figure, but it was based upon real kindness and concern for the welfare of employees. At Halls some vestige of the old family feeling survived even into the more sophisticated and formalized fifties and the directors were always approachable for advice and help. Retired members of the company remember the Saturday morning queues of people with personal problems in search of a solution; they brought their financial and matrimonial troubles, even difficulties with the law, to a director, knowing that their confidence would be respected. Before the days of formal pension schemes ex gratia payments were made to employees on retirement, benefactions being extended to widows to relieve the immediate financial burden or subsidize a child's education.

Touching evidence of Everard Hesketh's personal interest in his employees survives in his prayer book preserved in the company's archives. On the inside front cover he had written 'Used at the Funeral of . . .' followed by the name, date of death and age of deceased employees. He was a deeply religious man and felt it as a pious duty to pay his last respects to anyone who died while in his employment. An entry for O.J. Ellis recalls the tragic result of one of the hazards of the job. Ellis was the firm's chief designer who, working nights and weekends in 1894 erecting a cold-air machine in s.s. *Aberdeen*, fell down an uncovered hatch in the darkness; his body was found by the stevedores the next morning.

The company was ahead of most businesses in welfare policy and in some respects in advance of the new health legislation. The National Insurance Act of 1911 covered neither dependants nor people earning more than £160 a year, so in that year Halls set up a non-contributory Benefit Fund for past and present employees and their families to supplement the official provisions. Launched with a sum of £2,500 (increased to £6,000 in 1914), the fund was controlled by three trustees and administered by a committee consisting of eight members nominated by the employees (having one vote each) and four members nominated by the directors (having two votes each). The Chairman of the company or his nominee was to have the casting vote. This fund provided assistance to widows and orphans of deceased employees, to employees and their families in exceptional need, to employees retiring for reasons of age or ill-health and to apprentices with inadequate subsistence or desiring to proceed to higher education. It also paid for the services of a trained nurse to attend employees and their families during illness. The Fund was increased from time to time as the profits of the company permitted and in 1915 a dental scheme was added for boys under sixteen and men with over five years' service.

In addition to the Benefit Trust the company had bonus schemes for workers and staff, supplemented with extra payments on the strength of a specially strenuous or profitable year. All employees participated in special Christmas and holiday bonuses.

Charity extended beyond the company's personnel and the minutes of Board Meetings referred briefly to donations to a variety of causes – hospitals (especially the local Livingstone Hospital), survivors of the *Titanic* disaster, the Lord Mayor of London's Japanese Earthquake Fund, the YMCA, trade and professional benefit societies, and Dartford Technical Institute for prizes for students. Everard Hesketh was particularly concerned to improve educational facilities in Dartford, for he was aware that despite industrial growth it was still very much a country market town, poorly supplied with cultural facilities. In 1888 he founded the Dartford Free Lecture Society and became its first president. Its purpose was to provide lectures of a non-political and non-sectarian character, and classes in the arts and sciences, literature and music. This gave the townsfolk the same kind of intellectual fare as J. & E. Hall's employees had enjoyed for several years through the firm's Literary and Scientific Society and the associated library housed under the railway arches. When the firm heard that the town's Free Lecture Society intended to start a public lending library, Halls transferred to it their employee library with its 750 books. The public subscribed more books to the Society's stock and so established a nucleus for a municipal public library. Similarly the science and arts classes formed the nucleus of the higher education movement in Dartford, out of which arose the town's Technical Institute. In 1892–93 Hesketh was chairman of the Technical and Educational Committee; he was also elected president of the Dartford Working Men's Club and Institute which had been founded in 1885. The link with J. & E. Hall became even firmer as growth compelled the club to seek larger premises; in 1890 it took over Westgate House, Spital Street, which had been built by the first John Hall and had remained the family home until 1886 when his last daughter died.

Halls' bounty and Hesketh's personal contributions to civic improvement, recorded in detail in S.K. Keyes' voluminous *Dartford Further Historical Notes*, were evidence of company growth and of the directors' belief that whatever fluctuations might occur in the national economy, refrigeration in the long term could not fail. The payroll had grown from 275 employees in the centenary year 1885 to 850 in 1910, the company's 125th anniversary. The works were extended and equipped with electric power throughout. The refrigeration industry was already firmly established, whole fleets of cargo vessels had insulated and refrigerated holds, land use of refrigeration was spreading and the industry was served by several journals, some founded before the start of the century. The files of *Ice and Cold Storage*, *British Refrigeration and Cold Storage* and *Ice Trades Review* reported technical achievements, marine and land installations, controversial issues usually on the merits or dangers of ammonia, and international conferences of refrigeration suppliers and users at which Hesketh or one of his senior colleagues made a forceful contribution. Halls were able to claim in 1906 that they had produced more successful marine installations than any two other makers combined. They made every part of the machines in their own works and could supply some of the smaller machines from stock or within a few days of receiving the order.

In 1903 many specialized journals reported a feat of service which was exceptional even in those times before industry became overgrown and muscle-bound. On 29 April of that year Halls received an order for a large installation in a new Canadian Pacific steamer *Lake Michigan*, and the plans for the holds to be refrigerated were approved on 11 May. The company had no parts in stock and was obliged to construct the entire plant from scratch. Nevertheless, it was completed and tested on 20 May and was in place on board the ship in Liverpool within twenty-four hours of leaving the Dartford works. Erection and completion took another four days and the ship sailed with all complete on 26 May. The contracts had been fulfilled in twenty-five days or – deducting Sundays – in twenty-one working days from receipt of order to installation. If one deducts the twelve days when the plans were being prepared and considered, this leaves only thirteen days during which the insulation of the holds and the fitting of the brine pipe grids were completed. Stung by the prevailing jibes about the easy-going way of British manufacturers compared with those on the other side of the Atlantic, the reporters drew the moral that British firms were abreast of the American competitors in every way, including speed of delivery.

In some directions the Americans continued to lead, notably in the storage of fruit. However, as early as 1898 and again in 1902, J. & E. Hall conducted experiments in fruit storage for the Technical Education Committee of Kent County Council, under the supervision of the county's Superintendent of Agriculture W.P. Wright. In a special chamber fitted with brine walls and CO_2 refrigeration machines, and with galvanized wire shelves to hold the fruit, they tested many varieties of apples and soft fruits (strawberries, black- and red-currants, cherries and plums) and also hops and bulbs under varying conditions, recording the effects of storing at various temperatures and for varying lengths of time. It was found that strawberries could be kept for at least three weeks at a temperature of 30°F., but had to be protected with cotton-wool to preserve their fresh appearance. Less delicate soft fruits lasted well for four to ten weeks and apples for many months.

By the first decade of the twentieth century the nation's feeding pattern had been transformed and fruits and vegetables which had been rare and expensive were appearing on market stalls at prices the average shopper could afford. Thanks to refrigerated importation seasonal variations were disappearing from the greengrocery trade. Prejudice against chilled and frozen meat had virtually ceased to exist, and the growing popularity of canned foods had long ago confirmed the vision and enterprise of Donkin, Hall and Gamble.

Halls' output of refrigeration plant was considerable. In one year, 1904, they completed orders for eighty-eight marine and eighty-three land installations. Seven of the marine contracts were for ice-making in battleships and cruisers, eight for the Imperial Japanese Admiralty for hospital ships, and two for battleships under construction in the UK. Others were for meat, butter and banana cargoes, passengers' provisions and fish preservation in trawlers. Of land installations thirty-two machines were for cold storage and ice production, twelve for breweries, eighteen for creameries and butter factories, one for a small arms factory in India and others for chocolate cooling, oil cooling, bacon curing and hotel use.

Japan had only recently emerged from the Middle Ages into the orbit of the modern Western world. It had been a violent entry. In the Russo-Japanese War of 1904–5 the Japanese had captured the Russian naval base of Port Arthur and annihilated the Russian fleet. Eleven of the Japanese warships, including the famous battleship *Fuji*, had installed Hall refrigerating plant for ice-making and the preservation of provisions. In 1905 the warship *Kishima*, 8000 tons, built for Japan by Sir W.G. Armstrong, Whitworth & Company, was fitted with Hall refrigeration in conjunction with an installation of 'Thermotanks' to control the supply of cold air to the magazines. That was more than half a century before the Hall and Thermotank companies entered into a much more intimate association.

Carcases in a Belfast beef chiller. The air cooling units are mounted in the false wall on the left

Other navies and merchant marines were customers for Halls' refrigeration – Argentine, Mexican, Italian and Portuguese. An Argentine merchant bought a Hall refrigeration plant to extract heat from corn before shipment. Refrigeration was opening up trade in regions and for products which would have been unthinkable without it. For instance, a ship fitted by Halls which had taken a cargo of goods to eastern Siberia returned from Nicolaievsk with the first cargo of frozen salmon from the River Amur. Meanwhile, meat imports had settled into a routine and expanded enormously. The total number of carcases imported into Britain from Australia, New Zealand and the River Plate had increased in less than a quarter of a century as follows: 1880 – 400; 1885 – 777,891; 1890 – 2,937,908; 1895 – 5,033,629; 1902 – 7,219,854. Beef, mutton and lamb were the main but not the only meat products. In 1903 six million frozen rabbits were imported from Australia, an interesting case of a pest being turned into profit.

Meat shipments provided the bulk of Halls' refrigeration business, but other applications were building up at home and overseas. Cold stores at the docks were in effect an extension of the marine side; they not only kept the food in good condition until it reached the customer, but averted a steep fall in prices in the event of exceptionally heavy landings. Halls' refrigeration in a cold store in Tooley Street, London, protected large stocks of cheese, bacon and butter shipped from Australia, Canada and Siberia. A large installation was supplied for the London and East India Docks Joint Committee Cold Stores at Smithfield. The building had a capacity for 100,000 carcases, and the brine grid system in the ceilings of its sixteen chambers consisted of ten miles of two-inch pipes.

Three leading London hospitals, St George's, University College Hospital and the London Hospital, were large users of Halls' refrigeration. The installation at the London Hospital produced two tons of ice a day, cooled an ice store containing 150 tons of ice and pumped cold brine to large overhead galvanized cylinders in the freezing rooms. Frascati's and Claridge's Hotels were Hall customers and so were some hotels overseas, including the Apollo in Bombay where the machines were used for cooling twenty suites of rooms. Burmah Oil Company had installed ten 160-ton Hall CO_2 machines for oil cooling in Rangoon.

Leading brewers had large Hall installations for cooling water, controlling the temperature in fermenting rooms, preserving yeast, storing hops and chilling beer for bottling. There was a market also in spheres where only a limited amount of refrigeration was required, for instance in the smaller breweries, at butchers' shops, in mortuaries as an aid in post-mortem examinations, and for small marine purposes such as making ice and preserving provisions. British yachtsmen installed these machines, as did Americans in spite of high US import duties. Retail grocery and provision chains were springing up, particularly in London, in the early 1900s and Halls' small machines, economical and uncomplicated in operation, were becoming a necessary item of equipment. Specially interesting among the letters of appreciation that Halls

A Hall single cylinder CO_2 compressor installed in 1914 in a cold store for imported foods in London's dockside Tooley Street

received was one dated 27 September 1905 from the founder of another distinguished and still flourishing business, Mr J. Sainsbury, provision merchant, of 11 Stamford Street, London S.E.:

> I have great pleasure in testifying and herewith expressing my satisfaction with the small refrigerating machines fitted up at my branch shops. They have now been running for over 12 months without any trouble whatever, and it will further interest you to know that the working expenses, including depreciation, are much less than the cost of ice. You are at liberty to make use of this unsolicited testimonial in your ordinary trade price lists.

Halls' range of small compact CO_2 machines for these applications foreshadowed a more important development to come some twenty years later, which will be described in another chapter.

In spite of these efforts Halls were aware of their inferiority in sales of refrigeration for use on land. In 1906 the Board had planned to increase their land business by appointing correspondents in the principal towns to advise their agents of any likely orders; a general agency manager would be responsible for and keep in personal contact with agents and correspondents. But the company's share of land refrigeration had remained small: that was the price they paid for concentrating on CO_2 and dominating the marine business. Most of the big land installations had gone to makers of machines using ammonia as the refrigerant. The ammonia compression system had certain advantages for land application which outweighed the dangers – diminishing with improvements in design – inherent in the nature of the gas. The main advantage was that it operated at much lower pressures than the CO_2 system, making it possible for much lighter, less substantial and less expensive equipment to be used. It utilized considerably less power for the same refrigeration effect, and was much less bulky overall than an equivalent CO_2 system. In 1910 therefore J. & E. Hall decided to add ammonia refrigeration machines to their range, and sales increased rapidly in the land department. Improvements in design were halted when war broke out in 1914, but after the war Halls developed a high-speed enclosed type of ammonia compressor with forced lubrication which proved so successful that there were times, according to Lord Dudley Gordon, when land sales exceeded marine. That must have been very exceptional; the marine department remained the backbone of the business.

By 1905 J. & E. Hall had shed most of their jobbing work and were almost exclusively a refrigeration business. The situation had its dangers, for despite their optimism for the future the directors felt that the times were too precarious and refrigeration still too new for complete specialization with safety. The century had started well for them: turnover in 1903 had been a record and the profit of £41,000 was considered good. But a slump in shipping caused profits to fall in the next two years, and though orders improved by 1906 the company had already taken steps to diversify. They sought a second string in an equally new and even more exciting industry: motor vehicles. Private motoring was still a novelty, more so in Britain than in France and Germany. In Britain motor manufacture and motoring as amenity and sport were retarded by a regulation requiring the 'horseless carriage' to be preceded by a man carrying a red flag to warn drivers of horse-drawn vehicles of the alarming addition to the hazards of the road. By the time the restriction was abolished in 1896 France and Germany were well ahead in design and sales. Alexander Marcet had become one of the car-owning élite in 1900 when he bought a belt-driven Benz. He did not live to see his company become a motor manufacturer, but died in 1903 at the age of forty-four.

Halls were not interested in the private motorist, but chose the commercial sector as the more promising market. In 1906 they acquired a licence to manufacture chassis for buses, lorries and other heavy motor vehicles from the Swiss firm of Adolph Saurer, makers of internal combustion engines since 1888 but producers of commercial vehicles only since 1903. Halls called their vehicles 'Hallford', after the company's telegraphic address. By 1907 they had three or four prototypes one of which, a three-tonner, took part in the Royal Automobile Club's Commercial Motor Trials, gaining a gold medal (the highest award in its class) and a special diploma. With such an accolade progress was swift. Halls built a motor workshop north of their main works on a site of many acres which had once been the orchard and market garden from which John Hall senior supplied his stall at Covent Garden. By 1911 the company had replaced the Saurer patents with an engine of its own design and was producing a variety of models up to five tons' capacity.

The Hallford was a rugged but very adaptable vehicle. Public transport operators put a bus body onto the chassis and some of these buses appeared on the London streets under the Tillings banner. Another user fitted his Hallford lorry with hard slatted wooden seats and put a canvas cover over all to form a passenger char-à-banc which no doubt made up in utility what it must have lacked in comfort. But the vehicle was essentially a lorry. The leading brewers equipped whole transport fleets with Hallfords, which were also bought by haulage contractors, the London County Council and other local government departments, and by export agents for shipment to buyers in Australia and South-East Asia.

With the commercial motors as with refrigeration J. & E. Hall had a product which would stand the nation – and of course the producers – in good stead in the event of war. The inevitability of war between Britain and an increasingly aggressive Germany had been foreseen since before the Boer War, and prepared for by both sides with big rearmament programmes. The two countries were nearing naval parity when Britain launched her powerful Dreadnought class of warships in 1906. She formed her Territorial Army the following year for home defence in the event of the regular forces being fully engaged overseas. All that was needed was a spark to ignite a world-wide conflagration, and if Serbia had not struck the match with the assassination of the Austrian Archduke Franz Ferdinand at Sarajevo, another excuse would not have been long delayed. In 1913, in anticipation of wartime need, Halls enlarged their foundry and invested in a new cupola, a twenty-ton overhead travelling crane and electric hoists. Before the war, also, the War Office introduced a system of subsidies for privately owned commercial vehicles which conformed to certain regulations and had passed a number of rigorous road tests, the idea being that the vehicles would be at the government's disposal for war purposes. As it happened, war broke out before the scheme had become fully operational and Halls were obliged to produce lorries of all kinds at great speed and in quantity to satisfy the urgent demand for war transport from Britain and her allies. From 1914 to 1918 Hallford lorries carried the products of British munition factories to the Channel ports and ploughed through Flanders mud to feed the guns and tanks. There was another, coincidental, connection between Hallford and tank warfare which has a certain interest. Halls' chief commercial vehicle designer had been C.W. Wilson, inventor of the epicyclic gearbox and other important contributions to motor technology. He was also one of the inventors of the tank. Evidently Halls were still a magnet for outstanding engineers as in Trevithick's time.

When Halls, in common with most engineering businesses and many other kinds of manufacturer whose processes could be converted to the production of war material, became controlled establishments under the Ministry of Munitions in 1915, Everard

A week's output of lorries from the Hallford lorry shop, in 1914. The lorries provided war transport, could be adapted for public transport (as below), and remained particularly popular with brewers till the vehicle branch of the business was wound up in 1926

Hesketh called together his entire work force – swollen to 1200 – and explained what was expected of them in the national crisis. Engineering was not a reserved occupation in the First World War as in the Second, and a hundred men had joined the Armed Forces. More than three hundred women were recruited to fill the gap. It was the first time that women had worked in the heavy industries, but at Halls they became skilled crane-drivers, acetylene welders, operators of capstan and turret lathes and milling and drilling machines. Women's contribution to the war effort had important political as well as military consequences. The pre-war decade had seen repeated agitation and even acts of violence by the suffragettes campaigning on behalf of women's suffrage. They called a truce when confronted by a more sinister enemy than their native menfolk, but had no need to resume the conflict after the war: they felt they had proved their right to vote.

More than 300 women filled the gap left by male employees who had joined the Forces, and produced war material in the company's machine shops between 1914 and 1918

Among the members of the company who had joined the Forces were two directors: Colonel Gordon, who served with the Gordon Highlanders and was awarded the DSO in 1917, and Captain Guy Evans, head of the motor department. In a letter to Everard Hesketh dated 2 January 1916 Dudley Gordon paid tribute to the efforts of the workers and the fighters and the Chairman, a good public relations man long before the term was coined, had it printed for distribution to the employees.

> I was very pleased on my recent visit to the Works during my leave to see everyone so busily occupied in helping to win the war. Owing to the great efforts of those at home we are now superior to the Germans in equipment and munitionment, and it may seem strange to some that no forward move should take place. If there are any who think this, it is due to their ignorance of the conditions of trench warfare in wet weather. It would be bad enough to be out of doors anywhere in this weather for four days continuously night and day, but when those four days are spent in a trench knee deep in mud with constant shelling going on and constant vigilance necessary it becomes extremely arduous. Men at the end of it come back to their billets caked in mud from head to foot and so weary that they often drop asleep on the road . . . It is an interesting fact that in my own company alone the total pay received by the men is about £150 less per week than the amount these same men received in civil employment before the war. The men are so keen on achieving the object we all have in view and so proud of their regiment that several who are specially skilled have refused to join more highly paid branches of the service.

Halls' employees who helped to sustain the war effort at home were spared the horror of trench warfare, but Dartford did nevertheless come under fire. It was part of the outer defences of London and was armed against air attack. Air battles were fought above the town and bombs fell nearby. In 1915 a Zeppelin bombed Gravesend, and in 1916 gunners based on Dartford were decorated for their part in bringing down a Zeppelin in the Thames estuary. It was not, however, until the Second World War that London and South-Eastern England experienced a sustained battering comparable with that of the most heavily engaged overseas war zones.

By 1917 almost the whole output of the Dartford factory was taken by the War Departments: all the lorries (£5,000 had been spent on extra machine tools to increase production); bombs, bomb dropping gear and equipment for field guns; paravanes, a device for cutting adrift the mines that endangered shipping; and of course refrigeration plant for all purposes, especially in cargo ships and warships. The enemy's submarines were causing heavy losses at sea and the need for replacement put great pressure on the shipyards and sub-contractors.

Pressure on the employees was heavy, and the Board did their best to prevent or relieve distress. Food rationing, which was introduced by the government towards the end of the war, was not organized as efficiently as in the Second World War, and the company opened a canteen in order to ensure that workers who lived at a distance could have breakfast and a midday meal and indeed that no employee need go hungry. This was a more serious effort than the earlier provision of refreshments 'under the arches', and out of it has developed the present highly organized catering in the company's establishments at Dartford and elsewhere. Many years were to pass before a bar was

Men at work in the Dartford foundry in the early 1900s

added, but the desirability of stimulants (in moderation) had not been overlooked even by the sober Everard Hesketh. He must have regretted afresh that his pre-war experiment in restaurant ownership had been killed by vested interests. In 1902 he had built a restaurant next to the Works entrance with the intention of running it on the lines of the Public House Trust Movement, 'wherein the manager, while selling intoxicants, has no pecuniary interest therein, but gets his profits out of food and non-intoxicants. The house was therefore a bona fide refreshment house where the sale of intoxicants was subordinated to the supply of meals, etc.'* Named appropriately the North Pole, since it adjoined a factory making refrigeration equipment, it offered restaurant service and party facilities to the townsfolk as well as Halls' employees. Its dining room accommodated a hundred customers, and the service proved very popular. Unfortunately the venture aroused the opposition of the licensed trade and for two years Hesketh petitioned in vain for a licence. At the third application the restaurant was granted a licence for two mid-day hours only. It thus incurred all the restrictions of a fully licensed house, and this handicap forced a closure. The mock Tudor building was bought by J. & E. Hall in 1911 and still survives under its enticing name as part of the Works premises.

*As reported in *Dartford Further Historical Notes* by S.K. Keyes.

The J. & E. Hall directors were concerned over the poor pay of members of the Forces and the consequent distress of their dependants. From the start of the war the company supplemented the incomes of Servicemen's families with a sum equal to the official grant, that is, 1/1d a day for the wife and 2d for each child under the age of fourteen. These were not trivial sums at 1914–18 values, and the total outlay was substantial for a business of J. & E. Hall's size. The spirit behind the company's benefactions was expressed with characteristic forcefulness in an addition by Everard Hesketh to the statement of the Chairman, H.J. Ward, at the Company General Meeting in 1927. Reporting on the progress of the Social & Athletic Club, the Works Canteen and the Veterans Club, he said: 'I am not much concerned whether all this social work pays, though I feel sure the shareholders lose nothing by it, but the personal touch which we get thereby makes the work of all of us, directors, staff and workmen, more interesting and satisfactory, and is therefore very well worth doing.'

Hesketh and his wife indeed extended their personal charity wherever they saw a need, irrespective of the moral reward of good human relations. The earliest victims of the war in Western Europe were Belgians, some of whom found refuge in Dartford. Mr and Mrs Hesketh fitted up a café and social centre for them and many of their menfolk found employment in the town.

Having helped to provide the fighting forces with essential goods and services, the company emerged from the war in sound financial condition and with a healthy order book. It could afford new schemes for employee welfare and the most fruitful was the resumption of the plans, halted by the war, for a Social & Athletic Club. The company purchased a sports ground on the outskirts of the town facing the peaceful Kent countryside, but the members were not left in peace for long. In 1922 the local transport department decided to carry a new bypass road across the ground and resisted all pleas and arguments to modify the plan. However, Halls secured an adjacent piece of freehold land and the Club actually gained by the change.

Another project proved less fortunate. In 1918 the company had bought $6\frac{1}{4}$ acres of land adjoining Dartford Creek on which to build new workshops, but manning proved difficult because of a housing shortage in the town. The Board were reluctant to become owners of houses let to their workmen, knowing what complications could arise in the event of labour troubles, but at the time there was no alternative. The company therefore bought $14\frac{1}{4}$ acres of land, enough for at least 120 houses. They built the first batch of twenty-four houses of what was to be Hallford Village, and let some of them to company employees. But the scheme had begun to look formidable; Halls were not a Cadbury or a Lever capable of founding their own model industrial community and were forced to call a halt. The Chairman told the shareholders in his 1922 report, 'We spent altogether something under £30,000 and of course these buildings stood in our books at that figure, which is considerably above their real value; so we have taken the drastic step this year of writing down these buildings by £10,000.' They sold the bulk of the Hallford Estate in 1933, retaining a number of the houses for employees.

Those were fairly small troubles compared with the major dislocation that followed four years of exclusive war production. As suppliers of motor transport Halls had fulfilled their wartime obligations only too well. They and other motor manufacturers had produced vehicles in vast quantities under government control and at very little profit. The poor profitability was due to the government's practice of delaying permission to increase prices until the steeply rising costs of materials and labour had made those increases unremunerative. 'However,' said the Chairman, H.J. Ward, 'we have the satisfaction of knowing that we served the country well, and gave good value in its time of trouble without taint of profiteering.' When the war ended the producers were left with bigger stocks than the peacetime market could absorb. The Society of Motor Manufacturers and Traders had foreseen this predicament and, some time before the end of the war, had proposed to the government that each manufacturer should be allowed to recondition and dispose of surplus vehicles of his own make on the government's behalf for a nominal return. The scheme was turned down and instead, the government built a depot at Slough, and dumped tens of thousands of lorries, vans, cars and motor cycles on 600 acres of land. After long delay, incurring much adverse criticism, the government sold the land and all it contained to a company which was later to create the Slough Trading Estate, but which first launched what must have been the biggest bargain sale in the history of the motor industry. Thousands of people setting up in business after the war flocked to the site and some picked up a lorry for as little as £100, sometimes with a motorbike or two thrown in. The commercial vehicle market was in chaos and the motor manufacturers proper had no choice but to sit out the disaster, but J. & E. Hall – to whom the Hallford lorry was a sideline though a sizeable one – faced a very difficult decision.

The sideline had been on the whole successful and the brewers were still enthusiastic. But would there be a future for a revived Hallford enterprise? Owing to the Slough bonanza it would be some time before anyone would make a profit out of heavy commercial vehicles. The existing Hallford model was little changed from that of 1911, and new designs would now be needed. In the period during which Halls were half inclined to remain in the motor trade they produced and successfully tested an electric battery vehicle; but, said the Chairman, 'until trade improves generally we cannot hope for many orders. We have fortunately been able to write down drastically the value of stocks, and are in a position to meet competition when business revives.' The Board soon realized that business revival would not help and they would have to invest heavily in new designs and buildings, also replacement of worn-out machine tools. New production facilities, they concluded, would be better employed in the growing refrigeration business. After several abortive attempts to sell their lorry business as a going concern, the Board decided upon liquidation and the last of a total output of more than 3000 Hallfords was delivered to a purchaser in 1926.

That was not quite the end, however. The supply of spares had always been profitable and the company had an obligation to Hallford lorry owners. A company was formed in

1927 to take over the spares department under H.G. Turner, who had managed the motor production at Halls for many years. Guy Evans, the director in charge of the motor vehicle division almost from the start, retired.

Halls were fortunate enough to find compensation for the loss of the lorry business in the almost immediate acquisition of another form of diversification. From horizontal transport they switched to what they called 'vertical transport', which will be described in the next chapter. They were even more fortunate in coming through the war with their refrigeration business intact and in working order. Refrigeration is the same whether deployed for purposes of peace or war and peace actually brought extra work to repair the ravages of war. Losses of merchant ships by submarine attack and of warships in battle had been severe, and Halls benefited by the shipbuilding boom in the first three or four post-war years. Orders came not only from shipping companies replacing old refrigeration tonnage but also for installations in ex-German vessels bought by British owners. Trawler owners renewed their fleets and resumed fishing in distant waters, and Halls were among the earliest suppliers of plant for on-board freezing. In spite of trading difficulties – having to buy the main materials, as H.J. Ward put it, 'from hand to mouth', and to wait patiently for customers to resume suspended contracts – the marine department did well. In 1922 according to Lloyds Register over 50 per cent of the world's refrigerated cargo installations were by J. & E. Hall. By 1924, though the downturn had started in shipping and shipbuilding, the figure had risen to 54 per cent.

Refrigeration work on land expanded at home and overseas. In response to a demand for faster running compressors, Halls introduced in 1922 their 'high speed' vertical enclosed ammonia machines referred to earlier. Operating speeds ranged initially from 250 rpm to 400 rpm, which was very fast judged by the standards of the time; but within ten years the range of machine speeds had been increased to 500 rpm. These machines, which included the largest compressors ever built by the company, became world famous, being widely used for much brewery work and specialized industrial applications. They had been designed by George Charles Hodsdon, who joined Halls as an apprentice before the turn of the century and became their chief designer in 1907. In a working life lasting well into his eighties he contributed to the development of refrigeration from the cold-air machine, through the CO_2 era, to machines using methyl chloride and the halogens.

Throughout the war J. & E. Hall had maintained contacts with and fulfilled contracts for foreign customers. One such contract, initiated before the war ended, was a technical triumph which attracted great interest in mining and engineering circles. It came from the St John Del Rey Mining Co. Ltd, of Brazil. Their Morro Velho Gold Mine was the deepest in the world, and the temperature and humidity were so high that even the native labourers, accustomed to a tropical climate, found them intolerable. The owners had contemplated closing the mine, but they approached J. & E. Hall who sent Dr F.A. Willcox to study the problem with the mining company's engineers. Halls designed and supplied an air cooling and drying plant consisting of six ammonia compressors and

Two horizontal CO_2 machines supplied to a Truman's brewery in 1912 for beer processing

their accessories. The result was entirely successful. Not only were the working conditions now bearable, but it was possible to extend the workings to a greater depth.

Dr Willcox's earliest experience of mine refrigeration had been in experiments conducted with the famous scientist Professor J.B. Haldane at the very deep and hot Pendlebury Colliery near Manchester. They used a small CO_2 machine fitted with a fan which blew cool air on the miners' bodies, a primitive and not very useful form of refrigeration with little or no effect on the environment. An opportunity for a more sophisticated experiment came in 1914 from South Africa, when the owner of one of the wet mines on the Rand wanted a plant installed at the mine surface to cool 150,000 cubic feet of air a minute. There were only three available refrigerants: CO_2, which required more power than the mine could afford; water vapour produced in a high vacuum, which required more circulating water than the neighbourhood could supply; and ammonia, which was practical and economical but would be dangerous to the men working below if there was any leakage. The choice was beyond question: it had to be ammonia. Halls were confident that they could produce a safe as well as an effective machine even with that frightening ingredient, and so it turned out. The installation in fact provided a model for the later Morro Velho contract.

Land refrigeration offered other possibilities which the company was exploring well before the end of the century's first quarter. These would always be secondary to the marine business, but together with the new diversification they would help to minimize the effects of the slump which now seemed inevitable. The Board had prepared to the best of their ability for the troubled years ahead.

In 1920 the Duke of York, later King George VI, toured Hall's Dartford works in his capacity as President of the Industrial Welfare Society. Colonel Gordon, seen on the left in uniform, had with Everard Hesketh sponsored the company's membership of the Society

CHAPTER 7

The Troubled Years

The closing down of J. & E. Hall's major diversification coincided with the steep decline in the market for the company's main product. This double blow might have appeared a prescription for disaster, but in fact it was much less desperate than that thanks to the emergence of a double prescription for survival. Those two innovations were to carry the company through the unhappy twenty-one-year period between the two World Wars with less serious injury than most engineering businesses would suffer, and enable it to serve the nation throughout the Second World War with distinction and with its viability as an enterprise intact. Almost simultaneously with the extinction of the motor activity, a profitable successor outside refrigeration arrived and a new line in refrigeration evolved to compensate for the slump in the shipyards.

Halls already had a useful and steady non-refrigeration sideline: since 1922 they had been manufacturing the entire output of Todd oil-burning equipment in the UK. It was a system for burning oil fuel in steam boilers designed and marketed by Todd Oil Burners of America, and contracted to J. & E. Hall by Todd's British concessionaires. As oil fuel encroached upon coal, the market for Todd plant expanded from exclusive marine use to heating and steam raising applications in hospitals, breweries, cement works and other industries. The concession ran for decades and Halls took in their stride such refinements as ultrasonic atomizers, automatic controls and specially designed oil fuel pumping, heating and filtering units. The Todd assignment recalled the miscellaneous engineering contract work undertaken in the pre-refrigeration era.

Todd was however a special case and not a tentative reversion to general engineering. Neither was it a Hall subsidiary, though Halls had shares in the company. A very different and more substantial kind of diversification was vertical transport, which was no side-line but a major activity, running concurrently with the mainstream of refrigeration for more than thirty years. The following pages contain a brief outline of its development and progress, with some leap-frogging of chronology in the company story as a whole.

In 1925 the old established Medway Safety Lift Company offered the entire manufacture of its passenger and goods lifts to J. & E. Hall. Any doubts Halls might still have had about the desirability of pulling out of commercial vehicles were now resolved – here was a potential winner in place of what had become an irredeemable loser. There were, however, problems. Lift production could not simply be slotted into the gap left by the lorries; it necessitated redeployment of equipment, the establishment of an entirely new electrical department for the manufacture of the control gear and the organization of a special sales force. These changes could not be accomplished without close integration of the two companies. Halls acquired an immediate controlling interest in Medway, and themselves concentrated on manufacture while Medway handled sales. In 1932 they took the inevitable final step of liquidating Medway and marketing the products under the Hall name. Other forms of rationalization had already been accomplished; up to 1927 the lift business had operated from offices and a maintenance department in London, but separation from the factory was proving uneconomic and therefore most of the executive functions were transferred to Dartford.

Herbert Ward had foreseen that there would be a marine as well as a land market for lifts. In fact one of the earliest orders came from Harland and Wolff for the White Star liner *Laurentic*. Refrigeration contracts stimulated orders for Halls' lifts not only in passenger liners but also in warships. In the 1939–45 war Halls installed lifts in *Vanguard*, *Eagle*, *Majestic* and other powerful units of the Royal Navy. The land users were owners or occupiers of all kinds of tall buildings: offices, factories, residential blocks, colleges, department stores, hotels and civic buildings. Among the more newsworthy customers were the new House of Commons rebuilt after the Second World War, the Parliament building of Northern Ireland, the Royal Opera House at Covent Garden and the Royal Palace in Bangkok. Overseas sales mounted over the years and Victor Patterson, who had been a leading figure in the development of the vertical transport department, was congratulated on his export achievements in 1952 by the President of the Board of Trade. Canada was a particularly good customer, 'on the doorstep of our American competitors', as a Company Report boasted.

A curious feature of the lift business was the revival, briefly referred to earlier, of the continuously moving lift. Called the Paternoster lift, it was more handsome than but no different in basic principle from its poor relation of the early 1900s. It was better known and more readily accepted on the Continent than in the UK. Since it did not stop for the passenger to enter or alight, it looked alarming and sales at first were slow in spite of its advantages. It could handle twice as many 'up' passengers as the most advanced high-speed lifts of its time, and a comparable volume of traffic at the same time on the downward phase of the cycle. Halls installed a Paternoster lift in their Dartford office building facing the conventional push-button type, so that prospective customers could satisfy themselves that what was safe enough for Halls' staff was not likely to endanger their own.

The Paternoster continuously moving lift was a speciality of the vertical
transport department

Halls built a lift-testing tower on their Dartford site, introduced a variety of styles into their range and adapted the latest technologies to lift operation and control. They sent one of their electrical engineers to Schenectady to study the American General Electric Company's system of gearless drives for lifts, and obtained a licence to use the technique through General Electric's associate British Thomson-Houston Company. J. & E. Hall were the first to use transistorized controls for lift operation and devised a group supervisory system connecting a number of lifts installed in one location. The first contract was a system serving fourteen decks in the liner *Canberra*. Others were in twenty-floor office blocks where they offered a simpler and more reliable service than mechanical lift systems employing a multiplicity of relays. One of the features was a passenger weighing device in each car which, when the car was fully loaded, diverted further calls to the next available car. Similar facilities were introduced into goods lifts. William Ball designed pallet lifts for his brewery customers, in which a memory unit ensured that a pallet would enter only when the lift was ready to receive it. The company manufactured and assembled these systems in its transistor shop, which was equipped also with a simulator for testing to scale the operation of a multiple lift installation in a high-rise block.

Vertical transport was Halls' portmanteau term for both lifts and escalators. In 1931 – as it happened, in the depths of the national economic depression – Halls signed an agreement to manufacture 'moving staircases' under licence from the German patentee Carl Flohr. The timing could not have been more fortunate. Bentalls, the well-known department store at Kingston-upon-Thames, had just completed plans for a new building on lines never before attempted on this side of the Atlantic, a store in which escalators were not merely an accessory but an integral part of the design. They invited tenders for the installation and Halls won the contract. Bentalls' escalator hall became an architectural showpiece and new business for Halls followed from Harrods, Selfridges and other famous London and provincial stores, also from department stores in Canada and Australia.

Halls improved upon the original designs, establishing new standards of silent and vibrationless running. These qualities gained them a significant order immediately upon resumption of escalator production after the six-year wartime intermission for a set of escalators in the Oratory, Montreal, a unique innovation for a house of prayer and a tribute to Halls' achievement of noise reduction in their product. In 1951 Halls installed an escalator in the Dome of Discovery in the Festival of Britain on London's South Bank, which was believed to be the longest single escalator span without intermediate support. When it had served its original purpose it was transferred to the new London Underground Railway station at Alperton. Throughout the fifties and sixties lifts and escalators sold well. The company supplied a hundred escalators to the new underground railway in Montreal, manufactured locally under licence to Halls' design, and a further eighty-two were manufactured under a similar arrangement for the Paris Metro. At home, the Ocean Dock Passenger Terminal at Southampton and the new London terminal of British European Airways were important customers. The building industry helped to boost production of Paternoster continuous lifts as well as orthodox lifts and escalators: over 150 lifts were constructed for the hospital building programme alone. Halls were among the leaders in escalator production and installation. New types of escalator were added to the range, including 'packaged' escalators delivered in sections for assembly on site; glass-sided escalators ('Crystallators'); escalators with illuminated inner balustrades; and the 'Starglide', a passenger conveyor based on escalator principles.

Lift and escalator production continued until well into the 1960s. Orders were good but margins had begun to shrink and the effort devoted to vertical transport was needed for refrigeration production. In 1967 a subsidiary company, Hall Lifts & Escalators Ltd, was formed to handle sales and production, operating from the Group's Silex Street premises in London to release space in Dartford. The following year, consistently with a

In the 1930s Halls switched from vehicles to 'vertical transport' in the form of lifts and escalators. London Transport, the Festival of Britain, and multiple stores at home and overseas were among the customers

new policy to concentrate wholly on refrigeration and air-conditioning, the subsidiary enterprise was sold to the Otis Elevator Company Ltd. Vertical transport had served its purpose of supplementing refrigeration production in the bad times and adding its quota of profit in the good.

While lifts and escalators were taking much of the strain in the slump years of the century's second quarter, a new departure in refrigeration was establishing Halls in the relatively neglected market for small inexpensive machines. They had no intention of competing with strongly entrenched suppliers of domestic refrigerators, but the small commercial users presented a challenge. The company had marketed small machines with moderate success in the recent past; one of these was named the Wembley compressor after the Wembley Exhibitions of 1924 and 1925 where it had been exhibited. It was a smaller version of the company's ammonia machines which had gained a world-wide reputation. But neither ammonia nor CO_2 refrigeration was ideally suited to the needs of the small user; they worked at higher pressures and therefore necessitated heavier and more expensive construction than the businesses of small butchers, dairies and ice-cream retailers could justify. Halls therefore developed an entirely new range of small electrically controlled automatic compressors, using methyl chloride as the refrigerant. Methyl chloride was the first of the halocarbon or halogenated hydrocarbon refrigerants to be generally used; this group of gases was eventually to yield a more flexible range of refrigerants than any used in the past for almost all branches of refrigeration. It worked at low pressure, was not scarce or expensive and unlike ammonia was compatible with non-ferrous metals. Although toxic and inflammable, the small quantities used meant that those disabilities could be easily controlled. Halls introduced the new machines under the proprietary name Hallmark at the Shipping, Engineering and Machinery Exhibition at Olympia on 8–24 September 1927.

The demand for small refrigeration units had become more insistent as the new food preservatives regulations came into force. Refrigeration, unlike chemical preservatives, was not a contaminant and presented no health risks to consumers of the food. The laws of hygiene were on the side of the refrigeration industry. For instance in July 1956 new regulations required catering establishments to keep certain classes of perishable food at a temperature below 50°F., sales of refrigerated display equipment benefited. Selfridges' food department was among Halls' customers for cooling self-service display units.

As with lifts and escalators, the Hallmark venture entailed considerable reorganization in many departments. While the prototypes were undergoing tests the company adapted part of the works vacated by commercial vehicles and installed new machine tools. Since the small machines were in a different market from the large installations, they required a separate sales and service organization covering the country. Launching the Hallmark was a major operation, but less speculative than lorries, lifts and escalators. There were potential customers among large refrigeration users as well as in small establishments, at sea as well as on land, overseas and at home.

The most numerous customers were food retailers, especially butchers and fishmongers, many of whom were thankful for Halls' hire purchase facilities. J. Lyons & Co. ordered 360 Hallmarks for the conservation of ice cream and their Cumberland Hotel in London installed seventy-three for a variety of duties at different points throughout the building. Hospitals used them for making ice, laboratories for testing scientific instruments at very low temperatures, brewers and mineral water manufacturers for water cooling, ships and railway restaurant cars for provisions, medical institutions for blood plasma storage, the Army for refrigerating trailer bodies on active service and householders in very hot climates for air cooling and conditioning. Turkey, Venezuela and South Africa were good export markets.

Hallmark machines were welcomed by naval architects, shipbuilders and owners as a simple accessory to the elaborate central refrigeration installations, providing cooling at detached and distant points without the need to run brine pipe leads from the main plant. A small Hallmark machine could be tucked away in a bar cupboard or replace the ice-box in the provision store, making these locations self-contained refrigeration units. Trawlers used these small machines to maintain a more even temperature in the mass of ice and fish and also to slow, but not to prevent, the melting of the ice. The result was economy in ice consumption without prejudice to the quality of the catch. In fact the fish retained the 'wet' look which the customer demanded as a sign of freshness longer than when ice was used without refrigeration.

By the late 1930s Hallmark had become a standard requirement within its sphere. When the large initial demand had been satisfied, the annual increases in sales – sometimes as high as 50 per cent – settled down to a steady level. These small utilities did not suffer the fluctuations that caused havoc in the main marine sector. There was a brief boom in Hallmark sales in 1947–48 to appease the unfulfilled demand of the Second World War years, but a buyers' market soon followed. Increasing competition was met by improvements in design and by keen pricing.

Hallmarks had been, like vertical transport, a valuable standby in the critical years between 1925 and 1950 and remained an important feature of the refrigeration service. Marine sales generally rose and fell with the fortunes of the shipyards and shipping was one of the biggest casualties of the economic depression. Construction had started to lag in 1923. 'Builders are putting back delivery dates,' says the Company Report, 'as they cannot put our machinery on board the retarded ships and can rarely afford us storage under a roof, hence we are somewhat encumbered with finished machines at the moment and payments are correspondingly delayed.' Halls obtained the lion's share of whatever business could be found, and also maintained their share of the world's cargo refrigeration installations at over 50 per cent, but they kept within the narrowing margins only by skilful cutting of costs. 'The administration of our business provides no sinecures,' wrote Ward. By 1925 the world's ports and rivers were choked with redundant tonnage, and in spite of comparatively low wages the owners could not afford to replace the older laid-up vessels. Shipbuilders and owners resented others making profits while they themselves were barely covering expenses, hence they drove savagely hard bargains with suppliers of equipment.

To many industrialists the General Strike of 1926 looked as though it might prove to be the crowning disaster. More than two million workers were directly involved in sympathy with the coalminers' long-standing grievance over poor wages. A large proportion of Halls' employees joined the strikers but enough stayed at work to avert a closure. The General Strike lasted only nine days and ended in defeat for the strikers, but the miners' strike which continued for another six months did the greatest damage to industry, especially the shipyards. Halls had reason to be glad of their vertical transport and experience in land refrigeration. In the Annual Report for 1927 Ward counted his company's blessings.

> We have reason to be thankful that things have not been as bad for us as for many of those firms whose names have been household words in past years as steady yielders of dividend, and whose debentures, or even preference shares, have been considered almost gilt-edged investments. As if things in these days of post-war readjustment were not bad enough, when we are making a slow, very slow, recovery from the inevitable effects of the greatest calamity of human experience, followed by the economically disastrous boom, certain misguided sections of the people of this country must needs make a gigantic experiment to further ideals by holding up the industries and services of the realm. Although the consequences were soon realised by the wise heads among the labour leaders and the general strike called off, the after effects have been long lasting, the price has to be paid, and our balance sheet, among many others, shows what it means to disturb the essential and inter-related activities of the community.

This was a sober and not unsympathetic statement, and not levelled only against the trade unions. He complained that high taxation and other costs were inhibiting foreign trade, and keeping profits and the standard wages of skilled men lower than they should be, though 'in our case,' he said, 'the earnings of the majority of workmen are substantially improved by piece work and bonus payments.' He added:

> The returns of sixty-six engineering companies, by the British Engineers' Association, show that for 1926 the average profits earned on paid-up capital have been no more than 2.8 per cent, while the dividends have averaged 3.9 per cent, showing the extent to which reserves are being depleted. It is a grim commentary upon the ordering of human affairs that the monetary return for the technical skill, honest workmanship and careful finance which go to the make-up of well-run British engineering concerns should compare so unfavourably with that yielded by industries of much less importance to the general well-being, but so it is and so it always has been.

There were some compensations in the form of sizable orders for refrigeration plant from overseas. One was for a large installation at Cape Town Docks for the pre-cooling and storage of fruit, part of a big project by the South African government on behalf of the growers to cool the produce rapidly before shipment and, as it were, seal in the quality.

Further orders followed for the extension of this development and later a visit by a Hall executive to the West Indies procured orders for similar installations in several of the islands. Other Hall contracts included a large fur storage installation for the Hudson Bay Company in the City of London and many orders from brewers, one of which was for a larger and more modern machine to replace that supplied in 1895. The old machine was still giving good service after more than thirty years! That is not, in fact, as remarkable as it might seem, for refrigeration plant does not become obsolescent to the same degree as production machinery. Improvements in design and performance are introduced to serve expanding operations and new purposes, but many owners continue to find their old machines as useful as when new. The Hall factory in Dartford is still able to provide parts for installations up to forty years old or more.

Those orders in the later 1920s could not disguise from the Board the progressive deterioration of the nation's economic condition and the inevitable further effect upon their business. The General Strike had been a British sickness, but the great Depression which followed within three or four years was a world-wide epidemic which devastated industrial nations in the same way as war. Every industry suffered, but shipbuilding tells the story most dramatically from Britain's and Halls' point of view. In 1929 British yards were building 1,650,000 tons of shipping. In 1930 the figure had dropped to 950,000 tons, in 1931 to 200,000, and in 1932 to 72,000. By that date there were yards without a single keel. Ships were laid up uncompleted, the most vivid illustration for the people of the predicament of their country being the cessation of work on the Cunarder *534*, which was to win fame in peace and war as the *Queen Mary*. This took with it into temporary retirement a large Hall refrigeration installation and one of the biggest single marine orders for Hallmark machines.

Engineering companies dependent upon the shipyards laid off tens of thousands of workers. Unemployment at Halls was below the national average at its worst thanks to its Hallmark enterprise and diversified interests, but the situation was bad enough. Orders for the larger marine jobs were at a standstill, though there were a few orders from old customers for extensions involving a good deal of brine pipework and additions to existing refrigeration in order to increase performance. Maintaining the depots at the shipbuilding centres for erection work was becoming a heavy burden. Employees were put on short time, taking one week off in three and drawing unemployment pay for that week. The company also took on odd jobs of engineering in order to keep the plant active. When that potent personality J.D. Farmer, later to become Halls' marine director, gained an order from under the noses of competitors for refrigerating the 500,000 cubic-foot cargo installation in s.s. *Port Chalmers* the work was shared out in the drawing office to give every man a little relief from enforced idleness. A big land order, announced to the employees by Lord Dudley Gordon in a period of deepest gloom in 1931, was greeted with cheers. This was to supply to the Grimsby Ice Company four quadruple-cylinder vertical ammonia compressors, directly electrically-driven, to replace a miscellaneous collection of old steam-driven machinery. The plant, with a total output of about 1100 tons of ice per day, exceeded in capacity any installation of its kind placed in Britain or elsewhere. Grimsby was at that time the leading fishing port in Britain and perhaps in the world, and further orders came to Halls in later years from the same source.

Herbert Ward remained optimistic about the company's ability to survive and the future of refrigeration. 'Our company has been fortunate in its chief speciality,' he told the shareholders in 1931. 'Refrigeration seems perennially to renew its youth.' But it was not an industry in which production could be stepped up quickly and recovery achieved without a struggle.

> Unlike manufacturers of standard articles such as oil engines or electric motors [said the Chairman] we have to design separately the arrangements and various details of each refrigeration plant before estimates can be prepared and submitted, and in the existing conditions of trade the number of estimates in relation to orders received is exceptionally high. The preparation of these schemes involves an expensive staff if we are to maintain our position in the industry.

The toll taken by the depressed years figures as a delayed action in the mid-thirties balance sheets. In 1932, despite the Depression, the company managed to pay a dividend, though a reduced one. In 1934 the business made a loss and for the first time in twenty-nine years had to skip the dividend on the Ordinary shares. The Board decided upon a rearrangement of capital, returning 30 per cent of the par value of the Ordinary and Preference shares to the shareholders. The return of capital had reduced the company's liquid assets, but it was justified by its general effect on the financial position of the business. The reaction of the Stock Exchange in the valuation of the shares was favourable, and the Preference shares, on which the company had never failed to pay a dividend, were quoted at a premium. By 1934 staff salaries, which had been cut when the Depression was at its height, had been restored.

Recovery had come in time for a happy celebration of the company's 150th anniversary in 1935. Local acclaim on that occasion was as keen for the octogenarian 'second founder' as for the business which owed so large a stretch of its longevity to his energy and talents. Everard Hesketh had retired from the Board two years before, but his voice was still heard with respect in its deliberations. To Dartford he was an eminent and beloved citizen, and as we have seen a multiple benefactor. The latest benefaction had been a gift to the town in 1932 from Mr and Mrs Everard Hesketh of a building to house a massage and electrotherapy clinic. Electrical treatment had relieved his arthritis, he said, and he wanted other sufferers to have the same facility.

The revival in the shipyards (over one million tons on the stocks in 1936 and 1937) was reflected in Halls' order book. It was fortunate for the company that the largest category of new building – the big food-carrying cargo ships – was the one that called for the largest class of refrigeration installations. A change had been taking place in the refrigeration of perishable cargoes. Up to 1935 the cargo spaces had been cooled by

The Patterson Pavilion provides amenities for members of the Social and Athletic Club and their families. It was named after Victor Patterson, works manager and member of the board from 1925 to his death in 1957

brine grids with some assistance from fans, but that system was now gradually being replaced with one relying mainly on ducts to distribute the air through the cargo spaces, and with only minimal use of overhead brine grids in some circumstances. Those changes required corresponding improvements in the design and insulation of the refrigerated environment.

Another change at about this time was the replacement of steam drive by electric drive. The departure from steam, which had given good service for so many years, caused some regret at Halls because they had manufactured the steam parts themselves at a good profit, and now had to buy the electric motors which it would not pay them to produce in their own works. Nevertheless they recognized that electric drive had advantages, not strictly in refrigeration, which from the customers' point of view tipped the scales in its favour. There were other innovations still at an experimental stage. Before the trade recession Halls had supplied diesel drive for compressors to the order of the Nelson Line, and now other shipping lines were beginning to show interest. An installation of four electrically driven compressor units in the passenger and cargo ship

Orion broke new ground, for a London passenger ship at least, by using one of the units to ventilate the dining saloon. Air-conditioning was being increasingly included in marine refrigeration contracts. Run-of-the-mill work was also growing, including additions to the refrigeration in the *Queen Mary*, no longer a number in a paralysed yard but triumphantly at sea, the most spectacular symbol of economic recovery.

'Never before,' said the Chairman in his 1936 Report, 'has a more varied and representative output issued from our Works.' In the four years up to the outbreak of war the company supplied plant for the liquefaction of chlorine, for the low temperature testing of motor engines, for the manufacture of boot polish, matches and confectionery, and air-conditioning equipment for tobacco factories, cinemas, banks and public buildings. By 1938 air-conditioning was second only to work for the brewers in the land refrigeration department. There were increased orders for ice rinks, especially in Scotland, with the devotees of curling mainly in mind. Successive mild winters had prevented sufficient ice formation on the lakes and some curling clubs were losing members. Halls came to the rescue of the national sport with artificial indoor lakes which were independent of weather. The growing interest in ice hockey helped to

A modern ice skating rink under construction at Stirling. The company has supplied refrigeration systems for ice skating since the late 1890s

encourage this development further. Halls were specialists also in the gas storage of fruit, particularly in the maintenance of a controlled atmosphere for apples, and had helped to put Britain ahead of other countries in this branch of refrigeration. The USA was the world leader in quick freezing of foodstuffs, but Halls were prominent in promoting the technique in Britain. They had designed a rotary conveyor primarily for the quick freezing of herrings which had proved so successful that the Herring Board exempted herrings frozen by the machines from some of the restrictions imposed on the kippering of herrings.

Throughout the Depression Halls had kept contact with their overseas agents and gained a good proportion of what little business a world in crisis could afford. Economic recovery brought orders for general cold storage from Argentina, Malta, Lithuania and the Straits Settlements, and for air-conditioning from Canada and the Near and Far East. The company made special efforts to cultivate the Dominions and the vast Indian market. Some contracts, as always in export trade, were frustrated by local habit and prejudice. A contract for the provision of numerous cold stores in India was part of a scheme promoted by the Army to establish a central abattoir with distribution and cold storage facilities both for the military and, through private enterprise, for the civil population. At the last moment, however, political and religious objections were raised and the scheme had to be abandoned. There were fortunately no such obstacles to the fulfilment of a contract for cooling and ventilation plants in Indian gold-mines. An installation at the Ooregum mine in the state of Mysore proved so successful that it was soon followed by a similar order for the adjoining Champion Reef mine, and later by a third mine in the same group.

The gold-mine contracts demonstrate how refrigeration and air-conditioning can save lives as well as provide comfort and increased productivity. Ooregum mine, at 8330 feet, was one of the deepest in the world. At 8000 feet the rock temperature was 134°F. and increased 9°F. for each additional 1000 feet. 'There comes a point,' wrote J. Spalding and T.W. Parker (Halls' engineer on the job) in a paper delivered to the Institute of Mining and Metallurgy, 'when an increase of 1% in wet bulb temperature marks the difference between being just able to carry on and complete failure to do so.' In such conditions men are not merely inefficient but accident-prone. Ventilation by fans at the face had reached an economic limit, and the mine was so dry and dusty that it would have needed vast quantities of cooling water and water piping, which could be a source of danger in the event of a rock burst. It was less expensive and more effective to install an ammonia refrigeration plant at the surface capable of cooling 150,000 cubic feet of air a minute. The saving in compressed air and fan power more than repaid the operating costs of the conditioning plant. It made deepening of the mine possible and working conditions tolerable down to well over 10,000 feet. There was also a great reduction in accidents due to fatigue. 'No statistics,' wrote the authors of the paper, 'could adequately convey the transformation which had occurred underground in the general alertness and comfort of the labour and of the staff.'

Records and buildings were destroyed by a fire at the factory in 1937, and rebuilding was long delayed by the Second World War and its troubled aftermath

The revival of trade after the desperate early thirties had the appearance of a boom. J. & E. Hall enlarged their work force and by their 150th anniversay were said by Hesketh to be employing 2500 people in Dartford and in the branches and depots. Everard Hesketh, who retired to South Africa soon after the start of the Second World War and died there in 1942, had lived to see the payroll of the business he had rescued sixty-four years earlier multiply more than ten times. The Board were wary of regarding the trade activity that followed the great Depression as a boom; they had seen booms prove abortive before. There were nearly two million unemployed in Britain in 1938, a million fewer than in 1932 but not exactly a sign of national prosperity. It would require another war to reduce the numbers to a state of full employment in the widest sense – that is, leaving only the unemployable without work. The possibility of war with Germany had been in people's minds long before the Munich agreement of 1938 brought an illusory respite from anxiety, and the government's rearmament programme continued to keep the engineering industries alert to their responsibilities in those critical times. In 1937 Halls attributed only a small fraction of their output to rearmament orders, but they were aware that if the conflict came it would be an engineers' war and they tooled up in readiness. They modernized the workshops with mobile cranes and trucks, scrapped the rail-borne internal transport, installed overhead cranes and runways and improved lighting, heating and ventilation.

It is ironical that a business which was to escape damage from incendiary and explosive devices falling all around its buildings during six years of war should have suffered accidental damage before the external enemy had gone into action. On 7 September 1937 fire destroyed a section of the office building at Dartford and did £40,000 worth of damage. Fortunately it was restricted to the least valuable part of the premises; had it spread to the adjoining pattern store, full of wooden models of machine parts, the place would have blazed like a forest in a drought. Fortunately also there were no casualties and the worst loss was the destruction of all the records of three important departments. Employees had to search their memories to reconstruct the details, but otherwise there was hardly any interruption of work and no one lost his job. The staff moved into the canteen next morning, and the management acquired and adapted some empty cottages nearby for temporary accommodation. The word 'temporary' was stretched to inordinate length by the government's clamp-down on all but essential building while the war threatened and throughout the war years. The company had reason to be grateful to the three local fire brigades for prompt and efficient aid, but they learnt the lesson that a manufacturing business may have to rely on self-help especially in perilous times. By the time war broke out, they had organized their own fire-fighting unit and also made preparations for the vastly more extensive conflagration which would set the country ablaze and indeed change the shape and character of the world.

Refrigeration and air conditioning plant was supplied to the
Queen Mary before her maiden voyage in 1936 and greatly
augmented after the Second World War

CHAPTER 8
An Engineers' War

Unlike the First World War, the Second, which started in September 1939, did not find the nation entirely unprepared. There had been many warnings in the preceding three years. Hitler's unopposed occupation of the Rhineland in 1936 was the catalyst and the Spanish Civil War was a rehearsal for a worldwide conflict. The alignment of forces hostile to Britain and her allies continued relentlessly, with the alliance of Italy and Nazi Germany following the Italian conquest of Abyssinia, the German annexation of Austria and destruction of the Czech defences, and the Munich agreement of 1938 which gave the Nazis their first – and bloodless – victory in a war still to be declared. Among the violent and sinister events of those years only Japan's invasion of China remained for some years unrecognized in Western Europe and North America as a potential element in a global conspiracy of conquest and domination.

Britain had barely recovered in twenty-one years from the losses sustained in the First World War. Her territory had escaped serious damage, but the slaughter on the French battlefields had impoverished her manpower resources for a generation. Industries and other assets were lost mainly to the USA. In defence capacity and in moral and political authority among the nations, Britain was a considerably diminished force. The self-distrust which had bought a respite at Munich contrasted with the ebullience which had greeted the prospect of a fight in 1914. The mood in 1939 was one of acceptance but also of resolution, in the realization that there was no escape from the predicament except by defeating the enemy.

At Halls there was no abrupt transition from peace to war. Most of the company's work was in any case of national importance, and its products are relevant to war as to peacetime requirements. In the precarious peace that followed Munich, and the quiet months immediately after the declaration of war (known derisively as 'the phoney war'), such redeployment of men and machines as the circumstances demanded could be accomplished undisturbed by an enemy who was fully engaged in overrunning his Continental neighbours. That veteran of the First World War, Dudley Gordon, was now the Company's Chairman in succession to Ward who had retired because of ill-health. Apart from a brief shocked slow-down under the impact of Munich the engineering industries, including J. & E. Hall, were busy and in good spirits. Exports of machinery – in Halls' case mainly to the Commonwealth – had been in 1938 21 per cent higher by value than the high figure of 1937; and though the decline in shipbuilding had had some adverse effect upon Halls' speciality, the company was fortunate in that a large proportion of the new tonnage included refrigeration installations. Among important customers were Houlder Line, Union Castle, Shaw Savill, United Fruit Company and, understandably, the British Admiralty. A new Board of Trade ruling for provisioning cargo ships benefited sales of Hallmark machines. Breweries continued to head the list on land, but small automatic plants were also in demand for beer cooling in bars and restaurants, cellar cooling in public houses, ice-making in hospitals, very low-temperature testing of instruments and aeronautical research. Meanwhile installation of lifts and escalators continued for large passenger liners as well as for hospitals, public buildings and blocks of flats and offices. In the early stages of the war 'business as usual' seemed in most sectors to serve the changing national purposes.

Changes in the pattern of production came gradually as the Germans swept westward across Europe, and in Britain the 'phoney' image faded even among the cynics. Refrigeration installations in cargo ships became more selective, but an island nation would continue to depend on seaborne supplies. Work on ice rinks was shelved, vertical transport and small refrigeration machine production was cut to war essentials; and manufacturing space was released for such contracts as blood storage refrigeration, cooling meat foods and increasing existing defence work for home and export. It was in the national interest to continue exporting to British territories and friendly neutrals, especially to replace machinery formerly supplied by Germany. So important were the overseas commitments that a director, J.D. Farmer, was sent to South Africa to supervise contracts in hand and reassure agents that Halls of Dartford would not neglect them.

Completely converting even an already strategically important business to war production was still a laborious operation requiring much thought, time and expense. Defence against military attack was, however, even more pressing, because it had to be started from scratch. Air-raid precautions were taken on government instruction before war was declared. Halls called for volunteers among the male and female employees to organize the company's defences, trained them in fire-fighting, provided equipment for dealing with incendiary bombs and constructed air-raid shelters. While the country was still at peace the company held an exercise involving complete evacuation of the works with every employee under cover and all the control posts manned. Immediately upon the declaration of war all roof lights and windows were obscured, so that work could continue day and night undetected by raiding aircraft. War production was carried out under difficulties, but this was total war with no escape for civilians from the dangers and responsibilities. The whole country was in the front line and South-East England its most vulnerable sector. The workers understood the position and accepted the difficulties philosophically. Good relations between management and employees kept morale high. Among the instruments was the Joint Production Consultative and Advisory Committee set up as part of the regional organization of the Ministry of Production. Representatives of the workpeople elected to the committee met members of management to consider means of increasing and improving production, also to discuss working conditions and rewards.

In order to reduce loss of working time when air attacks were intensified during the Battle of Britain, the company organized a corps of roof spotters, and built additional shelters close to the working points to provide easy access when the alert sounded and enable the swift resumption of work immediately upon the all-clear signal. The shelters were built of steel and concrete to withstand an explosive charge; they were air-conditioned and had electric lighting and toilet facilities. The works were protected with sandbags produced on site by a special sandbag-filling machine. Equipment was available for dealing with casualties and for decontamination in the event of a gas attack. An air-raid siren blared its warning to the town from the roof of one of Halls' buildings. Dartford was in the flight path of German bombers making for London and the docks. Indeed, Kent was part of the outer defences of the capital, where RAF fighters intercepted the attackers and where, during the flying-bomb period in the later years of the war, the barrage balloons entangled and brought down those ingenious and destructive weapons. An official air-raid control centre for a large area including the town of Dartford was located in the Works and connected with Observer Corps stations. Its function was to track and report upon the flying-bomb assault, virtually a second battle of Britain. During that comparatively brief period the course of 4438 of these missiles was recorded in the control room, 2000 of them in the immediate vicinity of Dartford. And those figures did not include manned aircraft bombings inflicted at intervals throughout the war. Though Halls' buildings escaped damage some of their members were not so lucky at home; among these was Victor Patterson whose house was destroyed by bombs, but the occupants were uninjured.

Engineering was a reserved occupation and indeed many manufacturing occupations were no less vital than battle in the field. Some members of the company had, however, joined the Forces and Territorials and Reservists were called up. As in the First World War, the dependants of fighting men were at a disadvantage financially compared with those of the factory workers, and the Board supplemented the official separation allowance to correct the inequality. Many of those who stayed in the factory joined the Home Guard and trained outside working hours for defence in the event of invasion. Again as in the First World War, the factory was brought up to the strength necessary for an intensified war effort by the recruitment of women. This time, however, within certain age limits the entire adult able-bodied population, male and female, was subject to government direction into work of national importance and young women had to serve in the Armed Forces, the war factories, government offices and other officially approved occupations. Sex discrimination, whether on grounds of prejudice or chivalry, was one of many indulgences that society had now to forgo. Women worked alongside men on rough, exacting and dirty jobs and did them as competently.

The social revolution brought about by wartime conditions impinged upon some of J. & E. Hall's foibles. They had always been reluctant to employ married women, but now found it expedient to accept even wives of employees. The rule about employing both husband and wife had been rigid and when a girl married a fellow employee she had been compelled to resign. An even more shattering assault on traditions was that women factory workers wanted to wear trousers! Before 1940 'nice' women always wore skirts; but now nice women were machining metal, soiling their hands with grease, sweeping up swarf and worrying more about the risk of catching a rare pair of nylon stockings on a sharp corner than about comfort or fatigue. They won from a reasonable management the right to dress appropriately for a man-size job.

Male employees posed other problems. In peacetime smoking had been prohibited in the factory; but in war the men worked long hours, suffered nerve-racking air-raid alerts day after day and often many times in the day, and wanted a comforting smoke. As a concession they were allowed to smoke in overtime periods before and after normal hours. Otherwise they were permitted to light up when the air-raid warning sounded but had to stop smoking immediately upon the all-clear signal. To add to the confusion, smoking was allowed in some corridors but not in others. The standard escape from bureaucratic entanglement was to slip into the toilet with a cigarette, so the management saw sense and rationalized the 'no smoking' rules.

For the first time in the country's history factory workers maintained supplies to the troops overseas while themselves under repeated enemy attack. 'They have now been working long hours,' said the 1942 Company Report, 'with little opportunity for change and relaxation for more than two years, but their energy and application continue at a high level . . . Visitors to our Works have commented on the wonderful spirit of goodwill and enthusiasm.' The Board did everything possible to ease the burden, maintained a high standard of ventilation and hygiene in the strictly blacked-out and closely guarded buildings, improved cooking and food quality in the canteen for day and night workers as far as official food rationing permitted and ensured the continued activity of the Social & Athletic Club. Even under the stress of current circumstances the directors planned for the future of the employees. The Benefit Fund had been in existence for over a quarter of a century on a non-contributory basis, and there had been a form of ex gratia pension payments. However, the management were aware of the need for a regular scheme of retirement pensions, under which no one would be in doubt either as to what he would receive on retirement nor at what age or under what circumstances he would be able to retire. A scheme was being discussed before war broke out, and by 1939 a Staff Pension and Life Assurance scheme had been formulated and funded out of the general reserve of the business.

By 1941 J. & E. Hall were fully employed on war production and in common with all essential industries they came virtually under government control. Refrigeration was covered by the Machinery and Plant Control Order made by the Board of Trade under Defence Regulations, and therefore remained a high priority. Considerable rearrangement of the company's production programme followed from market changes affecting non-essential items. For instance, the prohibition of all building except for government departments and war factories cut lift sales, and the halting of retail expansion reduced the demand for small Hallmark machines. Space was thus cleared for a massive and varied war effort on two levels: large-scale refrigeration for marine and land-based purposes, and the engineering of weapons and war machines.

On the eve of war in 1939, the refrigeration side of the business had been enlarged by the purchase of the goodwill and certain assets of Liverpool Refrigeration & Engineering Ltd and its subsidiary H. J. West Ltd. That group, which had been a respected competitor of Halls in the refrigeration field for many years, had been taken over by an engineering organization whose non-refrigeration business had grown to the point where it seemed expedient to shed the refrigeration commitments. Within a year of the purchase Halls absorbed this acquisition wholly into their existing business and opened several new accounts on the strength of the additions to their product range. Among these additions was a diesel-driven ammonia-type compressor for marine use where ammonia was not commonly employed as the refrigerant. By that time Halls were developing the range of Monobloc compressors, so-called because the cylinders were cast in one piece. They had been produced to meet mainly foreign competition with machines of lighter construction and less elaborate motion work, and like the high-speed types they were adapted for full automatic control. Halls had in fact been in the forefront of the automatic control of refrigeration as far back as 1927, shortly after the introduction of their Wembley compressor.

Throughout the six war years refrigeration remained Halls' major contribution to national survival and ultimate victory. It is hardly less important in peacetime but is taken for granted and operates unnoticed like all other agents of amenity and well-being. In war, however, dramatic events result upon any breakdown of refrigeration: the production of war material can be halted, the food supply may fail, battles may be lost and wounded men be denied life-saving treatment. A heavy responsibility rested upon J. & E. Hall as the leading practitioners and suppliers in this key section of the war effort. They provided every kind of fighting ship from submarines to battleships with plant for controlling the temperature in living quarters and for preserving provisions. The Royal Navy operated in every ocean and under all climatic conditions, and would have been seriously handicapped without reliable cooling equipment for men and magazines; it was impossible to operate efficiently in the warm waters of the Mediterranean and the Far East without the aid of refrigeration. The loss of refrigerated merchant shipping had become acute by 1941, and Halls were asked by the Admiralty to provide designs for emergency refrigerated tramp shipping in a programme involving about twenty ships. The programme had to be made with the utmost economy: money is also a precious war material. It is interesting to note that in effecting this economy Halls adopted a general principle of design which had been current thirty or forty years before in some of the earliest refrigerated ships built.

Most of the merchant ships lost had been torpedoed by German submarines and a very large proportion of the cargoes had consisted of food. Those losses were reflected in the rationing of supplies to the home population. When it became feasible to release the details, other countries were impressed with the British government's skilful management of fluctuating stocks in the interests of public nutrition and health. Half-way through the war nine million tons of Allied and neutral shipping had been sunk, and the figure had doubled by the end of the war. If any major contributory to the struggle at sea had failed – the shipyards, the naval escorts of convoys, the refrigerating plant – Britain might have suffered the fate of her friends and allies across the Channel.

Ships in private ownership were also equipped under Admiralty orders to a restricted wartime specification, but in such a way that the refrigeration plant could be brought up to peacetime requirements after the war. Halls were also concerned with an interesting programme to enlarge the refrigerated capacity of existing vessels to the limit by utilising any margins in the existing refrigerating power. This increased the carrying capacity of the ships by many thousands of tons of meat or other perishable cargo.

As part of the preparation for war the government had established emergency cold stores throughout the country to ensure an even distribution of food in every region. Their capacity was $18\frac{1}{4}$ million cubic feet. Halls supplied complete equipment for 25 per cent of this total, plus refrigeration machinery for stores equipped by other contractors, which meant that 37 per cent of the nationwide storage capacity was cooled by J. & E. Hall machinery. Large-scale cold storage was also provided overseas, particularly for the Middle East and Far Eastern campaigns. In the later stages of the war mobile refrigeration units of a completely new design much in advance of anything previously seen were produced to supply the troops with food in refrigerated trains and in temporary cold stores. The company designed two sizes of self-contained air-conditioning units to produce tolerable conditions in living quarters in hot and humid climates. Nearly 2000 of these units were ordered, many of them manufactured to Halls' design by firms which had never before done work of this kind. Halls had seconded Charles R. Croucher to the War Office to help in organizing the ACRE (Air Conditioning and Refrigeration for the East) programme. Among its functions was to supply cooling plant to the Forces fighting in Burma, and to base hospitals in the Far Eastern theatres of war. ACRE required four times as much refrigeration equipment as Halls could produce, and many other manufacturers participated in supplying parts. One of these was Searle Manufacturing Company Ltd who were later to become a subsidiary of the Hall-Thermotank Group.

All those installations were intended mainly for refrigeration, or for air-conditioning, or for both simultaneously. In fact, the two cannot be sharply separated: every air-conditioning plant uses a refrigeration compressor and any refrigeration system can be adapted to treat the environment or its specific contents. The interrelation between the

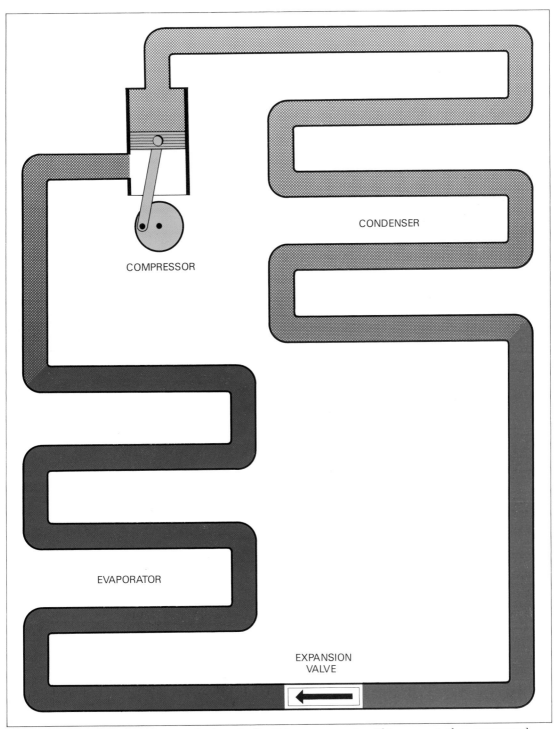

COMPRESSOR

CONDENSER

EVAPORATOR

EXPANSION
VALVE

Refrigeration is achieved by the vaporisation of a liquid in an evaporator. This vapour is then compressed, condensed back to a liquid and returned to the evaporator for further use

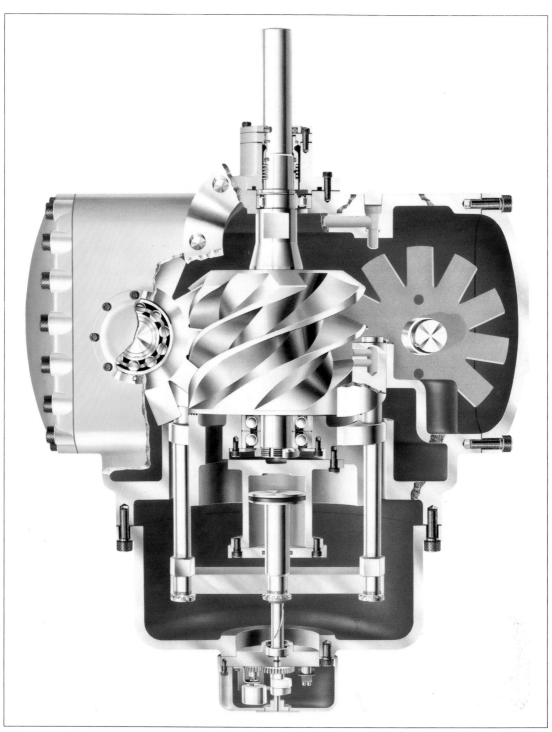

Cutaway sectional view of the Hallscrew refrigeration compressor. The machine, using a small number of moving parts, compresses the gas through the interaction of the star rotors which mesh with the single screw rotor

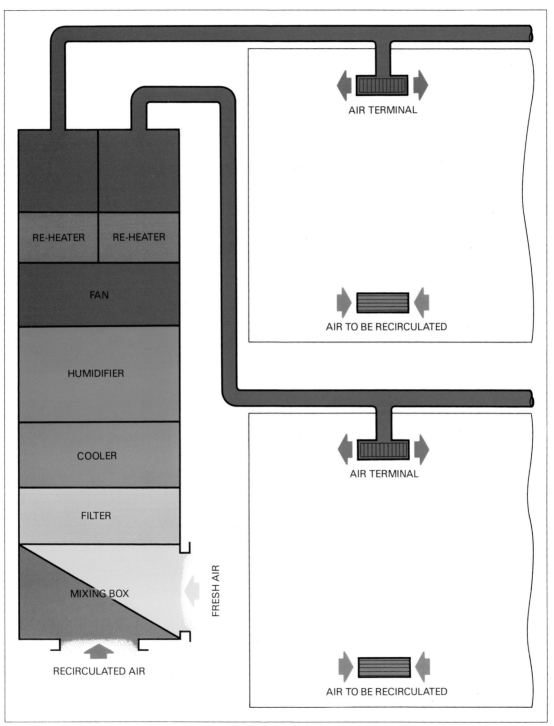

Diagrammatic illustration of a typical air conditioning cycle showing the mixing of recirculated and fresh air, the filtration, cooling, humidifying and reheating processes and the ducting of the treated air to air terminals serving the conditioned spaces

Aerial view of the factory complex in Hythe Street, Dartford, almost entirely rebuilt before the end of the 1970s

two and the areas of independence will be seen more clearly in the chapter describing the merger between J. & E. Hall Ltd and Thermotank Ltd. During the war Halls installed air-conditioning in some highly secret places; for instance, the government's Combined Operations headquarters and an emergency government headquarters deep under Horseferry Road, Westminster. A very interesting application of air-conditioning for which Halls supplied the refrigeration equipment was in a quarry at Corsham, Wiltshire, where valuable works of art from the British Museum were stored to save them from destruction by bombing. Refrigeration proved not only protective but curative, for the paintings had been removed initially to a store where they had suffered slight damage from damp. At Corsham they recovered and remained safe and in good condition throughout the war.

Where possible, manufacture of war material went underground for security against bombing. The war had halted the construction of an extension to the Central Line of the London Underground Railway, but the tunnel had been completed and rails laid for a four-station section. Given air-conditioning, this could be turned into a vast munitions factory. Halls were given the contract and installed four large marine-type refrigeration machines, one at each station, working in conjunction with air washers to control temperature and humidity and using CO_2 as the refrigerant for the safety of the workers. When the war ended the machines were dismantled and re-erected in their appropriate settings on board ship.

Refrigeration was employed to save lives as well as to destroy enemies, an important feature of the Second World War as compared with the first being the high percentage of recovery from serious wounds. One of the contributing factors was the blood transfusion service, which could not have been developed without the help of refrigeration. Halls provided a special type of refrigeration plant to produce plasma in powder form by extracting moisture from the blood under deep freezing in a high vacuum. This was one of the earliest applications of freeze-drying techniques, which are now standard procedures in medical and other scientific work and in some food processing. The two large plants equipped by Halls produced more than three-quarters of a million pints of plasma, representing blood donations from about one and a half million people. Halls also supplied small self-contained refrigeration units for insulated lorries used by the blood transfusion services in the UK and overseas. It was not unusual for blood to be delivered to forward units on Continental battlefields on the day it had been collected. Freeze drying was also used in penicillin production at temperatures as low as minus 120°F, and here also much of the plant for processing and air-conditioning was supplied by J. & E. Hall.

Large-scale refrigeration plant in conjunction with heat exchangers was also supplied to the heavy chemical industry for such purposes as the liquefaction of chlorine, the extraction of magnesium and the manufacture of tetraethyl lead and synthetic rubber. Hall refrigeration was used in the testing under low temperature of scientific instruments, tanks, guns and torpedoes. An important application was in aeronautical research. The equipment was used to remove the heat generated in the high-speed wind tunnel of the Royal Aircraft Establishment at Farnborough, and also to produce the low temperatures – sometimes in conjunction with low-pressure conditions – in which aircraft and their pilots would have to operate at high altitude.

All those highly refined uses of refrigeration are today accepted practice, but in the early 1940s under the stimulus of the national danger they were miracles of scientific invention. Refrigeration still produces its miracles, as will be seen, but they are perhaps less spectacular and less readily grasped by the lay observer.

The War Department made good use of Halls' long experience and technical quality as refrigeration specialists, but as engineers Halls could turn their hands and machines to a large variety of products unrelated to the speciality. They were however able to find a related purpose for one of their subsidiary products. The lift and escalator division started to produce ammunition hoists for warships from the beginning of the war; in all, 104 hoists were made and fitted in ships which included the famous destroyer *Cossack* and the Fleet Air Arm carriers *Implacable* and *Indefatigable*. Another demand from the Admiralty was for magnetic mines, which presented problems of design which were successfully overcome. They had to have great strength to withstand the shock of being dropped into the sea, together with light weight for carrying in the Swordfish aircraft of the Fleet Air Arm. By the end of the war in Europe 6130 mines had been produced. Other equipment produced by the company for the Royal Navy included 550 paravanes, 2800 mine-sinkers for harbour defence mines, 423 machine-gun mountings for the defence of ships against low-flying aircraft, and specially designed gun mountings for vessels of various types and sizes.

Among the war devices made by women employees of the Dartford works were over 15,000 firing pistols for controlling the detonation of depth charges at the desired level below the surface of the water. In another part of the works specially equipped for the purpose, more than two and a half million two-inch mortar smoke bombs were produced almost solely by female labour. These bombs were used for confusing and breaking up enemy infantry attacks or for screening attacks launched by British and Allied troops. Long after the end of the war, when that section of the works had reverted to its normal functions, it was still called the Bomb Shop and the name persists today among the old hands.

All this was routine conventional war production. An unusual and in application more exciting assignment was Halls' contribution to FIDO and PLUTO. FIDO (Fog Investigation Dispersal Operation) was a device to enable aircraft to land in thick fog, even at night. It consisted of a pipeline the whole length of the runway, with perforations at intervals. Fuel pumped into the pipes was ignited at the holes to provide a blazing flare path which released enough heat to thin the fog and provide visibility for a reasonably safe landing. Halls produced the steel pipes and delivered them welded and wound on drums. They provided pipework also for PLUTO (Pipeline Under the Ocean), a device for conveying liquid fuel across the Channel to France for the use of the troops fighting on the Continent after the Normandy landings. This was a safer method than exposing tankers to the enemy's bombers.

A year before the landing of British and American troops on the Normandy coast the turning point in the war had occurred with the victories at El Alamein and Stalingrad, the collapse of Italy and the rolling back of the Japanese in the Pacific. But there were shocks still to come in Europe, not least – from Britain's point of view – the havoc caused in London and the South East by the V1 missiles (flying bombs) and the V2 rockets which ceased only when the launching sites were overrun in the liberation of France and the Low Countries.

As far as the exigencies of war permitted, J. & E. Hall had tried to continue serving their civilian customers, but suppliers for that market were restricted and licences were required. There were concessions for the food industries, especially dairies, and for the brewing industry where equipment damaged by bombing needed to be replaced. In addition to refrigeration for the brewing processes, air-conditioning was being used increasingly in maltings. In total war it was difficult to discriminate between the needs of the Armed Forces and the civilian population, since the home territory was a war zone and suffered attack and casualties as did the Forces in foreign battlefields and on the seas. Food was in a sense war material. So indeed was beer. Halls not only supplied equipment to assist production of beer for the troops overseas, but installed refrigeration plant in specially equipped ships, in effect floating breweries, which brewed the comforting beverage on the spot for the forces in the Far East.

The company's war effort could not be revealed to shareholders until the war ended. There had been a succession of laconic reports, each in smaller type than the last. The Report for 1943 was a small single-fold sheet, evidence that paper was also a nationally important material and in short supply like other commodities which had to be brought in across submarine-infested seas. The first post-war Report, that of 1946, proclaimed the company's fine production record as described above. Two senior members were rewarded with a seat on the Board: A.G. Guthrie, who had headed the land department since 1919 and built it up from a comparatively unimportant position to one of the leading divisions; and R.P. Willcox, who had been since 1932 the company's resident engineer in South Africa. He remained in South Africa, joined the Board of Halls' agents there and gave help and guidance to the company's representatives in adjacent territories.

Halls had been throughout the war active members of their appropriate export group under the Export Council of the Board of Trade. The government appreciated that in a war for national survival the industrial companies that helped to make survival possible must be enabled to salvage the wherewithal to rebuild their fortunes in what they hoped would be the peaceful years ahead.

Board of Directors of J. & E. Hall Ltd in 1953. *From the left*
V.A. Patterson, Lord Dudley Gordon, H.W. Pasteur, A.
Greenfield, W. Ball, J.D. Farmer, E.G. Russell-Roberts, Dr F.A.
Willcox, R.P. Willcox

CHAPTER 9

Post-war Progress

J. & E. Hall emerged from six years of war service into a profoundly changing world. National boundaries had been redrawn and many obliterated. New affiliations were forming among the nations and power was being redistributed. Nazism and fascism had been defeated only to be replaced by a communist menace from Eastern Europe. Old empires – British, French, Dutch – had broken up and independent nations, especially in Africa and Asia, were arising out of the former colonies. As an international business Halls of Dartford had to adjust to unfamiliar conditions in the world at large, and at the same time work within the changes of political power in the world close at hand. Big public utilities in Britain (gas, electricity, coal and transport) with the addition of the steel industry were nationalized; the Welfare State, envisaged while the outcome of the war was still in doubt, had become a reality. There were temporary events which created problems for businesses hoping to resume normal operation quickly and smoothly: a labour shortage, inevitable while demobilization took its course; a dispute in the coal-mining industry which caused power cuts nationwide (though Halls were fortunate in having their own generating plant); restrictions on building which hampered physical reconstruction and growth, and on overseas travel and currency movements which complicated export trade. There was even some dislocation of the home food supply requiring bread rationing – unprecedented in peacetime and avoided during the war.

It was not until the publication of the 1947 Company Report that J. & E. Hall were able to announce that they had virtually completed their change-over to full peacetime production. Even so, they had fared better than most businesses, since both world wars had left them with their basic business interest unchanged. The customers had remained the same – shipyards and the merchant marine, the Royal Navy, the food and drink industries, manufacturers of various products, medical and scientific establishments. Even the company's buildings had survived intact under prolonged bombardment from the air. The post-war prospects were therefore favourable. But the war had

133

left individual business problems over and above the effects of the larger and deeper injuries sustained by the national economy.

Some of Halls' problems arose out of the nature of their wartime work. Their output of war material (and refrigeration machines were just as important a war material as bombs) was enormous and absorbed all the company's resources and energies. There was no room for business development or technical progress. Some useful experience was gained in improvisation, finding short cuts, and production economy, but the emphasis was on output and delivery in order to increase fighting power and replace losses. Profitability was in abeyance. In both world wars it was generally recognized that industry must not grow fat on the national emergency, and the government made sure by skimming off most of the fat. The main instrument was Excess Profits Tax (EPT), which was based largely upon the rate of profit the business had made before the war. While it was in principle an exercise in rough justice, it tended to weigh most heavily upon businesses whose profit had been hardest hit by the national and international economic disasters of the pre-war decade. Halls was one of these. As early in the war as 1940 the Chairman, Lord Dudley Gordon, in his Report to the shareholders referred to the provision he had had to make for 100 per cent EPT as 'an example of the difficulty of accumulating any special reserves to meet the inevitable period of readjustment after the war'. The company's profit before tax for the financial year ending September 30th 1937 had been, at £47,388, nearly £20,000 lower than that for the previous year owing to reduced margins on a healthy turnover. The profit for 1938 had risen to £69,280, but for 1939 it was about £10,000 lower, reflecting the cost of air-raid precautions.

In the event, the business was not squeezed too drastically. Profits (after tax) did rise progressively during the six war years from £65,841 in 1940 to £98,911 in 1945, but it was a residue after deduction of wartime extras such as war insurance premiums, National Defence Contribution, additional ARP expenditure and EPT as well as Income Tax. To take a typical example, the net profit before tax for 1943 was £235,000, of which 83 per cent (£195,000) was taken by EPT and Income Tax, 11 per cent (£26,000) was distributed to shareholders, and the remaining 6 per cent (£14,000) was carried forward to reserve. EPT was abolished at the end of 1946, and companies which had paid the highest (100 per cent) rate received a rebate. In Hall's case this amounted to £32,807 in respect of the financial year ending September 30th 1945, to be spent on developing and equipping the business.

The government was, on the whole, understanding in their treatment of the war industries. In 1943 they backed their optimism about the outcome of the war by forming a Ministry of Reconstruction, and encouraged companies to give some thought to the restoration of their fortunes after victory, without of course diminishing their war effort. They allowed Halls some latitude in keeping their normal markets alive at home, especially the brewing industry, and in helping their overseas agents to show the flag for Britain and for refrigeration, so that an important segment of the future should not become a casualty. When the war ended the J. & E. Hall Board of Directors called their overseas representatives to a conference to discuss the special needs of their markets.

Wars always leave a surplus of goods to be disposed of quickly, sometimes to the disadvantage of industries struggling back into production. The release of transport vehicles at the end of the First World War was an extreme and, for Halls and other motor manufacturers, a painful case. This time the circumstances for Halls were quite different. There was a government residue of refrigeration equipment which the company was glad to re-purchase in order to appease a six-year backlog of demand for refrigeration plant from old customers at home and overseas. The clamour would have created a boom if the war had not depleted stocks of raw materials and left a shortage of labour. Middle Eastern customers came to Halls with orders for refrigeration machines, ice plants and air-conditioning and the tussle between the home and overseas departments in the company for the limited production continued until the end of the 1940s.

The Merchant Navy, urgently in need of new refrigerated tonnage, was a major candidate, since losses from sinking by submarines and mines had been colossal despite all the precautions. Old hands in the company's London office which arranged shipping involving government contracts remember encountering ships whose names had been obliterated for security reasons and whose destination one did not dare inquire. The ships sailed in convoy under armed protection and tried to minimize losses by dispersal when attacked. Frantic wartime rebuilding in British yards, and the vast American mass production of makeshift Liberty ships, still left a deficit in 1945 of six million tons of merchant shipping, to say nothing of the need to restore the naval strength. All the new ships would need some refrigeration, if only for air-conditioning and crews' provisions, while many would have to be fully refrigerated for the meat and fruit trades.

In the two years following the end of the war a very large increase in business, combined with the effect of the falling value of the pound, made it necessary for the company to seek additional finance. This was provided by their bankers. By 30 September 1946 the company's indebtedness totalled £300,000 and was subsequently further increased up to the limit of its permitted borrowing powers. It was a tribute to the financial strength of the business that the bank made these large advances without demanding security. The directors felt, however, that temporary injections of cash by way of loans would not meet their long-term needs, and in 1947 sought a permanent increase of capital through a one-for-two rights issue of 224,000 Ordinary shares at £2.5s. They decided also that the time had come for their Articles of Association, which had remained unchanged for over forty years, to be brought up to date, particularly to increase the company's borrowing powers. Among the changes made, therefore, were the conversion of both classes of shares into stock and the increase of the company's Authorised Capital to one million pounds.

A further change in the capital structure of the company was made in 1954, when the Authorised Capital was increased to £1,500,000 by the creation of 500,000 shares of £1 each (128,000 Ordinary shares and 372,000 Undesignated shares), and by the capitalization of reserves totalling £336,000.

Halls' cautious financial policy was exemplified in their build-up of reserves for development and as a hedge against slow payers and other contingencies arising out of the vagaries of the shipbuilding industry. Dudley Gordon evidently felt that the nature of reserves was misunderstood by many shareholders as well as workers, for he took considerable space in his 1951 Chairman's Statement to explain in elementary terms why the reserves could not be distributed as wages or dividends without affecting the company's ability to trade and give employment. These reserves, he pointed out, were not in the form of cash or security but inextricably tied up in buildings, new machinery and the materials of manufacture. Rising prices made it essential to create large reserves for stock replacement and plant renewal.

The company's resources of money and men were stretched to the limit by the post-war replacement of the depleted Merchant Navy and the overhaul and refitting for civilian use of ships which had been taken over for war service. Between 1945 and 1951 orders poured in from all the most important shipping companies. Refrigeration machinery and equipment accounted for over 90 per cent of the company's total sales and half of this was for marine work, mainly for the carriage of foodstuffs. To achieve the programme the company had to enlist outside help; the works could cope with assembly, but had to call upon as many as twenty other firms for steel fabrication and heat exchanger manufacture, and to use the products of twenty-seven foundries. Meanwhile Halls explored ways of reducing what was threatening to become excessive dependence on others by research into improved manufacturing techniques, installation of automatic machinery, introduction of the latest management methods such as production control and work study and, with enthusiastic support from the trade unions, retraining key workers in the new ideas and systems. Those post-war years of opportunity and output under high pressure accelerated the company's progress towards a modern concept of engineering production.

The pressure on the marine department had eased by the end of the decade, and the changing volume of business was reflected in the rise and fall of profits from year to year. But the number of cargo ships fitted with refrigeration plant continued at quite a high level: thirty-three in 1950, falling to twenty-five in 1957. During those years there was a large increase in tanker building, but from Halls' point of view tanker owners were poor customers, ordering comparatively small-scale air-conditioning plants for 'comfort cooling' in the crews' quarters and refrigeration for preservation of their provisions. In the 1950s an increasing proportion of refrigeration in cargo ships and also in liners was being used for air-conditioning. The Chairman said, 'Air-conditioning, with the immense increase of ice consumption on all classes of ships, particularly passenger vessels, leads one to the conclusion that the application of cooling to the interior and exterior of human beings is likely in the future to form a not inconsiderable part of our business.' An interesting example was the Shaw Savill liner *Southern Cross*, fitted with ten of the latest type of Hall Veebloc compressors, only two of which were used for cold storage and general hotel service, and the remaining eight for air-conditioning. The installation was so arranged that the compressors could also act as heat pumps, taking heat from the sea to warm the passenger accommodation in cold latitudes.

This was not quite the first application of the dual purpose function in a ship. It had been used a year or two before when the newly designed high-speed Veebloc compressors were installed in H.M. Survey Vessel *Vidal*. The ship was designed for hydrographic surveying and charting in all climates from the Poles to the Equator, and its refrigeration plant could be used to extract heat even from water at Arctic temperatures. But the principle of deriving heat from a cold-creating machine was neither new nor even very remarkable. After all, an operating compressor converts suction gas at low pressure and temperature to delivery gas at a higher pressure and temperature. The reason for the compressor having had only limited application for heating is that the initial capital cost is high. It is worthwhile when, as in a ship, its main purpose is to cool the atmosphere, and instead of standing idle when heating and not cooling is required it can save the load on a direct heating plant by deputizing as a heater. It is particularly worth-while when its use is seasonal, as in a plant supplied to Ind Coope & Allsopp in 1950 which was used for malting in summer and as a heat pump in winter.

After the war quick freezing began to make headway mainly in the preservation of fish, vegetables and soft fruit. In this technique, too, J. & E. Hall had made early trials, as long ago in fact as the first decade of the century. The difference between slow and quick freezing is in the size of ice crystals formed from the water in the product. Slow freezing gives the crystals time to build up into sharp fragments of ice, which damage the tissues of the product and leave it mushy and unappetising when thawed. Quick freezing, down to 10° below zero F. (i.e. over 40° of frost) halts crystal formation while the particles are still small. Because of the low temperatures involved, transport of quick-frozen foods posed special problems of insulation and of ship and refrigeration plant design. The big development was to take place in the food processing factories and in the transport and storage of the products on land.

An important technical change in refrigeration practice had been the introduction just before the war of a new refrigerant. Up to that time CO_2 had been by far the most suitable refrigerant for shipboard use, and indeed held the lead until long after the Second World War. Ammonia was used as well as CO_2 in many land installations, and Halls had established methyl chloride with great success in their Hallmark machines. The new refrigerant was a near relative of methyl chloride, the first of the new range of halocarbon refrigerants developed in America by Du Pont and marketed under the generic trade name of 'Freon'. The producers did potential customers the further service of naming the first of these new refrigerants 'Freon 12,' as an alternative to its technical designation dichlorodifluoromethane. It differed from methyl chloride in being virtually harmless; its discoverer Thomas Midgley is said (by Isaac Asimov in his biographical

137

Encyclopaedia of Science and Technology) to have demonstrated its safety by taking a deep lungful and breathing it out over a candle flame, which quietly expired.* Freon 12 had other desirable properties: it had no taste nor odour, did not attack non-ferrous metals and could therefore be used in any kind of refrigeration system. Since it operated at relatively low working pressure it permitted a considerable reduction in the size and weight of the hardware. On the debit side was its high cost and, in the 1940s and 1950s, the difficulty of obtaining supplies. The position was eased when ICI started to produce the gas in 1948, under the brand name 'Arcton 6,' later 'Arcton 12,' with plant supplied by J. & E. Hall.

The halocarbon range of refrigerants, in various forms distinguished by numbers, are today almost the only gases used for the larger marine and, to a lesser degree, land-based refrigeration plants, occupying the place that CO_2 had held for a couple of generations. Its early application in the USA as well as in Britain was mainly in air-conditioning. Some of the fifty-three separate refrigeration machines which Halls installed in the *Queen Mary* used Freon 12 as the refrigerant, and its equivalent Arcton 6 was used in the ten Veebloc compressors in the *Southern Cross*. One of the largest marine plants using this refrigerant was supplied to the Swedish Shipping Company in 1952; it was capable of cooling 2000 tons of bananas in twenty-four hours, or maintaining a temperature of zero Fahrenheit throughout the cargo spaces.

The arrival of Freon 12 and its related halocarbons marked the beginning of the end of the long CO_2 era and it was partly with these new refrigerants in mind that Halls launched their Veebloc series of compressors. They occupied less space and used less power than the existing CO_2 and Monobloc compressors; they also operated at higher speed, initially up to 1000 rpm but in later years as high as 1750 rpm. Production of CO_2 machines was gradually phased out in the 1950s, but those in use continued to give good service and, indeed, many outlasted the ships in which they were installed. The Veebloc (so-called because the cylinders were arranged in the form of a V) was designed for use both with Freon – with marine needs in mind – and with ammonia, for land operation. With each of these refrigerants it served all but the very largest and smallest refrigeration purposes.

Prominent among those large-scale users were the big brewers and the Veebloc development coincided with important changes of scale in the brewery industry. Small maltings were being replaced by large mechanized units requiring delicate and dependable temperature and humidity control, which Halls' newly designed compressors could provide. There was a tendency in the larger breweries to centralize the entire refrigeration requirements in a single room, and Halls supplied Veebloc ammonia compressors with full automatic control for each individual service. The amalgamation of a multiplicity of small breweries to form the giants which dominate the industry today was well under way in the 1950s and proved very much to Halls' advantage. Halls were

---

*Midgley's experiment was more risky than he appears to have realized. Freon gas tends to decompose in the presence of a naked flame, forming phosgene, a highly poisonous gas.

represented in every branch and activity of the industry, and when mergers occurred it was often found that most or even all of the participants were already using their equipment. Almost inevitably in such cases Halls would be invited to extend and improve the installations. Popular taste was changing from draught to bottled beer and this also brought new opportunities. Halls designed refrigeration equipment for the bottling plants and stores and for cooling trays and shelves. Lager production, a big user of refrigeration, was also increasing in response to a demand stimulated by package holidays abroad. It is fermented at a lower temperature than ordinary beer and is then stored under refrigeration.

There was a market for compressors with even larger capacity than the Veebloc among leading brewers and other big users on land and at sea. For them J. & E. Hall developed a range of centrifugal compressors in cooperation with the British Thomson-Houston Company of Rugby using that company's steam turbine and air compression experience. Some of these plants, with data logging and other sophisticated devices, were supplied for the extension and modernization of fruit pre-cooling at Cape Town docks, where J. & E. Hall had installed the first such techniques many decades earlier. Centrifugal plants using Freon were installed in the deepest gold-mines in South Africa. Marine contracts for centrifugal compressors increased as more and more ships became air-conditioned throughout. These included well-known liners such as *Canberra* and *Oriana*, which were equipped additionally with Veeblocs and Hallmark compressors for low temperature duties.

Brewers continued to be the biggest non-marine users of Hall refrigeration, but others were growing in size and variety. Fishing ports which had been damaged by bombs during the war needed new ice-making plant. Orders came from chemical and dye factories, from Players and W.D. & H.O. Wills for their new cigarette factories in Nottingham and Newcastle respectively, from fruit growers for oxygen control in gas cold stores and from the broiler industry for poultry processing. The company supplied air-conditioning for comfort cooling in crane operators' cabs, also in the control pulpits in steel works where heat rising from processes on the floor can penetrate the glass screens to produce stifling conditions. Halls designed and manufactured large and complex plant to the requirements of the chief engineer of the Ministry of Works on behalf of the Atomic Energy Authority, to give programmed control of humidity and temperature over a very wide range of conditions. Another exacting customer was the aerospace industry and Fairey Aviation Company commissioned special low-temperature plant for testing stratosphere conditions. This was capable of reducing the temperature in the test chamber from 59°F. to minus 69°F. in eight minutes, and pressure from ground level to the equivalent of an altitude of 40,000 feet also in eight minutes. The lowest temperature obtained in the experiment was minus 100°F. Cryogenics, the science of low temperature, has made spectacular progress in the quarter century since those experiments, but the highest achievements of the J. & E. Hall machines in the 1950s still look impressive.

Those years were notable also for the energy the company put into building up its overseas connections. Export trade in the immediate post-war years was artificially inflated by the release of demand from a deprived world, and the problem was not to sell but to turn out the goods fast enough to supply. However, Halls were old hands in overseas markets and intensified their sales efforts as the backlog shrank and buyers began to call the tune. They were incidentally making a valuable contribution to the nation's balance of trade, whether it took the form of direct export or the installation of refrigeration plant in British-built ships. Conditions had become difficult in many ways: exchange control affected European sales, import and currency restrictions were widespread and competition had to be fought from local firms quoting lower prices, quicker deliveries and long-term deferred payments. The company was often able to beat the competitor on his home ground by shipping only a compressor instead of a whole installation and arranging through its agents to have the accessories manufactured locally to Hall standards. This worked best in those centres which had Dartford-trained technicians. To have been trained at Halls of Dartford was a coveted qualification and in one year alone, 1955, trainees came to the Dartford works from Italy, Yugoslavia, East Africa, South Africa, Australia, New Zealand, India, Pakistan, Hong Kong, Sudan, Iraq, Lebanon and Peru. Some were sent by the company's agents to acquaint themselves more intimately with the goods they had to sell. Others were nominated by their own governments under such arrangements as the Federation of British Industries scholarship scheme. The training took place in the works under the rough-and-ready conditions that preceded by many years the drafting of formal educational programmes and the establishment of a training school in its own premises, but there was nothing makeshift about the grounding that the trainees obtained in the science of refrigeration and the craft of installation. The company's current advanced facilities for internal and external trainees will be described later.

From the earliest years of the business it had been Hall practice to send directors and senior executives on extensive sales tours overseas. Everard Hesketh would have approved of the company's intrepid world travellers who visited every continent in the 1950s. One of them, J.D. Farmer, director in charge of marine refrigeration, even suffered shipwreck in the cause. He was returning from a tour of Brazil and Argentina in the Royal Mail vessel *Magdalena* when it foundered on rocks outside Rio de Janeiro harbour and finally broke in two. The distinguished passenger proved as durable as his company's products and both survived the disaster, though the ship itself was a write-off. It had been the largest of three Royal Mail Line ships equipped by Halls for the chilled-meat trade. The refrigeration plant was probably the most elaborate fitted in a ship up to that time; not only was all the cargo stowage fully refrigerated, but the whole of the first-class accommodation was completely air-conditioned, the design being carried out by Thermotank Ltd, later to become part of Hall-Thermotank Ltd Group. The finest quality passenger and engine-room lifts had also been installed by J. & E. Hall. To Halls' engineers and, one must admit, also to chance, goes the credit for the survival of the refrigeration plant. After the break-up the refrigeration machinery was located in the still intact aft portion of the ship and was started up on power drawn from the emergency generators. All the brine connections to the sunken forward portion of the ship were of course severed, but the cargo of meat and oranges was saved.

Few of the overseas tours were quite as dramatic as that, but they covered emerging countries and severe climates. William Ball toured Africa from the Cape to Cairo, renewing old contacts among brewers throughout the continent and bringing back orders for refrigeration installations in new breweries in Kampala and Khartoum. South Africa continued to be Halls' biggest overseas market for large refrigeration plant. When fire destroyed part of the big fruit pre-cooling plant installed by Halls at Cape Town Docks many years earlier, Halls were commissioned to supply a replacement. In 1949 Hugh Pasteur had spent three or four months on an exploratory and business-seeking world tour. He visited India, a market aiming at industrial independence and therefore difficult to breach; proceeded to Singapore where Halls had supplied ice plants for many years; then to Australia, impenetrable unless one bought an existing refrigeration business, which Halls were not yet in a position to do; and finally Canada, which had relied mainly on the USA for its refrigeration requirements, but where Halls had an agency in Vancouver and would before long establish a subsidiary company.

Among the agents and associates visited, Ellis Hardie Syminton of New Zealand were outstanding, 'the best appointment Halls had ever made' said Pasteur. The business was deeply entrenched in the country's meat and dairy industries and Halls, whose connection with them dated from 1938, participated in their prosperity. All three partners were engineers. By the time the firm had ceased to be an agent in the 1960s and had become a subsidiary of the Hall-Thermotank Group, it had bought thousands of Hall compressors but produced the coil work and other accessories in its own factory. Ian D. Syminton, the dominant partner, was a keen buyer, respected at Halls for his uncompromising insistence upon quality. This important company and other Hall developments worldwide are described in more detail in a later chapter.

Halls were alert to the potentialities of the Middle East as a market for refrigeration, and their representative visited the region in three successive years. One of these visits was to the British Trade Fair in Baghdad in 1954. The chief attraction was a Hall semi-portable ice rink, designed for use in the tropics and furnished with the indispensable sales aid of pretty girl skaters. It was the first ice-skating rink the city had seen, and for many of the local people their first glimpse of ice.

A project outside the general run of Halls' export business was undertaken in Yugoslavia in the middle fifties. It involved supplying a large number of refrigeration plants and a number of refrigerated lorries to help the country to develop an agricultural and meat exporting industry. Under the terms of the agreement the company had to provide technical information and training to enable the Yugoslavs eventually to manufacture locally many of the components of a refrigeration system. About thirty-five Yugoslav technicians were trained locally and at the Dartford works. This was a new sphere of land refrigeration for Halls and marked an enlargement of their export business.

Export had now become important enough to receive separate representation at Board level and in 1953 E. G. Russell Roberts was made a director with special responsibility for export developments. He was the grandson of Bernard Godfrey, who had carried the burden of the ailing business in partnership with Hesketh seventy years before. Halls had evidently remained a multi-family business! Russell Roberts had joined the company in 1923 and had served as technical and commercial representative on the staff of its Argentine agents from 1930 to 1935. In 1958 he moved from export management to management of the Marine Refrigeration Department, but retained his concern with overseas trade as chief executive of the newly formed Subsidiary Company and Overseas Branch Committee alongside Farmer, its chairman, and William Stanley Hayes, Halls' finance director.

Two subsidiary companies were established in Canada and Australia during the decade. A Canadian branch formed in 1953 became a subsidiary the following year, when W.S. Hayes negotiated the acquisition of Linde Canadian Refrigeration Company Ltd. Four years later the company took over the industrial refrigeration interests of John Inglis Ltd. The name of J. & E. Hall (Canada) Ltd was introduced in 1959; this was incidentally the last active company to keep the famous 'J. & E. Hall' designation. In Australia, Halls' company secretary J.W. McCarthy and export director Russell Roberts successfully arranged the launching of a wholly owned subsidiary, J. & E. Hall (Australasia) Pty. Ltd in 1957. Previously Halls' sales had been handled by agents, Amalgamated Wireless (Australasia) Pty. Ltd, who agreed to transfer their major refrigeration interests to the new company. The Australian venture also expanded by takeover when in 1958 it absorbed three subsidiaries of Daniel Scott Industries Ltd.

The parent business was cramped in its Dartford premises, but restrictions of new building imposed before the Second World War prevented the replacement even of the portion destroyed in the fire of 1937. A small extension to the works had been made in 1948 and the conversion of the light foundry two years later into a fitting and erecting shop, following a decision to buy the castings outside, had released capacity for more productive work. But staff were still housed in temporary accommodation which over the years had begun to assume an appearance of permanence. In this predicament the ancient 'Priory', as the old building at the west end of the works site is known in the locality, was a most useful standby. The latest of the varied roles forced upon it through the centuries was to deputize as a drawing office for Halls' lift and escalator department. It had seen better and worse times.

Halls had gained possession of what remained of the Priory when they purchased the freehold of the land on which it stood in 1927. It had been their neighbour since the first John Hall bought a piece of land to build a workshop from Peter Brames, who grew cabbages on the site for London greengrocers. When J. & E. Hall had the site excavated for the extension of their works, portions of buildings and a couple of skeletons were unearthed, also old foundations revealing the extent of the original settlement. The building that had survived the depredations of centuries was only a fragment, but it was sufficiently well preserved to constitute one of Dartford's few remaining antiquities, and to be both useful and a source of pride to the industrial purchasers.

The Priory was founded by Edward III for nuns of the Dominican Order in 1349. Endowed with many gifts of money and land, the Priory expanded and acquired fame not only as a religious institution but as the principal seminary for teaching the daughters of the Kentish nobility and gentry. In 1490 Princess Bridget, daughter of Edward IV, was placed there at the age of ten and later became a nun. Unfortunately most of the records of the life and work of the inmates had been destroyed during the dissolution of the monasteries by Henry VIII. In 1538 he demolished the buildings and used the material to build himself a manor house on the site. The building now in Hall-Thermotank's possession, though still called the Priory House, is in fact a surviving portion of Henry VIII's Dartford Manor. Edward VI granted it as a residence to Anne of Cleves, ex-wife of Henry VIII, and later Queen Elizabeth appropriated it as a mansion for herself. After that time the estate came into successive ownership in descending order of distinction, from Robert Cecil Earl of Salisbury in the reign of James I down to the twentieth-century farmers who sold it to Halls. For a time J. & E. Hall used the building as a pattern store, then converted it into offices and used it later as the town premises of the Hall-Thermotank Group's sports and social club. It has now reverted once more to office use.

There is a curious story about the adjacent 'Priory' walls, the only other substantial survival from Tudor times. Built into it, in addition to material from the fourteenth-century nunnery, are some black stones which had puzzled archaeologists since they could not have come from a British source. It is believed that they were brought to Britain from Baffin Island by the Elizabethan explorer Martin Frobisher who thought, mistakenly as it turned out, that they contained gold. The Queen had a financial interest in the search for gold and Frobisher was disgraced for the business failure.

It was not until twenty years after the 1937 fire that Halls' executives and draughtsmen, working in the old Priory, could be rehoused in a new office building. The number of employees was increasing rapidly – the figure announced at the Company's 175th anniversary in 1960 was 4000 – and the original four-floor plan had to be enlarged to six. The excavators struck the subterranean river Cran which had caused repeated flooding in the works when it flowed above ground along Waterside; it was still capable of delaying construction work for many weeks. The following year, when the office block had been completed, new bays were added to the plate and coil shops; the department making electrical control gear for lifts and escalators was extended, the iron foundry was modernized with new equipment and adjacent to it a new amenity block was built to provide up-to-date washing and drying facilities.

The company had taken the cost of the building programme in its stride, allocating £250,000 mainly for that purpose in 1954, and covering further work and the inevitable inflation costs without undue strain on its resources. The company's financial position was strong and the Board had made provision each year against a possible fall in the value of stock and work in progress. By 1953, the sum had reached £600,000 and remained at that figure up to 1958, when it was decided that the provision was no longer required and the sum was transferred to reserve. The balance sheet for that year showed that the net current assets, which included stock and work in progress, had increased to nearly £2.8 million.

The net profit before tax during that period reflected fluctuations in trade, but on the whole a sound condition. Between 1947 and 1950 the figure rose steeply, as the post-war spate of work mounted to a peak. Then came a slide to 1955, as competition hardened, shipbuilding slowed down and the company planned further capital expenditure on buildings and plant. There was a recovery in 1956, due in part to rationalization of production; the factory shortened completion and delivery times by offloading more of the work to outside contractors. By 1957 the Chairman reported the biggest trading profit in the company's history at £767,732, and that figure was substantially exceeded the following year.

Business expansion had made it necessary to enlarge the Board and to represent more of the executive functions at director level. The Chairman Lord Dudley Gordon had many business interests outside J. & E. Hall. He was a director of the Phoenix Assurance Company Ltd. and Barclays Bank, chairman of Hadfields Ltd and of Millspaugh Ltd, was at various times president of industrial, scientific and financial institutions and active in many social and charitable spheres. Consistently with long-standing Hall policy he delegated executive responsibilities to home-grown managers, who had risen to senior rank from apprenticeship or pupilage. He had relinquished the land refrigeration department in 1945 to Alexander Gordon Guthrie, his assistant for twenty-six years, one of whose special tasks had been the development of the company's contribution to the quick freezing of fish and soft fruits. Guthrie was succeeded as director in charge of the land department by Hugh Pasteur, who had served in both the home and the overseas departments before the new policy of sharper departmentalization had raised export to Board level under Russell Roberts. The brewery department had similarly achieved Board representation when its manager William Ball was made a director in 1948.

Because of the increase in the number of directors the Chairman thought it advisable to give one of the directors special authority to coordinate the work of the different departments. He chose for this key position Victor Alexander Patterson, creating for him – in addition to his existing authority as chief executive – the rank new to the company of Deputy Chairman. It was a wise appointment. Patterson had been a towering figure in the Hall hierarchy since long before the Second World War, and retained that eminence until his death in 1957. In physique and leadership he was a man built in the Hesketh mould, a powerful disciplinarian who like Hesketh maintained close personal touch with the departments both as monitor and friend. Whenever he chose to walk the shops the grapevine proclaimed his coming and everyone was assiduously at work, but he was well able to detect any shortcomings in performance behind the camouflage. Inside the strict manager, impatient with fools and incompetents, was a humane person, sympathetic and helpful to anyone in genuine difficulties, active both in company welfare and civic charity. He is remembered with respect and affection more than twenty-five years after his death in harness.

Patterson's death left a void which the Board had great trouble in filling and they decided that it would take two men to replace him. John Drummond Farmer was therefore appointed Deputy Chairman and joint managing director, and with him as joint managing director was Arthur Greenfield. Both had grown up in the business. Farmer had entered as a pupil in 1917, and worked mainly in the marine department until 1937 when he was made director in charge of marine and technical matters. As joint managing director he was responsible for the sales of all products and for the company's technical effort. Greenfield had started as an apprentice in 1906, and after qualification worked without a break in the manufacturing, installation and service activities of the company. He was appointed a director in 1947 in control of all the outside refrigerating erection and installation, and of the branch works of the company in the main shipbuilding centres. Both Patterson and Greenfield were able and highly experienced men and valuable members of the company singly, but as often happens the joint arrangement was not entirely successful. Farmer was thrusting and indeed brilliant at obtaining new business, convivial, unconventional in manner and tactics, not an easy 'organization man'. Greenfield was quite a different personality, no less brilliant in his speciality but with the almost clinical efficiency that the installation and erection of precise machinery demanded. Since Farmer was frequently based at the company's London office in his capacity as Deputy Chairman, it was found expedient to dissolve the dual control and Greenfield continued in Dartford as sole managing director.

While these management problems were being successfully sorted out, the Board were facing a situation that was much more difficult to handle, involving decisions which were to affect profoundly the future of the business. It was to prove a turning point as traumatic as that of 1878, when Everard Hesketh undertook the revival of a virtually extinct business. As on that earlier occasion, the event was to precipitate a prolonged crisis and put the company's vitality and leadership quality to a severe test. The circumstances were the merger in 1959 between J. & E. Hall Ltd and Thermotank Ltd, and the subsequent consolidation of the combined enterprise. This brought together two old businesses, deceptively similar in function but very dissimilar in structure and tradition, into an association rather like a kidney transplant struggling against rejection symptoms. The transplant 'took' only after drastic surgical operations in the late 1960s; but, as will be seen, the patient not only made a good recovery but emerged into the seventies with increased strength and promise.

The first Thermotank to be fitted on board ship, installed in
the Russian Volunteer Fleet vessel *Kostroma* in 1898. On the
right is A.W. Stewart, inventor of the machine and founder
with his two brothers of the Thermotank Company

CHAPTER 10

Merger Problems

In order to understand the events leading to the decisive change in the composition and status of J. & E. Hall in 1959 it is necessary to look back at the Company Report of 1948. On 1 July of that year a new Companies Act had come into force and in conformity with its requirements the Chairman was obliged to make public the fact, withheld from the shareholders until then, that J. & E. Hall was not an independent business. It had had a majority shareholder since 1920, namely the important shipping group Peninsular & Oriental Steam Navigation Company (P. & O.); in other words, J. & E. Hall was a subsidiary of P. & O. That fact, though no doubt surprising to the other shareholders, was neither alarming nor of immediate concern. P. & O. had been the most trusting of parents, who had neither demanded representation on the J. & E. Hall Board of Directors nor ever intervened in the running of the business. They had approved of its management, been satisfied with its progress and content to maintain the passive relationship.

That situation continued until late in the fifties. Halls were still a sound business, employing more than 4000 people and making a reasonable and steadily rising profit. There were, however, some darkening patches in the picture. Trade was becoming more competitive; the decline in the UK's proportionate share of world shipping and shipbuilding was accelerating; and, as was to appear a few years later, Halls had not read the signs with sufficient urgency. The revelation of weakness in the company's administration when Patterson's strong hand had been removed had shaken both Halls and P. & O., and indicated a need for stiffening the Board of this P. & O. subsidiary. An increase in the number and size of business takeovers in the late fifties and early sixties had resulted in some spectacular mergers and annexations. Big and apparently powerful fish were swallowed by even bigger fish and famous names disappeared in the digestive process. Halls would have proved a desirable and fairly easy capture if released from the parental hand.

P. & O. had in fact expressed a wish to reduce substantially their holding in J. & E. Hall, although they obviously had no intention of unloading a large block of Halls shares onto the market, neither did they intend to sell to the highest bidder. They had a more subtle plan for the solution of the shareholding problem. For the first time in nearly forty years of ownership they were represented on the company's Board, their nominee being John Frederic Earle d'Anyers Willis. His appointment was a departure from Halls' general policy of promotion from within, and was welcomed as a means of bringing an outside point of view to a directorate that had shown signs of becoming too ingrown. Willis was a businessman with great experience of trading in Asia; he was, at the time of joining J. & E. Hall, Chairman of the Anglo-Thai Corporation which had extensive interests in Canada as well as the Far East. The effect of the appointment was not only to strengthen the Hall management but to increase support on the Board for a merger between J. & E. Hall Ltd and Thermotank Ltd.

Thermotank was an old-established business, pioneer of air-conditioning in Britain and a leader particularly in its marine application. Air-conditioning and refrigeration are related techniques and Hall and Thermotank were old associates on many projects, Thermotank buying compressors from Halls and Halls calling upon Thermotank for the air-conditioning portion of a refrigeration contract. Their customers in shipping and brewing had often asked for a single quotation for the double installation. A merger between the two was therefore logical and potentially useful. Both companies were tied to the fortunes of shipping and shipbuilding, Thermotank almost completely and therefore more sensitive to adverse movements in those industries. As a private company Thermotank was even more at risk from takeover than Hall, and had been talking with UK and USA suitors; but in the end the Board considered they had more to gain from an arranged marriage with Hall, especially in view of the latter's association with shipping in general and P. & O. in particular. P. & O. as the marriage broker had other supporters on the Hall Board besides Willis. Hayes and Farmer were in favour and there was no very forceful opposition to the fusion of the two veteran businesses into a new entity, the Hall-Thermotank Group of Companies.

Hall and Thermotank in harness held the leading position in both refrigeration and air-conditioning on the seas. The original Thermotank had been installed in a ship many years before the term air-conditioning was coined in America for adoption by every English-speaking country. The machine was invented in 1897 by a young Scottish engineer, Alexander William Stewart, and patented by him the following year. It is described in the patent specification as 'a ventilating and heating or cooling apparatus for use on board ship . . . its object to provide improved means whereby the cabins or living quarters of a vessel may be efficiently heated in cold weather or cooled while the vessel is in a warm climate, and the holds of cargo vessels may be cooled and ventilated.' As heater and ventilator combined, it represented a great improvement on existing practice. Ships had been heated by steam pipes which were subject to leakage, could cause accidental burns, distributed warmth unevenly and inefficiently and made no provision for cooling, instead of heating, when required. The Thermotank was a closed vessel to which steam at any required temperature was passed, and from which the warmth was distributed by fans through ventilating gratings to the compartments. The provision of ventilation from the same instead of from a separate source was a valuable innovation in itself. When cooling was required, cold brine or expanding gas instead of steam in the Thermotank provided cool air for delivery to the cabins.

A.W. Stewart, chief electrical engineer with G. & J. Thomson of Clydebank (later part of John Brown & Company Ltd) soon had an opportunity to test his invention under operational conditions. The Russian Volunteer Fleet steamer *Kostroma* was being refitted at the Clydebank Engineering Company's yard (another eventual John Brown acquisition), and the officers agreed to have a Thermotank installed for comparison with conventional steam-pipe heating in the sister ship *Moskva*. The results were conclusively in favour of Thermotank. In a quarter of an hour the Thermotank on board *Kostroma* had raised the air temperature by 11°F., whilst a rise of only 1°F. was created by the steam-pipe system in *Moskva*. Within four hours Thermotank had registered an increase of $32\frac{1}{2}$°F., while within five hours the steam-pipe system had achieved only 8–9°F.

Orders followed from other ship-owners and in 1901 A.W. Stewart resigned from his job to form the Thermotank Ventilating Company with an office in West Regent Street, Glasgow. He was joined by his two younger brothers: William Maxwell, a consulting engineer, and F.C. (later Sir Frederick), a chartered accountant. Before forming their company they had supplied Thermotanks for heating only. In 1901 they installed a cooling version for Nippon Yusen Kaisha in their liner *Kumano Maru* which is believed to have been the world's first marine air-conditioning plant. The fact that it was made possible by refrigeration techniques which had preceded it and provided the indispensable compressor does not detract from its importance as an achievement in its own right.

Whereas refrigeration creates cold, air-conditioning creates a climate; it is the deliberate provision of a comfortable environment by control of temperature and humidity. Excessive heat, especially when accompanied by high humidity, debilitates both body and mind, thus diminishing performance and efficiency. Throughout the ages people at work have had to contend with bad or even poisoned air, as well as excessive heat and cold. In its modern sophisticated manifestations air-conditioning removes dust and fumes, adjusts temperature and humidity to the desired level, changes the air at regular intervals and maintains the required condition with a precision that nature cannot equal. The Stewarts had made a historic contribution to those human benefits.

Up to 1908 the Stewarts were contractors and designers, but did not manufacture the product. They had become well-known and respected in the shipping world and had supplied heating and ventilation for the two famous Cunardars *Lusitania* and *Mauretania* as well as cargo and naval vessels. The demand was now great enough to justify going into production and they opened a factory in Govan, Glasgow. A very detailed Thermotank catalogue of about that time shows the range of equipment already available and the functional versatility achieved in a comparatively short time. There were three types of marine heating and ventilating Thermotanks (top suction, bottom suction and 'tween decks), devices for extracting foul air as well as supplying fresh treated air to the living quarters on board ship, evaporative cooling and air-washing units, coolers employing chilled brine circulation and methods of cooling and removing explosive gases from magazines in warships. Even at that early stage the equipment incorporated facilities for temperature control, humidification, drainage of condensed moisture and other refinements which were later to become standard features of air treatment and conditioning systems.

When war broke out in 1914 the company concentrated entirely on Admiralty and War Office contracts for air-conditioning plant, and in response to the urgent need for ammunition built a new factory in Helen Street, Glasgow to manufacture shells. After the war the company's main production – including manufacture of centrifugal and later axial-flow fans – was moved to this factory. A.W. Stewart turned his inventive brain to problems of air distribution in marine ventilation and heating plants, and in

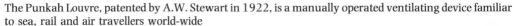

The Punkah Louvre, patented by A.W. Stewart in 1922, is a manually operated ventilating device familiar to sea, rail and air travellers world-wide

1922 patented the revolutionary Punkah Louvre. This is familiar to sea, rail and air travellers as the ball valve which can be turned manually in its socket in any direction to deliver a stream of air wherever the passenger wishes. Various types of Punkah Louvre are now fitted in ships, trains and aircraft throughout the world. After adoption by P. & O. for their liners on the Far East service the Punkah Louvre quickly became virtually a standard method of air-distribution aboard ship. The airlines followed later and a range of Punkah Louvres was developed to suit various needs; Thermotank produced special designs for Concorde's flight and passenger decks.

By the 1920s the word ventilation no longer adequately described the increasing subtlety of the company's air-conditioning service, and the business name was simplified to Thermotank Ltd. The service was extended to industrial and other land-based users – for instance the textile industry, the new automatic telephone exchanges, hotels and offices. Before the Second World War Thermotank installations were operating on the London Underground and in mines overseas, notably in South Africa where a subsidiary company had been formed. Marine work however continued in the lead, and the *Queen Mary*, *Queen Elizabeth* and *Normandie* were merely the most spectacular examples among whole fleets of customers.

W.M. Stewart died in 1926 and A.W. in 1933, leaving the surviving brother F.C. as Chairman at the head of a reorganized board. W.A.F. Stewart, elder son of W.M., joined the company in 1938, but died soon after the outbreak of the Second World War. His brother Iain was recalled from the Forces to fill the vacancy in this vital war industry – a decisive appointment for this young engineer was to grow with the business, succeed his uncle as Chairman of Thermotank Ltd, play a major role in the merger with J. & E. Hall Ltd and, as Chairman of the new group, lead it through its most troubled years to record prosperity.

Wherever the fighting forces and supporting services were accommodated, at sea and under water, on land and underground and in the air, Thermotank provided air-conditioning. The locations ranged from battleships and troopships to minesweepers and cargo vessels; from the War Cabinet room in Downing Street where Churchill and his Service chiefs laid down the strategy for victory, to the floating 'Mulberry Harbour' which was the springboard to the Normandy invasion; from the supply of exhaust fume extraction plant for the first large ocean-going tank transports and landing craft, to atmospheric controls in munition factories; from the air-conditioning component in refrigerated food stores throughout the country, to ventilation in coal-mines and air-raid shelters. Thermotank was consultant to the Ministry of War Transport on troopship ventilation and was represented on official government air conditioning panels. It was inevitably an official target for the enemy and after the war our occupation forces in defeated Germany found a captioned map of part of Glasgow on which the Thermotank offices and factories were described and marked for destruction.

Fulfilment of the massive war programme forced Thermotank to expand its production capacity and additional offices and works were established in London,

Liverpool and Newcastle. The company had matured under the heavy responsibility of war production, and made further progress in the immediate post-war years under the guidance of Iain Stewart and his Board of six able long-serving executives: W.H. Glass, J.B. McNair, D.D. Blackwood, J.K.W. McVicar, A.D. Third and F. McPherson. By 1951, when the business celebrated its jubilee, it had established its first four branches – in the USA, Canada, South Africa and India – and had agents in all parts of the world.

In common with J. & E. Hall, Thermotank Ltd was involved in the vast post-war programme to rebuild and equip the merchant navies of Britain and her allies. Air-conditioning of crews' living quarters became standard practice in ocean-going vessels and accompanied the restoration of refrigeration. The long-standing working arrangement between the two companies became even closer and their cooperation extended beyond marine work – for instance into the provision of complete air-conditioning and refrigeration plants in maltings and in every branch of brewing. Most installations were designed to fit individual cases and in their research laboratory Thermotank had constructed a test cabin enclosed in an environment in which the most extreme tropical conditions could be reproduced. This was used for research into marine air-conditioning problems and for demonstrating to customers the effect of air-conditioning in realistic circumstances.*

In the decade that followed the end of the war the company enlarged considerably the range of its operations and its technical expertise. One of the largest marine air-conditioning plants up to that time, incorporating a Hall centrifugal compressor as noted in the previous chapter, was installed by Thermotank in the P. & O. liner *Canberra*; its $17\frac{1}{2}$ miles of ducts carried 50,000 tons of air per day, 5000 tons greater than the weight of the ship. At the other end of the scale there were self-contained units no bigger than a suitcase for installation in an individual cabin or small office. The company provided equipment for cargo spaces in addition to passenger and crew accommodation. They developed 'Drihold' to prevent condensation which could damage cargoes and the ship's structure. Another development was Thermal Injection, a technique for dealing with condensation in cargo spaces adjacent to refrigerated holds.

Computers were increasingly coming into use in the 1950s, and Thermotank supplied the controlled climatic conditions that these delicate instruments demanded. Non-marine installation accounted for some of the company's most interesting product diversification. Air distributors of many types were designed, square diffusers and grilles, also continuous strip diffusers for walls and ceilings and weatherproof diffusers for exterior walls. A range of water-cooling towers was evolved incorporating an ingenious light-weight plastic fill. The company also designed powerful fans up to 180 inches in

---

*The demonstration was followed by an initiation ceremony for the customers, who were mainly ships' engineers and sometimes the owners themselves or their captains. They were admitted to membership of 'The Scottish Swelterers Society' and crowned with a tartan topee – a special hat decorated with the three Stewart tartans, the Royal Stewart, the Dress Stewart and the Hunting Stewart. Initiation into this society, now referred to as the Swelterers' Society, still continues and it has a large and growing membership.

At an initiation ceremony customers for air conditioning plant who have been subjected to a climatic 'ordeal' in the company's test laboratory qualify for admission to membership of the Swelterers' Society

diameter for the ventilation of collieries, and special low-speed fans for use where silent running was essential. They did research into noise and space problems in high velocity air-conditioning systems and evolved new techniques which they applied successfully in an audacious assault upon American dominance in land applications of air conditioning.

The Americans had taken the lead in air-conditioning on land by virtue of their enormous home market, covering many climates and subject to seasonal extremes of temperature. Iain Stewart, believing that his company's system could beat the American competitors on their own ground and also ward off the competition from New York and Montreal, formed a subsidiary company in Detroit on the doorstep of the motor industry. This company proved his point by winning a $2 million contract to install their pioneer high velocity, twin-duct air-conditioning plant, manufactured at the Glasgow works, in a large part of the General Motors Technical Centre in Detroit. The plants had two major advantages over the conventional American product: it saved considerable space by using smaller ducts, and it included devices which reduced outlet velocity, pressure and noise to those of ordinary low-velocity systems. There was little profit in the American venture, but so long as the motor industry flourished it did not make a loss. Unfortunately its business outside the motor industry was very small and when the demand for automobiles slumped in 1956 so did Thermotank Incorporated.

Excessive dependence upon a single market was a matter of concern for the parent company too. In spite of its success with brewers and maltsters its industrial and commercial work was a minor part of the business and subject to strong competition. Adverse winds were rising even in the marine sphere. Thermotank led the world in marine air-conditioning as did J. & E. Hall in marine refrigeration, but since 85 per cent of their order book depended on shipping and shipbuilding they were less secure against a shipping decline. Shipping in the UK had, in fact, become less efficient than that of overseas competitors and even British owners were placing orders in foreign yards. Thermotank's profits had fluctuated over the previous five years and had on the whole declined, mainly due to losses by the subsidiary companies, while Halls' profits rose steadily in the same period. Thermotank was the smaller business, with 1500 employees against Halls' 4500, and had remained a family concern at a time when many other such businesses were being taken over or going public. It was a less closely knit business than Halls', having some of the characteristics of a conglomerate. Both groups had establishments overseas, some of them languishing, but Thermotank's American subsidiary was running at a loss and German and Scandinavian competition was pressing hard against the company's interests in Europe.

The merger brought together under one heading twenty-six companies employing more than 6000 people at home and overseas. They comprised, in addition to a holding company, eight trading companies in the UK and seventeen overseas, of which five were at that time dormant. There were three major manufacturing companies: J. & E. Hall Ltd, Thermotank Ltd, concerned with marine air-conditioning, and Thermotank

Engineering Ltd which handled work for maltings and other land users. Five subsidiary companies were involved with products and services which had only a tenuous relation to air-conditioning – these were the 'conglomerate' element in the package. Two of them were plastics manufacturers. Arnoplast Ltd was started in 1946 to supply thermoplastic sheet materials and fabricated products which were used in the food trades for trays and containers, in the building trade for wash-basin and sink units, in lighting fittings and refrigeration plants. The other plastics subsidiary, Thermotank Plastic Engineering Ltd, concentrated on reinforced plastic sections such as bearings, ducting, tubes and piping. Air-conditioning and refrigeration used its products.

Lumenated Ceilings Ltd, another Thermotank diversification formed in 1954, introduced the suspended luminous ceiling into the UK for offices, shops, showrooms and factories. Built up of translucent plastic panels lighted from above, these ceilings provided a diffused shadowless lighting like daylight in quality. The company did not long enjoy its initiative – and monopoly – as the first in Britain to supply this product, for big electric lighting manufacturers quickly saw the possibilities and creamed the market. Two acoustic companies, Sound Control Ltd and Acoustical Investigation & Research Organisation Ltd (AIRO), completed the tally of subsidiaries. Thermotank also brought into the Group their overseas companies in South Africa, Canada, USA, Australia, West Germany, Norway and Iraq; most of them had subsidiaries of their own. There were in addition manufacturing associates in Italy, Yugoslavia, the Netherlands and Spain, and agents in every continent.

This complex package was merged with J. & E. Hall Ltd on 22 June 1959. Halls financed the deal by increasing their issued Ordinary capital from £1,008,000 to £1,512,000 by the issue of £504,000 Ordinary capital at a premium of £1,134,000 to the shareholders of Thermotank Ltd, in exchange for the share capital of that company. The issued Ordinary capital was further increased to £3,024,000 by the application of the share premium of £1,134,000 and the capitalization of £378,000 out of general reserve. By the merger P. & O. reduced their shareholding in J. & E. Hall from 52.3 per cent to 35.6 per cent. Thus at the moment of absorption into Hall-Thermotank Ltd, J. & E. Hall ceased to be a P. & O. subsidiary.

While the directors of Hall and Thermotank were considering the merger, they also discussed bringing into the Group another company whose products were complementary to their own. This was Vent-Axia Ltd, with whom Halls had had a long business relationship and in which J.D. Farmer was a shareholder. Vent-Axia was better known to the general public than either Hall or Thermotank, because of its familiar window ventilators used in offices, restaurants and domestic kitchens to remove stale air and odours and suck in fresher air from outside. The founder of the company, J.C. Akester, had introduced into the UK in the later 1920s the axial flow screw-pressure fan for marine use, and in 1932 formed a company called Axia Fans Ltd to exploit it commercially. He soon realized that the axial flow principle could be applied in a small window-fitting fan to ventilate rooms in buildings simply and inexpensively. In 1936 therefore he formed a second company, Vent-Axia Ltd, to manufacture and sell his new invention. Not only was it the first time that an axial flow fan had ever been fitted into a window; the fan was also the first to be made of plastic and to be sold as a packaged article. The public were slow to accept it as a means of changing the air in kitchens and the first users were mainly offices, restaurants and pubs. During the Second World War it was fitted in air-raid shelters, mobile X-ray units and operating theatres. By 1953, when the first reversible window fan was launched, (i.e. a fan capable of supplying or extracting air at the touch of a switch), householders had begun to appreciate it in its smaller versions as a home utility. The more powerful units spread widely in the manufacturing and the service industries for ventilating poultry houses, laundries and workshops, and for valve cooling in electronic equipment.

Vent-Axia Ltd had become the major partner in the business, with Axia Fans Ltd as a subsidiary. The latter was a competitor of Thermotank, and the new Hall-Thermotank Group's main purpose in taking over Vent-Axia Ltd was to acquire the subsidiary company. The Group saw revolutionary possibilities in the axial flow screw-fan for circulating air in refrigeration systems in food-carrying ships. These fans were also used for engine-room ventilation in place of the more cumbersome centrifugal fan which

An office fitted with the well known Vent-Axia ventilating unit. Vent-Axia Ltd entered the Hall group at the time of the merger with Thermotank

occupied valuable deck space. Axia Fans Ltd provided complete installations for ventilating machinery spaces in ships, and water turbine driven units for gas freeing in tankers.

With the approval of the Thermotank Board and the endorsement of P. & O. as the majority shareholder in Halls, the directors of J. & E. Hall Ltd made an offer to acquire all the 3,936,000 issued Ordinary Stock units of 1s. each of Vent-Axia Ltd and its wholly owned subsidiary, Axia Fans Ltd, at 10s.6d per unit in cash. This offer was conditional upon the merger between Hall and Thermotank becoming effective. The deal was financed by an issue of £2,250,000 Unsecured Loan Stock at £99.10s. per £100 stock.

On 22 June 1959 therefore the newly re-named company Hall-Thermotank Ltd confirmed the threefold merger. Hall-Thermotank Ltd was not a trading company but a holding company only, acting mainly as a banker to the enlarged Group. As the Chairman Iain Stewart said in his report to the shareholders on 29 March 1960, 'It also acts as a binding and co-ordinating force, in that virtually all Group companies are represented through their directorates on the Board of the holding company.'

Inevitably the old Board had to be drastically overhauled. Lord Dudley Gordon's long and distinguished service was signalized by his election as President of the multiple business. He retired at the end of the 1960–61 financial year after fifty-three years with the company, twenty-four of them as Chairman of J. & E. Hall, Iain M. Stewart was appointed Group Chairman. Five former Hall directors – R.P. Willcox, H.W. Pasteur, W. Ball, E.G. Russell Roberts and C.R. Croucher – resigned their directorships and were appointed on the same day to the Board of what was now the Hall-Thermotank Group's J. & E. Hall Ltd subsidiary. John Drummond Farmer, Arthur Greenfield and William Stanley Hayes were joined on the main Board by James MacVicar and Finlay McPherson, both of Thermotank, and (until his retirement in 1962) Joseph Akester of Axia Fans and Vent-Axia. The three main constituents of the merged Group were thus represented on the Board of the holding company. So also were P. & O., no longer the owners of the business but still a substantial shareholder, one of whose directors, Ford Geddes, joined the Board of Hall-Thermotank Ltd.

Before the end of the financial year there were further changes on the Board. Iain Stewart, after only a few months in the Chair, found it necessary for domestic reasons to resign that position and was succeeded by the Deputy Chairman Willis, but he remained a member of the Board. As Chairman of the Thermotank Group, Stewart had been energetic and persuasive in promoting the merger. He had brought with him a profitable business, with weaknesses in some of its minor subsidiaries and one failure which had no prospect of recovery; that was the American company, which the new Board wanted to be rid of. Unhappy at having saddled them with a liability which he had neither the time nor opportunity to straighten out, Stewart made a voluntary gift to the Group of £100,000 to cover what was estimated to be the sales value of the US subsidiary.

The Board were aware that the provision of a holding company and of a financial base for the Group was only the start of a formidable task of rationalization and integration.

157

SIR IAIN STEWART
Chairman of the Hall-Thermotank Group 1964–79, wearing
the insignia of the Worshipful Company of Shipwrights, of
which he had been prime warden in 1972–73

158

Immediately after the merger they established several committees through which all the Group companies could formulate and convey to the main Board their opinions on the financial, technical and commercial problems. During the vital stages in the merger negotiations, the employees in the factories and offices had been kept fully informed of the reason for the operation; now through the continuing liaison between the Group Boards their representative committees helped to ensure that the changes which were bound to arise from time to time were understood at all levels. But in spite of these efforts at coordination and communication the Group continued to be for many years a collection of companies instead of a coherent business. J. & E. Hall remained in name and activity the self-contained unit it had always been and this was equally true of Thermotank. In fact, it was not until 1962 that the division into two companies was abolished and Thermotank Engineering Company Ltd was absorbed into Thermotank Ltd.

In some respects the slow consolidation of the Hall-Thermotank merger is understandable, for in old and respected businesses there are local loyalties which are not easy to convert into a feeling for a new and arbitrary amalgamation. Hall-Thermotank had not only to create a common ground for Halls of Dartford, Thermotank of Glasgow and Vent-Axia of Crawley. Each had sales organizations and agencies in various parts of the country, sometimes in the same town, and marriages at gun-point would not have been tolerated. Mergers overseas were especially difficult because there were companies with vested interests which needed tact and time for their liquidation. While Iain Stewart was still Chairman, he and the Deputy Chairman J. Willis made personal visits together or separately to Europe, America, India, East Africa, New Zealand, and other parts of the Commonwealth, where the Group either had established interests or saw new possibilities.

For two or three years the Hall-Thermotank collection of companies seemed to be settling down. Multiple establishments in Australia, South Africa and Canada were trimmed by liquidating or amalgamating the smaller units. Halls' old and valued associate in New Zealand, Ellis Hardie Syminton Ltd, was taken into the Group. The United States business was sold in 1963. A subsidiary company, Hall-Thermotank Overseas Ltd (now a holding company only), was formed to undertake refrigeration and air-conditioning contracting in territories where the Group was not represented by a company of its own; it opened its first branch in Nairobi to serve East Africa and the Red Sea region and the second branch in Hong Kong. There were promising developments in most of the minor UK subsidiaries.

However, the picture was not so bright with regard to the Group's main activities. Conversion of the older ships from simple ventilation to air-conditioning was coming to an end. There was also a shortage of new ship construction and American and European competition for the available jobs was increasing. The situation was relieved in part by government loans to shipowners. The Royal Navy placed some orders for guided missile ships and the land refrigeration division had work in hand for breweries, maltings, fruit growers and meat stores, also for flake ice-making plants. The tall office blocks with large window space which were rising in all the big cities and requiring internal temperature control and elimination of noise and dust, presented new opportunities for air-conditioning. While the Group had designed and installed air-conditioning on a 'made to measure' basis for many years for marine and industrial users, demand on the land side had been too small to justify installing machinery for the manufacture of standardized equipment on the lines adopted by American manufacturers. The Board therefore decided to make use of American facilities and formed an association with Westinghouse Electric Corporation to distribute all the products of that company's air-conditioning division in the UK and also to manufacture under licence certain Westinghouse products with an option on the rest. This opened up for the Group a useful market for packaged air-conditioning units in shops, offices, hotels and restaurants.

In 1962 the Group made a valuable addition to its list of constituent companies by acquiring for cash the whole of the issued capital of Searle Manufacturing Company Ltd. Searle were manufacturers of heat transfer products used in refrigeration and air-conditioning installations and both Hall and Thermotank were old customers. The business had been built up by Leslie W. Searle from the small workshop inherited from his father, and it proved to be one of the few bright spots in the gloom that descended upon Hall-Thermotank in the middle sixties. The purchase was largely financed by the creation of £500,000 7 per cent Cumulative Preference shares, the Group's second issue of Preference shares in two years. It brought the issued capital of the business to £4,546,000, that is, £1,320,000 7 per cent Cumulative Preference shares of £1 each and £3,226,500 in Ordinary Shares at 5s. each.

Two fortunate acquisitions – Searle at home and Ellis Hardie Syminton overseas – and a consistently good performance by Vent-Axia were insufficient to dispel the depression that descended on the Group in 1962 and deepened in the five subsequent years. There was no single cause for the crisis, which was due partly to external circumstances but in no small measure to weaknesses within the organization. The external factors were recurrent and only too familiar: stagnation in the shipyards; increasing competition for the decreasing business; the effect of the credit squeeze upon customers, contractors and all the suppliers of goods and services in between; rising wages and the shortage of skilled labour; harsh new company taxation; all these laid a severe multiple burden upon businesses. They were however old enemies, which Halls had always found ways of defeating. The company's internal troubles were a less easily discernible enemy, too close at hand to detect until plunging profits sounded the alarm. Profit before tax for 1959–60, the first full financial year of the merged Group, was £1,261,035. In 1960–61 the profit rose to £1,378,916 but in 1961–62 it fell sharply to £953,385. Thanks to the return on the investment in Searle Manufacturing Company Ltd, there was a brief recovery to £1,139,097 in 1962–63. Then followed four disastrous years with profits of £772,381, £804,181, £424,804 and £474,242 respectively. In the last but one of those years, ending 30 September 1966, no dividend was paid on the Ordinary shares.

Packaged water chilling units in the works awaiting delivery for use in Royal Naval vessels

The main source of loss in the Group was the J. & E. Hall subsidiary, the largest of the contracting companies, in which about half the capital was invested but which in 1964–65 contributed only 28 per cent of the total Group operating profit. Iain Stewart defined the trouble as the 'totally unsatisfactory state of profitless prosperity which exists in certain of the Group's operations in the marine field,' which represented 20 per cent of the turnover of the business. He had resumed the Chairmanship in 1964 upon the resignation of J. Willis, and followed up his predecessor's efforts in diagnosing and seeking a remedy for the Group's ills. J. & E. Hall were exceptionally vulnerable to adverse conditions of trade because of the nature of their operations. Accustomed to handling up to a thousand contracts in a great variety of types and sizes at any one time, this involved holding large stocks and gave rise to the problems of a complex production schedule. When, as a result of the credit squeeze, customers asked for delay in the completion of contracts, the company faced the double disability of over-stocking and of idle machines. In 1964 contracts to the value of nearly £2 million had to be carried forward, and since material and labour costs rose continually and prices already quoted were fixed, the company could not look forward to a substantial deferred profit.

These circumstances were partly bad luck but also bad judgement. Many long-term fixed-price contracts, accepted between 1962 and 1964 in order to fill the order book and in some cases to avoid redundancies, proved unprofitable. Record orders and low margins amounted to profitless prosperity. Halls' profit in what the Chairman called the thoroughly bad year of 1963–64 was the lowest for sixteen years. Land work fell short as well as marine and Thermotank was in little better plight. The cost of some major land contracts, said the Chairman, greatly exceeded estimates.

To some extent therefore the failure was attributable to management deficiencies over a long period. 'Part of the problem at J. & E. Hall,' said Iain Stewart, 'stems from a failure to discern in earlier years the changing trends in a field where the company had for so long been, and still is, an acknowledged leader.' He followed up his diagnosis with recommendations for a course of treatment including 'a more commercial attitude towards our sales pricing – new techniques for the control of inventory, production and costs – more and better use of our skills in engineering research and development.'

Some of the measures adopted in the hope of halting and then reversing the decline were drastic and inevitably there were redundancies. Dead wood had to be chipped out and – again inevitably – some sound timber was damaged. A sad instance was the closure, fortunately for little more than a year, of the J. & E. Hall Social & Athletic Club. Opinions differed on the value of the closure as an act of retrenchment, but it did bring home to everyone the seriousness of the company's condition and the need for strong medicine. At the same time the Board had more constructive policies in mind for the revision of the Group's structure and for ways of dealing with the weaker subsidiaries. They also decided to seek the advice of a business consultancy whose report, delivered in 1965, confirmed many of their views. The main recommendation was to reconstitute the Group Board as a non-executive policy-making body acting through the Group managing director, who became the only full-time executive member. The managing directors of the operating companies were to be responsible to him for their own profit performance, and he would be answerable to the Board for overall results. The reason behind the change was that executive directors were too deeply immersed in departmental responsibilities to give the necessary attention to policy matters, and the enlargement of the business and its multiplicity of problems made the separation of functions urgent.

The managing director of the reconstituted main Board was Donald MacPhail, who had joined in 1962 as a member of the Group Board and also as executive Chairman of Vent-Axia. In 1964 he had in addition been appointed Deputy Chairman upon the resignation of J.D. Farmer, but relinquished that position a year later to Sir Laurence Menzies, newly appointed to the Board. Sir Laurence was an adviser to the Governor of the Bank of England, an appointment which had included a period of secondment as Secretary of the Export Credits Guarantee Department. The other newcomers to the Board in 1965 were Sir Leslie Robinson, a distinguished public servant, formerly Second Secretary at the Board of Trade; H.K. Roseveare, who had directed business operations of a similar kind to Hall-Thermotank's, particularly overseas; W.F.C. Schaap, who brought valuable experience of engineering and other technical subjects; and in 1966 an appointment from within – L.W. Searle, who thereupon relinquished his executive duties in the subsidiary company Searle Manufacturing Company Ltd. As a result of the reorganization W. Ball (who had been reappointed on 1 September 1962), F. McPherson, J.K.W. MacVicar and W.S. Hayes resigned from the Group Board but continued to act as executive directors in the operating companies.

MacPhail was given the task of reorganizing J. & E. Hall, the subsidiary in greatest trouble. The Board were well aware of the long and painful haul that lay ahead. The predicament of the subsidiary reflected that of the Group as a whole, since profit had fallen disastrously, the Group had reached the limit of its overdraft and no more help could be expected from the banks. Indeed, Hall-Thermotank needed a swift rescue operation to avert bankruptcy and this operation was begun in 1967 with a new appointment to the Group from outside the business. Donald MacPhail and H.K. Roseveare having resigned, the Chairman Iain Stewart brought in David Kenneth Fraser to take over immediately as Group Chief Executive and gave him a mandate to stop the rot. Fraser had held top management positions in leading engineering companies, was a member of the Ministry of Technology's Advisory Council on Technology and the Advisory Board on Relations with the Universities, and was on the Council of the British Welding Association. His new assignment presented some formidable managerial problems.

What had gone wrong with the business? The new Chief Executive summed up the crisis of the sixties as 'lack of money, poor uses of resources, absence of definition in the business'. The lack of definition had caused a drift into diversifications, when what the business needed was concentration. One of the less fortunate effects of the merger had been to turn the Group into a conglomerate and further accretions at home and overseas increased the load. This form of empire building was fashionable in some business circles at the time and some large groupings came to grief as a result. Fraser regarded it as his main duty to use the company's resources for organic growth, reverting to the traditional functions and natural markets from which the Group had been diverging to its cost; concentrating, that is, on refrigeration and air-conditioning which, with heating and ventilation, accounted for 93 per cent of the business. This would involve a massive structural reorganization of the Group and would take several years to accomplish. To begin with, there would have to be a ruthless excision of subsidiary companies and diversified interests at home and overseas which were losing money and were not worth saving.

The new Chief Executive visited overseas subsidiaries and found that, nearly a decade after the merger, there were still countries where former Hall and Thermotank companies behaved like unrelated businesses. The first act in the interests of integration and development was to make changes in the top managements. At home there was a slaughter of sidelines. Arnoplast went into voluntary liquidation in 1967. Hall Lifts and Escalators Ltd, as recorded in an earlier chapter, was sold to Otis. In 1968 Colneside Windows Ltd (formerly Sound Control Ltd) was liquidated; and the manufacturing activity of Axia Fans Ltd was sold to Airscrew Weyroc Ltd. In the same year the Group Board decided that it would be more economical for Hall-Thermotank to buy than to make its own heavy castings and they closed the foundry.

In addition to defects in structure and organization the business was deficient in technological expertise, so two new appointments were made to strengthen research and development. Dr S.C. (later Sir Samuel) Curran joined the Group Board in 1968. He had been successively Chief Scientist of the United Kingdom Atomic Energy Authority, Principal of the Royal College of Science and Technology in Glasgow, and Principal and Vice-Chancellor of the University of Strathclyde. As a member of the Advisory Council on Technology, Chairman of the Advisory Board on Relations with Universities (both Ministry of Technology bodies) and Chairman of the Advisory Committee on Medical Research, he provided a valuable link with government, universities and medicine. Shortly before, Professor Geoffrey G. Haselden, Brotherton Professor of Chemical Engineering at Leeds University, Chairman of the British Cryogenics Council and Vice-President of the International Institute of Refrigeration, had joined the Board of J. & E. Hall Ltd as a non-executive director and chairman of the company's technical and development committee. He brought to the Group wide experience of low-temperature processes and applied thermodynamics, and guidance on the transition from traditional spheres of refrigeration to the application of sophisticated technologies.

In 1969 Derek James Palmar, a distinguished merchant banker, formerly industrial adviser to the Department of Economic Affairs and a director of a number of industrial companies, joined the Group Board. He had been from 1966–68 associated with Iain Stewart in a remarkable experiment to save the old-established Fairfield Shipbuilding

Company of Glasgow from closure. Hall-Thermotank had been indirectly concerned. In 1965 the Board had made provision amounting to £140,000 for possible losses resulting upon the appointment of a receiver and manager at Fairfields. The following year Hall-Thermotank's Chairman became also Chairman of the ailing shipbuilding company. Supported by an equally enlightened management team, sharing his ideas on employee relations, he instituted a novel system of all-ranks co-operation which, within less than two years, restored the vitality and prestige of the company. Among these measures was investment in equity shares by several trade unions who changed their rule books to enable them to put up the money. The innovations were eventually submerged in the government-sponsored amalgamation of Fairfields with John Brown and three other companies to form Upper Clyde Shipbuilders Ltd. When Iain Stewart resigned it was with a knighthood in acknowledgment of his enterprise but without the satisfaction of carrying the experiment to a triumphant conclusion.

Since the Hall-Thermotank Group Board, with the exception of D.K. Fraser, was non-executive, Fraser initiated a system of Chief Executive's Reports, to keep the directors informed of the current situation in all sectors of the business. The reports drew the Board's attention to such matters as progress in business negotiations, manpower

Hall refrigeration plant for Billingsgate fish market

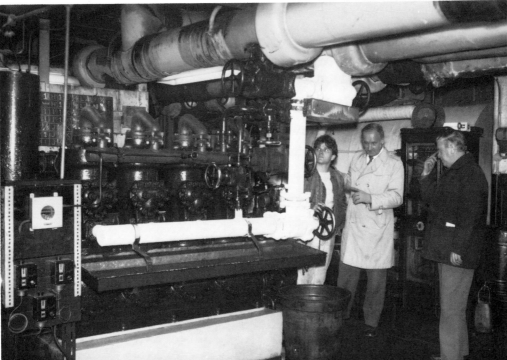

problems and plans, labour relations, the possible effect of proposed legislation upon the business and the difficulties of overseas subsidiaries in specially sensitive parts of the world. Inevitably, the Chief Executive had to face some opposition to the upheavals he had precipitated in so many sections of the business, but confidence grew when it became apparent that they were yielding positive results. Even before the end of the sixties the results had become apparent in contracts that were being completed at a profit. J. & E. Hall were out of the red. The company had contributed to the refit of the *Queen Elizabeth*, had supplied refrigeration equipment to four large refrigerated ships, seven freeze trawlers, fruit carriers and submarines. Contracts on land included freezing plant for Buxted Chicken and refrigeration and lifts for a Birds Eye Foods cold store. A major contract which was to expand during the 1970s into one of the Group's most spectacular achievements was a refrigeration system for the Container Terminal at Tilbury. The Group's range of products and markets was also enlarged by two acquisitions in 1970. One was a comparatively new company, Paracon (Air Conditioning) Ltd, manufacturers of packaged air-conditioning equipment, which was incorporated into the Thermotank Products division of the company. The other was the heavy industrial refrigeration equipment business of Sterne Ltd, acquired from Prestcold Ltd, which with its installation, service and spares activities was incorporated into Sterne Industrial Refrigeration Ltd as a wholly owned subsidiary of Hall-Thermotank International Ltd.

Overseas, the surviving companies showed improved results. There had been an important addition as well as some necessary subtractions. In 1968 a company was formed called Hall-Thermotank Equatorial Ltd, by combining the East African branch of Hall-Thermotank Overseas Ltd with the refrigeration installation and servicing division of A. Baumann & Company (Kenya) Ltd of Nairobi, who had been the Group's agents. The new company covered a territory comprising Central and Eastern Africa and the Red Sea region. At home the sole remaining diversifications, after the sale of Lifts and Escalators, were Vent-Axia and AIRO, though it could be argued that both had peripheral relevance to the Group's main interests.

Major surgery and skilled aftercare had pulled the Group through the crisis of the sixties to a position of financial strength and renewed technical progress. The profit before tax for the financial year 1967–68 at £1,199,921 was more than two and half times greater than in the previous year. In 1968–69 the figure was just under a million and a half. The Chairman summed up the achievement when he attributed the improvement to 'changing policies, changing attitudes, changing methods and improved techniques. And,' he added, 'there are more to come.'

CHAPTER 11
Reconstruction

Of all the troubles that beset the Group in the 1960s, the one that had caused the deepest shock to the Board was the virtual collapse of the J. & E. Hall subsidiary. Hall was the ancestral member, inheritor of the world-wide fame built up during more than a century and a half of technical innovation and business enterprise. It was still much the biggest subsidiary, much the biggest employer of capital. Upon its revival depended the existence of the major activity, the *raison d'être* of the business. J. & E. Hall had therefore to be the subject of the most urgent scrutiny and ultimately the area of most radical change. The problem was in the dual character of the company as both manufacturer and contractor. Superficially the combined functions seemed logical, since J. & E. Hall was a self-contained organization, taking on contracts, designing refrigeration and air-conditioning systems, manufacturing the hardware, erecting and installing the equipment and providing after-sales service. But the operation was unwieldy for a reason that had long gone undetected – namely that contracting and product manufacture were two distinct businesses requiring a different approach and therefore proving incompatible under the same command. They would have to be separated financially and administratively.

In order to avoid excessive disruption the separation was phased over four or five years, the first phase being a divisional rearrangement in J. & E. Hall in 1968. Three divisions were formed: a products division, to identify, develop, manufacture and market the product needs of the refrigeration industry; a contracts division, to design, procure and supply complete refrigeration-based turnkey projects; and a supporting erection and service division, to serve the outside activities of J. & E. Hall and Thermotank and those taken over from Axia Fans. In 1969 J. & E. Hall Ltd was renamed Hall-Thermotank International Ltd, and its structure was further rationalized by dividing the company's activities into two groups: a contracts group consisting of two divisions, HTI Engineering dealing with systems design, engineering and installation and HTI Services dealing with after-sales service and repairs; and a production group

The Hall-Thermotank Gold Medal Award was instituted in 1977 to mark the centenary of the company's involvement in refrigeration. The Gold Medal is awarded annually through the Institute of Refrigeration to the person considered to have made the most noteworthy contribution to the advancement of refrigeration for any practical application. The winner of the award holds the Gold Medal for one year and retains a solid silver replica

comprising three divisions, J. & E. Hall Products, Thermotank Products and Searle Products, trading under their individual business names and each responsible to its own divisional managing director. The separation was completed in 1973 with the reorganization of Hall-Thermotank International Ltd to carry on the business of the engineering and services divisions only, and the formation of a new company, Hall-Thermotank Products Ltd, to take over the manufacturing business of J. & E. Hall Products and Thermotank Products.

The separation was not a simple matter of hiving off a few divisions but a surgical operation not unlike that of separating Siamese twins. The Group's biggest constituent part, containing most of its vital organs, was split down the middle so that each half would have to grow independently of the other. The operation was more disrupting for the Products than for the Contracts segment. Hall-Thermotank International had an established marketing department and a number of sales outlets to provide a base for advancement; but Hall-Thermotank Products, left with a large factory and no sales staff, was in a serious plight. One of the purposes of separating the contracting facility was to put production into direct contact with its markets. Hall-Thermotank Products now

Compressor assembly in the Dartford works

faced the urgent task of creating a marketing and sales structure, finding new outlets, organizing a research and development department and redesigning its product ranges to suit the increasing competition. Since a large part of the factory was long overdue for replacement, Hall-Thermotank Products had the additional burden of maintaining profitable production while completely rebuilding its premises on the existing site around a work force of some 1200 people. The building programme, to be described later, was the biggest in the history of the business; it had to be on that scale in order to help in transforming the rump of a products division into a dynamic business in its own right.

Hall-Thermotank Products and Hall-Thermotank International were separated physically as well as functionally. The former took over the entire factory complex and the adjacent offices in Hythe Street, Dartford, and an office block was built for the latter in Home Gardens close by the factory complex.

There had been misgivings in some sectors of management about the wisdom of detaching production from the contract work which made use of the products. Some thought this destructive and their opposition was understandable. It is unusual to divide so sharply what are, in effect, the two halves of a single operation. However, the policy was logical in the Hall-Thermotank context because the business had become too inward-looking. Its production plant was capable of serving a much larger clientele than its own contracts partner offered. The products divisions had had a struggle to show a

169

good enough return on the substantial capital employed. Clearly, the products side could not subsist satisfactorily on the single internal customer and in order to maximize resources Hall-Thermotank Products had to seek business outside the fold, even though this would involve selling to Hall-Thermotank International's competitors. In effect, separation of the two sides into virtually independent businesses enlarged enormously the sales horizon for each of them, but especially that for Hall-Thermotank Products.

Thus the two companies became both associates and competitors. Hall-Thermotank International has remained Hall-Thermotank Products' biggest single client, but the bulk of Hall-Thermotank Products' output now goes outside the Group. By the same token, Hall-Thermotank International is free to buy hardware wherever it chooses. The recovery of the Group from the setbacks of the recent past to a position of greater profitability than ever before justified this bold and imaginative policy. It is true that by trading with the opposition the Group had given a hostage to the fortunes of the industry as a whole, but that is in any case one of the risks of specialization.

Morale improved as the wounds of separation healed and production began to boom at Hall-Thermotank Products. In the desperate years of the sixties many engineers had left J. & E. Hall, where they could see no future. Now, in the new buoyant conditions, executives found job satisfaction and as much responsibility as they wanted, and they had an incentive to stay.

Hall-Thermotank Products and Hall-Thermotank International had their own boards of directors and each was represented on the Group Board by its senior member. D.K. Fraser was Chairman of both companies during the formative period, and through him the Group Board was firmly in control of the reorganization. He continued as Chairman of Hall-Thermotank International Ltd for some years after succeeding Sir Iain Stewart as Group Chairman, but relinquished that position when he shed all his executive functions in 1979. Archie MacDougall became Managing Director of the Hall-Thermotank group and Chairman of both Hall-Thermotank Products and Hall-Thermotank International. He had joined Thermotank Ltd in 1946 after serving an apprenticeship with John Brown & Company Ltd, shipbuilders of Clydebank, the same stable from which had come A.W. Stewart, the founder of Thermotank. Hall-Thermotank Products' Managing Director George Robert Connor joined the company in 1969 from the machine tool industry, and was the manufacturing manager before being elected to the divisional board. The Managing Director of Hall-Thermotank International is Peter W. Ball, son of William Ball; he joined J. & E. Hall Ltd as a pupil apprentice in 1948 and became a Director in 1963.

Primarily a manufacturing business, Hall-Thermotank Products is a more compact organization than Hall-Thermotank International. The company designs, manufactures and supplies refrigeration and air-conditioning equipment to contractors, distributors, agents, and other engineering manufacturers. The products include piston and screw compressors, valves and fittings, condensers, heat exchangers, chillers, cooling towers, special ducting and air terminal equipment. The company also supplies complete chiller packages from stock or made to order, and a 'matched product' service for specific applications such as cold stores and block ice manufacture. Hall-Thermotank Products' markets cover the whole range of land and marine applications including merchant shipping and navies, breweries, dairies, food stores and food manufacture, the petro-chemical industry and other industrial processing.

DAVID KENNETH FRASER
Appointed Hall-Thermotank Group Chief Executive in 1967,
he succeeded Sir Iain Stewart as Group Chairman in 1979,
and retired in 1980

171

Thermotank cooling towers being delivered to Harrods for cooling condenser water for
the store's air conditioning plant

By the nature of its work Hall-Thermotank International has to be more widely spread geographically than Hall-Thermotank Products. It relies upon the latter for much of its equipment, builds the units into refrigeration and air-conditioning systems for thousands of users with its erecting and installation facilities at depots throughout the country, and follows up with maintenance, repairs and spares.

As part of the reorganization the Group's regional network was brought into line with the general policy of functional rationalization. Most of the depots were situated in port areas, since marine work had predominated, but the slump in the shipyards brought about an increase in the proportion of non-marine business such as brewing, industrial and cold store refrigeration. Market changes and hardening competition necessitated a thorough overhaul of local organizations, involving the retraining and improvement of managements and the separation of what were seen as two incompatible functions, namely construction work and the servicing of existing installations. The result was a more profitable regional operation, the extension of the local depots and offices to some thirty locations and in many cases their achievement of a large measure of local autonomy.

To support the chain of regional service, a separate spares organization was formed to concentrate in one centre the stocks formerly dispersed among the depots. Housed in Derby, the new Halltherm Materials Centre prospered because it was able to respond swiftly to a customer's urgent need. An item of equipment could be located immediately and delivered anywhere in Britain within twenty-four hours. From its inception the Centre has held spares for a number of other suppliers of plant in addition to Hall's regional service organizations. In fact, its trade counter is open to any maker of refrigeration equipment, even business competitors.

While organizations and policies were undergoing decisive changes, an operation of comparable magnitude was in progress in the bricks and mortar of the Group, since the reorganized and technically advancing business could no longer be housed in antiquated buildings. Some parts of the Dartford factory dated from before the start of the century. As the company grew new buildings had been added, and the inevitable result was lack of cohesion, interrupted work flow, excessive handling and uneconomic duplication. There were two machine shops and three fitting shops where one of each, built and equipped specially for current needs, would have sufficed. Moreover the fabrication shop was in Victoria Road Works on the other side of the railway line. An external consideration was that the local authority had a road-building scheme which would impinge on Hall-Thermotank land. In 1970 the Group therefore embarked on a project to rebuild the whole factory complex, reducing the area by some 40 per cent but using the main location more productively. It was to be financed entirely out of the Group's own resources, derived mainly from the sale of unwanted factories in a rising property market but helped also by the increased profitability of the business.

Phase 1 provided a new machine shop on the site of the old foundry and the lift and escalator factory. The Victoria Road Works were sold and replaced in Phase 2 with a new fabrication building on the main site. Phase 3 extended the fabrication facilities and added a new assembly shop. The new buildings have wider bays than the old; these span 80 feet and are served by larger capacity overhead cranes. Hall-Thermotank has taken its own medicine and provided the new buildings with the most advanced ventilation – a fresh-air heating system designed on novel lines. Contrary to the usual process, warm air is blown in from the roof and extracted at floor level in order to eliminate the fumes produced by a large amount of welding.

Retooling had started before the new building, an outstanding feature being the purchase in 1968 of a machining centre which was only the third of its kind in the world. It was a numerically controlled machine tool of an advanced type which could perform automatically the functions that normally required several conventional machine tools. Numerical control of machining is a spin-off from the computer industry. An operation, for example the machining of a compressor crank case, is programmed in minute detail and a punched tape prepared to convey the instructions to the machine. The work then proceeds without human intervention – quickly, with extreme accuracy and with a much reduced need for inspection of the product.

Before such highly productive automated processes are installed the need for these advanced techniques is discussed with the trade unions. Throughout the years of rebuilding and redeployment, the plans were drawn up with the cooperation of the shop floor, the shop stewards and the safety committee. The transfer from the old to the new workshops was scheduled and drawings pinned on notice boards to ensure that everyone knew the moves and his own position in the scheme.

Within a decade the Group rebuilt almost every factory, totalling over 600,000 square feet. The rebuilding at Dartford accounted for the largest segment of a capital investment of £6,400,000 during the five years 1970–74. The cost of other building was £300,000 for Vent-Axia at Crawley, £318,000 for Searle at Fareham and £290,000 at Govan. The title to all land and buildings in the UK and the Irish Republic was vested in a separate property company, Axstane Properties Ltd, set up in 1974.

Several smaller items in terms of expenditure made important contributions to other interests than improvement in plant and production. One of these involved the Priory House, which was incorporated into the new factory complex with the least disturbance to the few surviving roof beams and the ancient walls. The only unfortunate casualty among the relics was an old mulberry tree, whose destruction evoked protests from some local conservationists. Certain sections of the Press branded the developers as 'the rapists of Dartford'. How the shade of that early unscrupulous resident on the site, Henry VIII, must have chuckled over the hyperbole!

Improvements of premises and amenities have also been made at the J. & E. Hall Social & Athletic Club's Patterson Pavilion and Sports Ground. The Club is well patronized by employees who at the Pavilion can enjoy dancing, squash, darts, table tennis and the bar facilities; and in the 25-acre grounds, tennis, bowls, cricket, football and 'pitch and putt'. A popular feature is inter-departmental competition in various sports, with over

600 entries each year and trophies for the winners. The Club is self-governing and to a large extent self-supporting and self-financing.

Another department that has benefited by the improvements in accommodation and organization is the Technical Training Centre at Dartford which has three lecture rooms and a cinema which can if need be serve as a fourth. The lecture rooms are equipped with modern instructional aids, while another building houses equipment for practical training, facilities for which are arranged in five sections. In the basic refrigeration section the student is familiarized with simple refrigeration plant, sectional components and a variety of models. The main refrigeration section is equipped with a large selection of refrigeration plant, most of it fully instrumented, incorporating the latest micro-electronics to enable the student to log the data necessary for technical calculation. The compression section displays the range of J. & E. Hall and other manufacturers' machines; these can be dismantled and reassembled and some are shown in section and others in 'exploded' form. The air-conditioning section incorporates an air-handling unit employing a secondary refrigerant and a packaged direct expansion unit in an air-conditioned room. Fan test and air flow measurement rigs are included. The fifth section is an electrical laboratory containing examples of the various types of electric motors, electrical control panels and other components. The Technical Training Centre has its own staff to cover the standard courses, but practising specialists from within the company can be coopted to assist at certain high level courses. An area in the machine shops is also available for the practical side of training.

The company has always regarded craft and technical training as a vital element in its progress and as the biggest refrigeration business in Europe has recognized the importance of designing its own training system and building it up within the company's own resources. There are two broad classes of beneficiary: the company's customers and its employees, present and future. The courses thus provide a thorough competence in refrigeration and air-conditioning, together with the associated electrical technology for a large number of practitioners and for the industry in general. In addition to craft and technical training there are courses for managers who do not work directly with refrigeration and air-conditioning plant, but whose work demands an intelligent acquaintance with the associated technicalities.

Tailored courses can be arranged to suit customers' special requirements. Many of them find that in order to obtain the best results from their installations it is worthwhile to have their engineers and operators trained in what is acknowledged to be an exceptional school of its kind. Clients often follow up the instruction of their employees with 'on site' training, where those who have taken a course at the Centre can have the training applied to their particular plant at their place of work. That form of training has also been made available overseas and has been greatly appreciated.

Besides customer training, the company trains all its own engineers, technicians and craftsmen in order to ensure the maintenance of its design and manufacturing standards. It also sponsors undergraduates and provides them with industrial training

Customers' engineers considering some of the finer points of compressor design at the training centre

Facing page: The company's training centre ensures a succession of skilled refrigeration engineers. The illustrations show apprentices receiving practical instruction: Admiral Sir John Fieldhouse during a visit to Dartford discussing a project with a group of students, technicians and craft apprentices

during their academic studies. Each student has a chartered engineer appointed to be his or her tutor and the instruction – approved by the Engineering Industry Training Board and the Institution of Mechanical Engineers – is intensive. Graduates can become refrigeration engineers in their own right and many of them eventually join the company's sales design or research and development teams.

In order to ensure a supply of trained employees the company also has an Apprentice Training Centre where the technical and crafts grades start their training. They learn their craft skills both externally under the guidance of permanent instructors and in the workshops under the supervision of a foreman. Technicians are trained in a specialized branch of their choice – for instance, design and drawing office, standards department, technical estimating, planning, production engineering, and production control. Training is a continuing activity and established members of the organization keep up to date with the latest techniques, developments and legislation by attending specially prepared courses internally or at approved outside training establishments.

From the start the company's technical and craft training was years ahead of any that the engineering industry as a whole could offer. Its quality continues to enjoy the approval of the Engineering Industry Training Board which exempts it from official supervision. During the decade of upheaval in the business, the prestige of the Technical Training Centre and the demand for its services grew to the point of almost complete financial self-sufficiency, where in the past the cost had been met wholly out of the company's resources. This comparatively modest achievement is symptomatic of the pay-off in the wider sphere. As the business approached the centenary of its pioneering contribution to refrigeration, the success of the reorganization was reflected in the profit record. Between 1971 and 1978 profit before tax rose consistently from just under £$1\frac{1}{4}$ million to a little over £$4\frac{1}{4}$ million. 'We wanted the business to be a major influence in its market place,' said D.K. Fraser, 'and this we have achieved.' The world-wide extent of the market place, and what it has gained from this pioneer of a great technological and social revolution will form the substance of the next two chapters.

CHAPTER 12

Hall Overseas

The Hall 'market place' has been a two-tiered edifice since the early years of the bicentenarian business, when the founder sent his eighteen-year-old son Edward, just out of his apprenticeship, to represent the family ironworks in Europe. For nearly twenty years, while his brother John partnered their father in Dartford, Edward carried the Hall reputation as far as Russia from his base in Paris. It would hardly be an exaggeration to say that when the two sons took over their inheritance on the death of John Hall senior, they brought into the top management of the business an international outlook which was to persist and flourish throughout all the metamorphoses undergone in the century and a half to come.

By the 1970s the family business had expanded into a family of businesses. Direct exports and the overseas companies accounted for between one-third and one-half of the total Group turnover. But as we have seen, the merger with Thermotank had brought duplication into the overseas activities and the interests of the two sides had to be reconciled in order to secure a happy and workable partnership. This process took some years and involved tough decisions, but it was a fusion rather than a massacre. A series of local mergers brought the outlying companies into line with the newly enlarged parent organization, the broad purpose being to match in the overseas businesses the resurgent enterprise that powered the reorganization of the Group as a whole.

Maintenance of a strong overseas representation was vital and its enlargement by advance into new territories was part of the plan. This was not easy to achieve amid the disturbing political and social conditions in so many otherwise desirable markets. Establishing a branch in an unpredictable and sometimes hostile environment was costly, and casting one's bread upon the waters had to be supported with continuous vigilance and exceptional management skill. There were frustrations to contend with at home as well as in foreign fields; for example, exchange control regulations which threatened to starve the overseas companies of expansion by demanding the remittance of too high a proportion of their profits.

179

Africa continued to offer worthwhile opportunities as well as problems. There had long been a substantial Hall and later Hall-Thermotank presence in South Africa, and the establishments in the Republic are still much the biggest employers among the overseas companies. In 1973 the holding company, Hall-Thermotank Overseas Ltd, took under its wing the Australian, New Zealand, Canadian and South African subsidiaries, together with Hall-Thermotank Equatorial Ltd, incorporated in Kenya, and its subsidiary Hall-Thermotank Zambia Ltd. The chain of enterprises then spread to Asia and Hall-Thermotank Medafric Ltd – incorporated in Gibraltar in 1973 but operating first from Athens and then from Dubai – was formed to undertake refrigeration and air-conditioning business mainly in the Middle East. In 1978 Pernas Hall-Thermotank Holdings was formed jointly with Pernas Trading and Wong Brothers in Malaysia. There were also new establishments nearer home: Hall-Thermotank Ireland Ltd and its subsidiary Irish Insulation (1974) Ltd; and a useful acquisition also made during 1974 in West Germany, Assmann & Stockder GmbH, which gave the Group an entrée into Europe. The record of Group reconstruction and consolidation would not be complete without a more detailed account of what has been achieved in the far reaches of the business around the world.

It is not surprising that Halls' most extensive overseas interest should be located in South Africa, since the Republic is economically the strongest and industrially the most advanced nation in the continent. It is also climatically and occupationally a natural market for refrigeration and air-conditioning. To the north there is now a vast area divided up amongst emergent nations – former British, French and Portuguese colonies, some already Hall customers but most with immense potential which Halls' technology and products can help to release. Hall South Africa presents an object lesson in what can be achieved. While retaining much of the parent company's philosophy it is in a special sense a South African organization, identified with the special needs of the country's basic industries. These include fruit and viticulture, meat and poultry production, mining and brewing, fisheries, and marine and land refrigeration and air-conditioning, in spheres almost as varied as those served by Halls of Dartford.

Halls appear to have had substantial customers in South Africa before the start of the twentieth century. A catalogue published in 1902 names agents of J. & E. Hall in Cape Town and Johannesburg, but cold storage and ice-making plant had already been supplied to hotels and clubs in South Africa and Rhodesia (now Zimbabwe) from Dartford. By 1919 dairies, breweries and abattoirs had installed Hall refrigeration to protect their products against the searing heat of the South African summer and it was clear that there was enormous potential for refrigeration in the country's fledgling industries. In that same year Jan Smuts became prime minister of South Africa. He was not only a great statesman but a notable botanist under whose influence the Cape fruit-producing industry flourished. In 1922 the country became the first British Dominion to establish its own pre-cooling plants to keep fruit in good condition for shipment to England in Union Castle vessels, whose own refrigeration plants had been installed by

Halls of Dartford. The order for this pre-cooling plant had been handled personally by Lord Dudley Gordon and proved so successful that during the ensuing twenty years pre-cooling plants from J. & E. Hall were erected throughout South Africa in Port Elizabeth, East London and Cape Town, also in Lourenço Marques (now Maputo).

In 1932 R.P. Willcox, nephew of Frank Willcox, a director of the parent company, came to South Africa as the J. & E. Hall representative attached to Sturrock S.A. Ltd, Halls' local agents. He rose to be managing director of the Hall subsidiary in South Africa and retired in 1964 after nineteen years as a member of the main Board. Willcox led the company during the difficult years of the Second World War, which inevitably affected the relationship with the parent firm. Hall South Africa became increasingly committed to local mining industry for which it fulfilled two important cooling contracts. One of these involved the erection of one of the largest ammonia plants in the world at the time, using 50 tons of ammonia refrigerant.

Because of the wartime breakdown in communications with Dartford in England, the local company had to develop its own techniques and buy from local manufacturers. After the war, eager to take advantage of big new opportunities, it joined forces with the

Refrigeration plant room at Cape Town Docks. Hall's South African subsidiary helped to restore the fruit pre-cooling terminal after the disastrous fire of 1958

leading engineering business of Reunert & Lenz, and for the first time set up its own engineering division with its own designers and erection team. The association was long and fruitful. It was during that period that a disaster in the port of Cape Town presented Halls with a challenge that confirmed the company's commitment and ability to serve South African industry.

On 29 January, 1958 the pre-cooling sheds in the Duncan and Victoria Docks were almost completely destroyed by fire. The damage to the buildings alone was enormous, but the industrial predicament was even more serious. A newspaper described it as 'the gravest disaster in the history of the Union's perishable export trade'. Halls, in co-operation with the Perishable Products Control Board and the engineering department of the South African Railways worked for forty days and nights to restore the situation and save the fruit crop. Cooling coils which had been ordered from Halls for Port Elizabeth were diverted to Cape Town and the erection team worked round the clock to meet its deadline. Not surprisingly, further important contracts followed for Halls.

In 1960, after the merger of J. & E. Hall with Thermotank the long and happy association with Reunert & Lenz was severed, and in the following ten years the company achieved advances in technology and trade which paralleled the dramatic changes at Dartford. The company's Durban branch acquired contracts for refrigeration and engineering work at the Rainbow Chicken organization which produces one and a half million birds a week for local and export markets. In Cape Town Halls introduced refrigeration into the wine fermentation process. Fermentation normally creates heat, but the process is liable to accelerate in the South African summer temperature and affect adversely the flavour of the product. However, refrigeration can extend fermentation for as long as three or four weeks to suit the wine producer's requirements. Climatic conditions have also influenced the spread of comfort cooling in office blocks, and prominent among Hall customers has been the large Cape Town Civic Centre complex.

Two recent contracts of which the company is particularly proud are in the marine sector of the nation's industry. One is the company's contribution to South Africa's most sophisticated fisheries research vessel, virtually a floating laboratory. This demanded very accurate temperature and humidity control because of the specialized and delicate equipment aboard. In addition, a blast freezer had to be designed and built for freezing sample fish and sea-water from different depths. The other noteworthy Hall achievement has been the installation of the plant for the Refrigeration Container Terminal in Table Bay Harbour, which had a capacity for storing and cooling 500 containers and facilities for extension to a total 1200 containers. The refrigeration contract was the largest ever handled by a South African company.

Hall-Thermotank Africa Ltd was joined by a second Hall company in 1964, Searle-Bush Africa Ltd, and both became subsidiaries of a newly formed group called Hall-Thermotank Southern African Holdings Ltd. Searle-Bush is a manufacturing company and Hall-Thermotank Africa an engineering and contracting company. By the mid-

1970s the African group was the biggest Hall overseas employer, with more than 1200 people on its payroll and operating divisions covering the country with marine and land-based refrigeration and air-conditioning services. The original policy was that Searle-Bush would sell its output to the group contracting company, but this was found to be too restrictive and Searle-Bush started trading in the open market. The company was modernized and tooled up with the most up-to-date machinery to meet foreign competition in world markets. Most of the equipment manufactured is procured locally; in fact, only items requiring high volume production are imported from overseas. The company employs half of the total production work force engaged in the manufacture and supply of refrigeration and air-conditioning equipment in South Africa.

Searle-Bush has grown from a payroll of six in a corner of a workshop to more than 370 employees. The company acquired the Dunham-Bush franchise, and after obtaining a manufacturing licence equipped its factory for highly mechanized production. Searle-Bush designs and manufactures products for a variety of altitudes, climatic regions and purposes in the residential, military, marine and transport spheres. Among these have been air-conditioning for large office blocks and hotels and equipment for airports, electrical power generation and steel manufacture; notably, in the last category, the cooling and de-watering of producer gas used in the production of stainless steel. The company has also pioneered the local use of specialized environmental packages for control purposes and application in computer rooms. It exports its products to many parts of the world, including Indian Ocean islands and even as far as Ceylon (now Sri Lanka).

In addition to the two substantial companies under South Africa Holdings, Halls have also penetrated the continent successfully in its eastern reaches. A market for refrigeration opened there as long ago as 1916, when an ice-making plant from Dartford was installed in Zanzibar. Expansion really got under way soon after the Second World War with the influx of farmer settlers into Kenya and the strong development of an agricultural industry. J. & E. Hall compressors and other equipment were installed in the Kenya Co-operative Creameries, Kenya Breweries, the cold-store at Mombasa port, Kenya Meat Commission and Upland Bacon Factory. Initially the company was represented by a trading firm G.B. Nicholas & Company, but soon after the appointment of a Hall resident representative in 1952 the agency was transferred to A. Baumann & Company Limited. When Hall-Thermotank Equatorial was formed in 1968 it absorbed the refrigeration division of A. Baumann, who became minority shareholders in the company and have remained so under its present name APV Hall Equatorial Limited.

The first air-conditioning plant installed by Halls in Kenya was in the new Stanley Grill Room, now the Bacchus Club. This plant, commissioned in 1960, was the forerunner of many air-conditioning installations in Kenya, Uganda and Tanganyika (now Tanzania). Since Kenya achieved independence there has been a major swing towards air-conditioning in the country and Halls have equipped nearly all the leading hotels including the Nairobi Hilton, the Intercontinental and the Mombasa Beach Hotel. The company has been widely associated with developments both industrial and agricultural in Kenya, including such diverse applications as the underground Gitara Hydroelectric Power Station near Mount Kenya and the Kenya Extelecommunications Satellite Station near Mount Longonot.

Halls' penetration into Africa contrasts strikingly with that of their other major overseas establishment half-way round the world in New Zealand. The common factor has been the need for refrigeration to develop basic industries; but in New Zealand the initial impulse came from within in the form of a dramatic event and of developments accelerated through the initiative of a vigorous and far-sighted local business. The historic event occurred over a century ago when s.s. *Dunedin* set sail from Port Chalmers in South Island with the first refrigerated cargo of sheep and lamb carcases from New Zealand to England. The local business was the engineering company Ellis Hardie Syminton, through whom Halls have become an important local enterprise as they have in South Africa. It is fair to claim that s.s. *Dunedin*, EHS and Halls constitute three of the main elements in the emergence of New Zealand from a remote pair of Pacific islands into one of the world's great producers of essential foods.

When Ellis Hardie Syminton Ltd – the trading name was later simplified to EHS Engineering – was registered in New Zealand as a private company on 1 September 1939, the time was ripe for the injection of vigorous enterprise into the country's generally sluggish refrigeration business and for the replacement of outdated equipment in the user industries. The date was also significant for another reason: the Second World War was about to break out in Europe. No one could foresee at the time that the conflict would spread as far as New Zealand's doorstep, or that a hungry post-war world would clamour for the produce of primary food producing countries. Refrigeration was to be a vital factor in fulfilling the *Dunedin* promise on a large scale for New Zealand, and who better to supply the plant than Halls of Dartford via EHS.

The three EHS executive directors – J.S. Ellis, J.G. Hardie and managing director I.D. Syminton – were able engineers with experience gained in a variety of machinery manufacturing and selling enterprises who were fortunate to have the Hall representation from the start. The business was formed to provide an engineering design, manufacture, supply, installation and repair service, with emphasis on medium and large-scale industrial refrigeration for New Zealand's primary producing industries, mainly meat and dairy produce, and also in the early years a good deal of brewery work. It was an ambitious programme for a business with no more than ten office staff and a small factory, but EHS embarked on growth without delay. Having acquired the New

Facing page: Breweries in Britain and countries throughout the world remain major users of Hall refrigeration. The pictures show: *above:* a 4-cylinder NH3 compressor supplied to Molson, Canada, in 1959 for beer processing; and *below:* a package refrigeration unit being prepared for despatch to a Guiness factory in Cameroon

Zealand interests of J. Wildridge & Sinclair (NZ) Ltd, a branch of an Australian refrigeration engineering business, they launched immediately into manufacture, producing ferrous finned coil for ammonia refrigerators, shell and tube heat exchangers and some general engineering equipment. For refrigeration compressors and spares they looked of course to Halls.

From the start EHS were innovators, having devised a dry compression system with pumped liquid refrigerant circulation which had wide acceptance among users of refrigeration and gave New Zealand a world lead in the large-scale application of the method. Other innovations followed. From the country's meat exporters there was an increasing demand for boning out and cartoning, and EHS designed a very efficient large capacity carton freezing tunnel. They achieved further successes with a novel lamb blast-freezing system, and with slaughterboard equipment for sale to abattoirs at home and abroad; and co-operated in the development of a downward pulling beef hide-stripper and a new type of viscera conveyor.

At the time when Halls merged with Thermotank, EHS had been thinking of forming a public company. Instead, they accepted an offer from Hall-Thermotank to become a wholly owned subsidiary of the Group. Both sides have been happy with the outcome, not least the new parent. By the time of the transaction EHS had installed 446 Hall refrigeration compressors exceeding 5 tons standard rating in a country which had then barely two and a half million inhabitants, an impressive example of market coverage.

Apart from the formation of a short-lived subsidiary company in Fiji, EHS have remained largely a New Zealand business, well satisfied with the scope that the country continues to offer and enjoying a large measure of autonomy consistent with the happy British affiliation. EHS are now established in five centres in both North and South Islands. At their factories in Auckland and Christchurch they make almost all their own refrigeration hardware except compressors and motors.

It was obvious that Halls would follow up their strong base in New Zealand with a second establishment in the South Pacific. Like New Zealand, Australia was a major exporter of meat and dairy products to the UK and received regular visits from refrigerated ships, many of which were equipped with J. & E. Hall refrigeration plant which would need expert servicing. Such facilities were in the competent hands of Amalgamated Wireless (Australasia) Ltd, whose service vans plied along the wharves of Sydney Harbour to attend to the marine radio and other instrumentation needs of the visiting vessels. AWA were Halls' agents in Australia and had a full time organization of about thirty staff and operatives to handle the business. Those arrangements continued until 1957.

Australia had become an increasingly difficult market and the abrupt impositions of import restrictions had for some years given J. & E. Hall considerable concern. They therefore sent out a director to investigate local conditions and following his report a subsidiary company J. & E. Hall (Australasia) Pty Ltd was incorporated in New South Wales. This remained dormant for some months, but in August 1957 the Hall parent

Board decided to bring it to life and by a friendly arrangement with AWA that company's Hall agency organization was transferred to the new Hall subsidiary.

In the following year J. & E. Hall (Australasia) purchased the Australian refrigeration business of Richard Wildridge & Company Pty Ltd, refrigeration compressor manufacturers and engineers who were also well-established as suppliers of processing equipment and services to the dairy and food industry. Halls took over the premises of Richard Wildridge in a Sydney suburb, from which they continued to provide a service to shipping and in addition designed, installed and commissioned refrigeration systems. These transactions established Halls firmly in Australia.

A small business transaction which took place in Australia in 1951 is interesting in view of the subsequent history of Halls of Dartford. In that year Thermotank Ltd of Glasgow, which had formed a close working association with Halls in the UK, established a small subsidiary in Melbourne by the purchase of a plumbing business, Guy & Company. Eight years later Hall and Thermotank merged in the UK and set in motion a chain of local mergers wherever in the world the two companies had subsidiary organizations. In Australia their respective offspring combined under a new title Hall-Thermotank (Australia) Pty Ltd, with headquarters in Melbourne, a branch in Sydney and the former Thermotank company's managing director in command. In 1962 the company moved to a 5-acre site at Box Hill, Victoria, where they fabricated air-conditioning accessories.

The air-conditioning of offices became more popular from the 1950s onwards, coincident with increasing activity in the building industry. By the 1970s Hall-Thermotank had extended their establishment in Australia with an office in Canberra, and were recognized as major air-conditioning contractors. They had been responsible for installations amounting to some (Aust.) $40 million in important buildings, which included the National Library, the Australian Mint, the Parliamentary House of Assembly, the Australian Government Printing Office and a number of hospitals.

Popularity had, however, brought about severe competition in the air-conditioning market, and in consequence Hall-Thermotank changed the direction of the business from manufacture to procurement, followed by the cessation of major contracting which was diminishing rapidly. The Board decided to concentrate on commercial, industrial and marine service. They had made an agreement with James Howden in 1965 to sell Howden refrigeration screw compressors, which were just being introduced into the Australian market. Substantial contracts followed, notably one for the equipment of twenty vessels under construction for the Royal Australian Navy. The equipment had to be installed in spaces four feet high in which a man could only crawl, but every item was accessible for maintenance. Other contracts were for the air-conditioning and refrigeration of passenger and container vessels.

Further change was to follow for the Australian company, as for the parent company and its home and overseas subsidiaries almost a decade before the Hall enterprise attained its 200th birthday. That major event, the incorporation of the entire Group into the larger APV organisation, will be featured at appropriate length in the final chapter of this history.

Canada presented a market comparable in area with Australia, but very different in character and in business prospects for J. & E. Hall. Some of the details have already appeared in earlier chapters. The technical sophistication and trading strength of the USA in refrigeration and air-conditioning tended to inhibit competition from the UK in Canada, and it was with what Halls called vertical transport that they made their initial and successful entry into Canada, despite the fact that Canada and the USA were the most advanced manufacturers of lift and escalator equipment in the world. From 1949 onwards a senior member of Halls' lift and escalator department in the UK explored the Canadian market intensively, carrying out market research and contacting architects, contractors and potential users. Canadians seemed to favour trade with Britain provided deliveries and prices were satisfactory, though they had highly competitive suppliers nearer home.

A substantial order for escalators from Simpsons of Toronto, one of Canada's largest department stores with branches in many other cities, encouraged Halls to set up a small Canadian subsidiary company. In 1953, with management drawn from Dartford and office and technical staff from local sources, they opened an office in Toronto and a branch in Montreal. Despite production problems in the UK, aggravated by shortage of materials, they were able to complete their contracts in time and to a high standard. Orders then followed from retail stores, breweries and government departments.

While at first lifts and escalators dominated the business, a sales manager for refrigeration was appointed within a year and obtained orders for compressors from food companies and breweries. The refrigeration side was expanded by the acquisition in 1954 of Linde Refrigeration Company Ltd, a long-established company with a good reputation which had a small factory in Montreal. Renamed Linde-Hall Refrigeration and operating as a branch of J. & E. Hall of Dartford, the company set up its headquarters in Montreal and appointed representatives in all the main Canadian cities. Three years later the refrigeration business was further expanded by the acquisition of the refrigeration and air conditioning division of the John Inglis Company Ltd.

At this stage Halls' Canadian venture struck difficulties for which no satisfactory solution could be found when an alleged infringement of patents prevented the company from offering for sale certain types of lift controls. This virtually barred them from participation in some of the larger and technically most advanced projects, and it became expedient to restructure the Canadian business and withdraw representation from some of the Provinces. By that time the business was operating through a separate subsidiary J. & E. Hall (Canada) Ltd, and functioned from Montreal and Toronto instead of through a network across Canada.

Drastic reorganization eventually restored the Canadian enterprise to profitability. It continued to provide refrigeration and air-conditioning equipment and its lift and escalator business survived the phasing out of that diversification in the parent Group.

Mention of its big contract for the Montreal subway has been made in an earlier chapter. The Canadian subsidiary is unusual among the overseas companies in conducting its affairs in two languages, being established in the heart of a province that is bilingual in French and English.

It may seem odd that Halls should have settled in three continents, and gained a foothold in Asia to make a fourth, before looking to the UK's nearest neighbours, though the company had exported to Europe consistently since Edward Hall's time and exchanged knowledge with European innovators in refrigeration and other engineering technologies. They had been looking for a suitable opening some years before the UK joined the European Economic Community and had in fact set up an office in Rotterdam so that they could watch events from a suitable springboard. The opportunity came with the takeover by Hall-Thermotank Overseas Ltd of the refrigeration business of Assmann & Stockder KG of West Germany, which company had been established in Stuttgart for many years and had supplied refrigeration equipment mainly to the brewing and food industries. A new company was formed, Assmann & Stockder GmbH, in which Hall-Thermotank Overseas Ltd subscribed 60 per cent of the share capital and Assmann & Stockder 40 per cent.

As the UK's nearest neighbour and a fellow member of the EEC, the Irish Republic was another obvious choice for a Hall-Thermotank subsidiary. The Group's branch in Dublin merged its functions with those of Irish Refrigeration Ltd to form Hall-Thermotank Ireland Ltd. Membership of the EEC contributed to a large increase in Irish industries using refrigeration – for example public cold stores, blast-freezing, brewing and chemical processing, which brought business to the local Hall-Thermotank company. Contracts were also received from leading meat processing plants for the fast chilling of meat carcases under strict EEC regulations and the company became the biggest commercial and industrial refrigeration supplier in the Republic.

As the record has shown, Halls' overseas interests have not been an unqualified success. Expansion has been achieved under difficulties local and worldwide, and profits have fluctuated with economic conditions under which bigger and more powerful businesses have also suffered. But the vitality of the enterprise after two centuries in business is beyond question. Its contribution to industrial progress and human amenity has spread from Dartford literally to the ends of the earth, as this chapter has tried to show, and continues as human needs become more insistent and the technology to satisfy them becomes available. The next chapter will focus upon some of the links in that chain of human betterment.

Heat pump for a French nuclear power station

CHAPTER 13

An Engineering Revolution

In order to appraise what Halls had accomplished by the time they had celebrated their 'Refrigeration Centenary' (barely a decade before the bicentenary of the business) it is worth while to look again at the eighteenth-century beginnings. What stands out is the remarkable continuity of policy and fulfilment stretching from the middle of a historic industrial movement to within sight of the twenty-first century. Two essential facts emerge. First, in an age of unprecedented innovation, the ingenious John Hall chose to remain simply an engineer. A tide of revolutionary ideas swelled around his little workshop and some of it washed over his doorstep, but he refused to be beguiled into specialization. He saw his function not in manufacture but in the provision of an engineering service. The inventors needed the engineer and their successors do so still. Second, when Everard Hesketh took over the remnant of the business and revived it with the new techniques of refrigeration, the engineering concept persisted. Hesketh and all the generations of engineers who followed him in his historic business have viewed refrigeration in an engineering context, as a means of promoting man's control over his environment and improving the human enjoyment of the products.

In a sense Halls have contributed, as have other distinguished businesses, towards the prolongation of the Industrial Revolution far beyond the limit conventionally placed by historians somewhere near the middle of the nineteenth century. The revolution had not lost its impetus by the arbitrary date; it had simply sought new directions, scored new channels. For instance, the channel of refrigeration engineering had penetrated into ever-widening fields of industrial processing and social need, and every advance locates fresh and desirable applications. The range is already vast, taking in abattoirs, mortuaries and blood banks; fighting ships and fisheries; almost every kind of manufacture, from cement to lipsticks; the clinical control of atmosphere in computer rooms and comfort cooling at work and recreation; deep mining and environment conservation; offshore oil platforms and nuclear power plants; bakeries and breweries; heat recovery, freeze-drying of foodstuffs, and the most delicate scientific research.

Engineering may be defined broadly as the application of scientific principles to the benefit of mankind, and the history of Halls is in effect a record of the way in which the most varied technical discoveries and developments have been enlisted into the service of refrigeration towards the achievement of those ends.

The development of the motor car offers many parallels with that of refrigeration. When Nicolaus August Otto produced the internal combustion engine in 1876 (about the time when Everard Hesketh was looking at Giffard's cold-air machine at the Paris Exhibition) he had established a principle upon which Daimler and many others were to plan and build the 'horseless carriage'. In the hundred or so years since Otto's inspired achievement, the engine has been applied in such ways that the modern motor car with its automatic transmission, hydrolastic suspension, air-conditioning, pneumatic tyres and subtleties of steering bears little relation to its earlier antecedents. Equally, the modern refrigeration system bears little similarity to Giffard's primitive machine. Each is part of a system: the motor car as one medium of transport in a comprehensive effort to produce easier and more rewarding accessibility of every part of the earth to human penetration: and refrigeration as a means of harnessing any relevant branch of technology to the better control and utilization of the earth's resources. It is with systems design and development in that sphere of application engineering that the staff of Hall-Thermotank International Ltd (later renamed APV Hall International Ltd) has been concerned since its formation.

The scope of these developments in refrigeration has been vividly highlighted by two events, almost a century apart and both, by coincidence, centred upon the Falklands Islands. The first was the visit of ss. *Selembria* (described in Chapter 4 in a contemporary extract from *The Times*) to bring back from those South Atlantic islands in 1886 a cargo of 30,000 carcases of frozen mutton. This was for its time a remarkable achievement with far-reaching implications in the opening-up of remote sources of food. The second event occurred in 1982, when Argentina tried to implement by force its long-standing claim to sovereignty over that British possession. The campaign provided object lessons not only in modern defence but also in the part played by refrigeration in the naval contribution. A Task Force of more than 100 ships and 28,000 men, operating 8000 miles from the UK and 3500 miles from their nearest base on Ascension Island, fought off a hostile navy powerfully supported from the air, landed 10,000 men on very difficult territory under fire from an entrenched enemy and achieved complete victory in a little over three weeks. At that distance from its source of vital supplies the British naval force had to be self-sufficient in fuel, food, water, and military equipment. It had to carry adequate stores of chilled and deep-frozen food, fresh vegetables and beer for a campaign of unpredictable duration; provide cooling for weapons in store and for the enormous heat generated in operations; protect medicaments against deterioration and ensure comfort and safety for the sick and wounded on improvised hospital ships; maintain accurate temperature control for instrumentation and efficient living and working conditions in the Antarctic climate. Without refrigeration on such a scale and of such

HMS *Invincible*, a command cruiser which took part in the Falklands campaign

technical sophistication, it might have been impossible to undertake the Falklands campaign at all.

It is because of the special characteristics of the Falklands event that it claims more extensive treatment in these pages than its brevity might seem to warrant. The marine complement presented virtually a cross-section of world shipping and therefore an immense variety of problems and tasks for the supplier of refrigeration as for the naval command. The engineering as well as the defence services derived important lessons from the performance of their contribution in the testing circumstances of modern warfare. It was after all on the seas that refrigeration first demonstrated how it could help mankind, mainly in peaceful and life-enhancing directions but at need as a protective adjunct in war. Of the 110 ships deployed in the Falklands campaign forty-four ships were of the Royal Navy, twenty-two from the Royal Fleet Auxiliary and the rest almost every kind of merchant ship with volunteer civilian crews. The naval and auxiliary vessels included frigates, guided-missile destroyers, aircraft carriers, assault ships, landing ships, minesweepers and tankers and salvage vessels: among the ships taken from trade were passenger liners with world-famous names – *Canberra, Queen Elizabeth II, Uganda* – general cargo ships, tankers, a container ship, a cable ship and even 'banana boats', all chosen for special duties in a multiple and skilfully planned operation. Many of the merchant ships had been considerably modified and the *QE2* had had an extensive refit and upgrading of her passenger air-conditioning. The *Uganda* was one of the few passenger ships still using the safe and reliable CO_2 as a refrigerant, an example of the useful survival of earlier methods and materials alongside the new. The *Canberra* was among the first ships to have large centrifugal compressors, and used the more modern Refrigerant 22. The *Geest Bay*, withdrawn from the banana traffic for Task Force service as a supply ship, had been equipped with the most modern Hallscrew compressors and a Redicon electronic temperature control.

The company had equipped many of the naval vessels and fleet auxiliaries with ventilation systems and with cold storage chambers for food and drink. In many cases the ships' own domestic food lockers were Hall-refrigerated and the ferries, borrowed from British Rail for use as accommodation vessels, had the car decks ventilated by the company's Thermotank department. Car ferries provide a small but interesting example of application engineering by the adaptation of long-used techniques to the solution of new kinds of problems. When cars and heavy lorries are being unloaded carbon monoxide and other dangerous fumes can collect below the deckhead and the use of a number of small ventilation units was not entirely satisfactory, because they still tended to leave pockets of gas. In order to disperse the gases quickly and safely the Halltherm Stirvent was devised, employing the principle of the Punkah Louvre invented more than fifty years previously. This uses a single high-velocity air jet which mixes the air and blows out the lurking gases, a method similar to that used in hospitals to mix bacteria-laden air for swift and complete dispersal. It demonstrates the way the engineer looks at a problem, focusing upon the need rather than the hardware. Stirvent is not limited to vehicle ferries but can be used with advantage in other special ventilation applications as, for instance, in some shipboard machinery spaces.

Intense involvement in the marine sphere has required expertise not only in the design of refrigeration equipment but in the training of the craftsmen to install it. Over the years the company has developed its own standards of welding, especially in the brazing of non-ferrous metals, which have led to contracts for hydraulic pipework. It is in the support equipment that the company has made some of its most important contributions. Among such developments have been special glands for carrying pipework and air-conditioning ductwork safely through water-tight bulkheads, and also the upgrading of a range of fire dampers for use in this ducting. These fire dampers are also used for work on offshore oil rigs where the fire risk is a prime consideration. Another example is a well-proven seawater control valve, originally designed and activated by outside suppliers but with the controls further improved by the company's own electronics department.

Inevitably the marine aspect of the Falklands campaign dominates the story, but the vital importance of support for the land and air forces must not be underrated. Here too the company was able to provide valuable aids to victory. Its Glasgow regional office had developed a close control system for the Barr & Stroud optical factory, which not only produced the periscopes used in underwater vessels but also the infra-red sights which served the troops with such good effect in their struggle against an inimical terrain under fire from entrenched enemy forces.

While most of the triumphs of refrigeration for industrial and defence purposes have had a marine setting, with land a good second, it must not be forgotten that the air has also presented important challenges and contracts. Among leading examples have been the Royal Aircraft Establishment at Farnborough, where many large wind tunnels have Hall refrigeration systems, and the National Gas Turbine establishment at Pyestock where there is a very big test bed for testing Rolls-Royce RB211 engines. In the latter case, a refrigeration system was specially designed and installed, using very large Howden screw compressors and an ammonia circulation system. The heat exchangers incorporated must have been, at the time, the largest designed for refrigeration duty.

Oberon class submarines, fitted with direct expansion air conditioning using spot coolers distributed in strategic positions throughout the vessel

Some of the most telling lessons to emerge from the Falklands campaign have stressed the continued importance of improvisation. In engineering as in warfare the mother of invention, immensely fertile though she has been in the past, actually increases the numbers and quality of her offspring. Here again a backward glance at conditions in earlier times is illuminating. An 1896 Hall catalogue shows two shipping photographs, the 'old style' (pre-refrigeration) expedient of hauling live cattle ashore by the neck, and the 'new style' of unloading frozen meat in a net. The second picture may appear to have only the most tenuous connection with the growth of container traffic three-quarters of a century later, but it prefigured a system of organization, transportation and supply which belongs to a different world.

Superficially the container might appear to be a form of gigantic packaging, a steel box which replaces a multiplicity of goods in small packets of miscellaneous sizes and shapes or a variety of unpackaged goods in bulk. The refrigerated container is in fact the basic module in a system of transportation, an integral part of the ship in which it is carried, requiring specially designed vessels and compatible dockside storage and handling equipment. It is the answer to a human need which had exercised the ingenuity of engineers for generations, to evolve an integrated scheme of long-distance international food supply for the benefit alike of the supplier and the consumer. All the past improvements in the export and import trade of refrigerated foods may be said to have led to containerization.

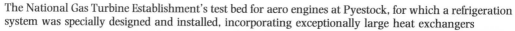

The National Gas Turbine Establishment's test bed for aero engines at Pyestock, for which a refrigeration system was specially designed and installed, incorporating exceptionally large heat exchangers

Envisaged originally to serve the New Zealand and Australian frozen meat trade with Europe, the containerization idea has spread widely throughout the world, with Britain as a prime food importer understandably high on the list. J. & E. Hall had realized the possibilities for refrigeration of containers as early as the 1950s, when they designed and equipped a number of containers which were tested and approved by Lloyds and gave good protection for the perishable contents.

In 1964 leading British shipping companies, realizing the potential of containerization for their Australian trade, formed two specialist organizations – Overseas Containers Ltd (OCL) and a consortium, Associated Container Transportation Ltd (ACT) – to develop the business, HTI collaborating closely with ACT in the original

The container depot at Tilbury, where the Halltherm Unicore system is installed to provide refrigeration for assemblies of containers

container ship design. The container area is an integral part of the ship, not a space into which containers are loaded. The containers are stacked up to eight high, and the tolerances required in locating them within the ship's framework are exceedingly tight. Although special couplings were developed for the cold-air distribution there is a limit to the amount of play which even they can tolerate. The original container installation at Tilbury in 1968, the beginnings of Britain's initial container terminal, was a building much like a ship's hold, containing 360 insulated containers stacked from floor to ceiling. The next phase, at a cost of £2,500,000, was to enlarge the company's commitment to 1200 refrigerated containers housed in the open, with the aim eventually to build up to 1500, making this the largest refrigerated depot in the world. The logical accompaniment in the new circumstances was to evolve the Halltherm Unicore method of module construction.

The Unicore system consists of a prefabricated engine room containing compressors, control gear and forced draught air condensers, built into a 20-foot container module, with three-high stacks of air distribution 'mother' units which supply cold air by means of ducting to a complex of up to seventy-two containers. The system is flexible and can supply differing degrees of cold simultaneously to containers carrying goods with different cooling requirements. Unicore has a small daughter, the Minicore, a self-contained unit designed to support two containers which has particular relevance to fruit farms, where probably only two to four containers are required but need to be kept cold until ready for collection. There are small Minicore installations in Continental ports, but the large expected sales to the banana market suffered a setback through disastrous hurricanes at the farms.

There is also a portable clip-on refrigerated utility which can be fitted to an individual container for transport from the container base to the customer's store. This is a small link in an integrated circuit which illustrates more vividly perhaps than any other aspect of refrigeration how the engineer has extended a scientific discovery into a connected system of food supply covering a vital human need in a vast environment stretching from the farming source across the world to the ultimate consumer's table. Thus, perishable goods protected by refrigeration in store are transferred into refrigerated containers, conveyed by refrigerated road or rail haulage to the quayside, loaded on to ships equipped with a built-in refrigeration system, unloaded on arrival at the container terminal and similarly protected against deterioration of the contents until removed to the refrigerated warehouse and eventually passed on to the consumer. The retailer's display case and the domestic freezer where the journey may end are the only locations outside the chain of industrial refrigeration.

Almost inevitably technical advances bring with them new problems which require the talents of the engineer and perhaps the enlistment of other technologies for their

Facing page: Above: A refrigeration container ship and *below:* Halltherm Searod, a vertical duct system for maintaining refrigeration in container holds

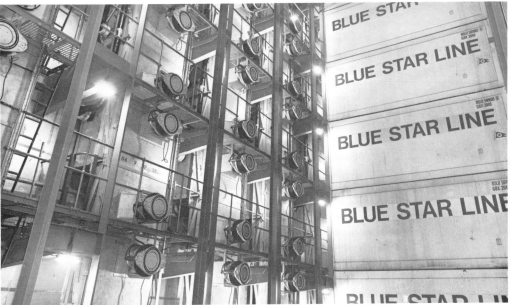

solution. The container site is so extensive and the straddle carrier traffic used for handling the containers so dangerous for pedestrians that personal inspection and control are out of the question. Special remote control telemetry systems have therefore been devised for coupling and uncoupling the containers and electronic methods are also used for continuous remote monitoring of container movement and condition. In a control room at the Tilbury depot a visual display unit no bigger than a television screen logs the temperature of each container every forty seconds, indicates an empty space in an assembly where another container can be slotted in, shows if the container has been satisfactorily coupled to the refrigeration system and flashes an alarm if anything goes wrong. A record is typed automatically on an adjacent printer. There is two-way communication with the straddle carrier driver and cross-checking with the yard as a safeguard against error or breakdown in the instruments.

Halls' historical role as pioneers in shipboard refrigeration, together with their expertise in container refrigeration techniques, has been demonstrated by the increasing number of the world's largest container ships which incorporate the company's plant. Typical of these ships are the five built by the German shipyard, Bremer Vulkan, during 1975–78 for the Australian trade and fitted with over £4 million-worth of refrigerating equipment supplied by Hall. The 44,000-ton *New Zealand*

Hallscrew package supplied to the Bremer Vulkan shipyard for the Shipping Corporation of New Zealand

Pacific with its central refrigerating plant provides controlled cooling for up to 1200 containers carrying a variety of cargo at temperatures ranging from minus 25°C. (minus 13°F.) to 13°C. (55°F.).

Marine refrigeration for naval as well as civil purposes has gained from the development of packaged units. The package is a device for preparing as much of the assembly as possible in the factory as well as on site, in the interests of speed, economy and efficiency for the benefit of supplier and customer alike. It reduces the space needed for cooling machinery and the time and labour required for its installation on board ship. One example, the Halltherm Provpak, is designed to provide refrigeration for two to five insulated provision rooms. A more extensive unit is the Provstore, a completely packaged and containerized provision room. Similar in principle but more specialized is the Halltherm Seascrew, a range of screw compressor packs assembled, wired, instrumented and tested in the factory to facilitate direct mounting on board. These are rationalizations, not accessories, fulfilling a modern constructional need. Refrigeration and air-conditioning are not bolt-on extras but an essential part of the total design and liaison with naval architects and marine engineers at an early stage is vital. Many of the marine department's refrigeration engineers have been at sea themselves and understand the problems and the environment in which they occur.

Although the environment is similar, work done on North Sea oil rigs is regarded as 'industrial' and is therefore handled by the land department. An early assignment was to design a method of chilling – and therefore drying – North Sea gas as it was piped ashore at Easington, near Hull. Originally the North Sea rigs were closely tied to American design, but gradually HTI designs were recognized and now some of the company's largest tailor-made packages are for the oil rigs.

Some of the more recent Hall marine contracts have included installations in Iolair, semi-submersible emergency support vessel for patrolling the North Sea, equipped with highly sophisticated fire-fighting equipment for use in emergencies involving oil. Hall designed, supplied and installed air conditioning for officers' and crew and independent units for the control bridge, the computer and power supply rooms, the galley, and the machinery control room

For many years the company has served the chemical industry where process cooling plays a vital part. In 1967 they installed AEI centrifugal compressors at ICI Castner Kellner Works in Runcorn to cool and liquefy chlorine gas for use in the manufacture of refrigerants. This type of work culminated in 1978 in the design and installation of equipment worth £4 million for a complete PVC plant in Poland; its purpose was the pre-cooling prior to liquefaction of oxygen and nitrogen, cooling and liquefaction of chlorine, process control of vinyl chloride monomer and final temperature control of exothermic polymerization reactors. Skid mounted packages were used, which were manufactured under very stringent quality control requirements and designed to be knocked down to shipping size for transport to Poland. A substantial part of the plant operates in the open during the winter and this called for sophisticated steam tracing of much of the equipment and special care with instrumentation. The temperature ranges from 40°C. in summer to minus 40°C. in winter. The inflammable nature of many of the solvents used also called for special design knowledge, which had been built up during many years of collaboration with the petrochemical industry.

A solvent with no such problematical side effects has emerged in the form of comparatively new uses for CO_2, a by-product and ingredient in brewing and also, as we know, an early and in its day very successful refrigerant. It is still used as an essential agent in carbonating beer and excluding air during bottling and other processes, and as dry ice in non-brewing industries, but now serves also as a solvent for a variety of essences in food and chemical processing. In liquid form it acts as a carrier for hop extract and other essences in solution and there may be possibilities for further applications of a similar kind.

Modern brewing has proved to be an ideal field for the application of electronic controls on the largest and most comprehensive scale. Its processes have been transformed into a highly coordinated operational system, served by a fully automated refrigeration plant and amenable to linkage and control by telemetry techniques. Electronic applications have occupied the HTI development staff for many years and have advanced as the micro-chip has pointed the way. One of their earlier applications was Halltherm Redicon, first used in marine refrigeration installations for temperature control and measurement and later extended to food stores on land and to breweries. It consists of a range of modules, one for each point of measurement, connected to a control unit, and permits temperature control to the very fine limits of plus or minus one-tenth of a degree Centigrade.

Control by microprocessing techniques has now been tightened yet further, an interesting example being the Sentralink system installed at the Park Royal brewery to enable the already considerable refrigerating plant to cope, particularly with increased lager brewing facilities. Sentralink is in effect an extension of Redicon; the refrigeration

Facing page: Features of the construction work for a large PVC complex built for Poland. *Above:* a water chilling package unit and *below:* welding pressure vessel for the chlorine plant

Plant employing CO_2 in liquid form to serve as a carrier for hop extract

plant has been controlled by mimic diagrams on traditional control panels containing instruments and certain control gear. The adoption of Sentralink permitted parts of the circuit to be displayed in colour on a screen like that of an ordinary television receiver. These displays, which can be interpreted in plain English on a typewriter keyboard attached to the visual display unit (VDU), show the various operating parameters such as temperature, pressure and flow rate which are normally displayed on an instrument face. Further, the state of the mechanical plant – whether it is running, shut down, under maintenance and so on – can be indicated by means of colour coding. The keyboard can accept commands to start and stop equipment, or to open and close motorized valves, and so enable the plant to be properly controlled from a simple work desk. Emergency alarms are set to override other displays in preference to the historic arrangement of buzzers and flashing lights. Moreover (and not the least of the advantages) by the use of telemetry techniques a simple 4-core cable is all that is needed instead of the expensive multi-core cable used for normal type instrument panels.

This latter advantage is particularly significant because it bears out a valuable function of the engineer, to find better ways of achieving an end not only technically but

204

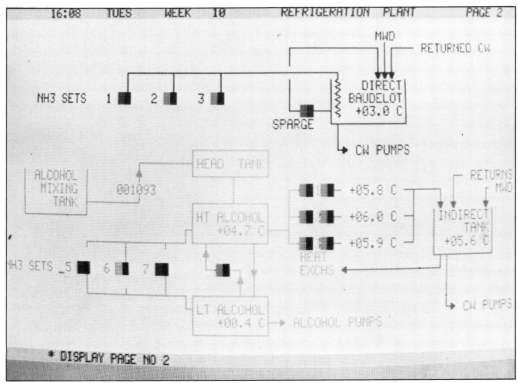

Visual Display Unit (VDU), installed at Guinness Park Royal Brewery, used to log information about actions and conditions at a distant plant site

more simply, more economically in the use of materials, space and effort. Equipment and accessories have tended to get out of hand as more functions have been pressed upon them, wiring lengthening to miles, control panels becoming vast and parts of the record remote. A reduction in size and complexity has accompanied increased efficiency – that is true of Redicon, Sentralink and the extension of the operative principles into Rediopt. For instance, some sections of highly automated procedure, as in a modern brewery, may become overloaded while others are under-utilized, or a high-powered machine may be in use where low power would be adequate. The purpose of Rediopt is to select the optimum compressor configuration for lowest power utilization. The control circuit includes built-in safeguards for maximum power demand and start-up procedures and in fact any requirement the operator may specify can be built into the computer's memory chip.

The electronics team is now working on computer-aided design so that during the design and specification stages of a new installation the effect of changing the many operating variables can be easily quantified. Formerly a design/sales engineer would use his experience to fix the size or nature of many variables, so that the total design equations become more easily soluble. With the computer the effect of varying any parameter can be quickly seen and thus the installation can be more accurately sized to the client's exact requirements. The next step will be on-line monitoring of the whole plant performance, calculating the heat transfer achieved and comparing with the original design parameters. This could facilitate decisions to clean or replace equipment. While on-line monitoring has been achieved to a limited extent on mechanical equipment, the application to whole plant operation has yet to come.

Nowhere has the economy of refrigeration been more urgent than in the direction of energy conservation. During the 1970s and 1980s fuel costs, especially those of oil, swelled to critical proportions worldwide, with political accompaniments which aggravated the economic problem. The need for greater fuel savings became one of the major concerns of the refrigeration engineer who, with his applied thermodynamic knowledge, was well-placed to meet the requirements. Halls formed an energy conservation department to handle heat recovery and energy saving in industrial, commercial and social applications, and to design and provide facilities for heat energy transfer from air to air, air to water, water to air and water to water. The service has given particularly good results in environments such as swimming pools where a great deal of heat can be lost to the atmosphere. The equipment, incorporating high-temperature heat pumps and run-around coils, can be built into the structure or supplied as a self-contained package unit. Both the refrigerant gas and the oil impose a limit, currently about 105°C., to raising the temperature in the heat-pump circuit, but these problems will be overcome and a steam generating circuit will become a practical proposition.

Energy conservation, vital in itself, is one consideration among many in what has been, in the culminating decade of the Hall bicentenary, the revolutionary re-thinking of the structure and performance of the compressor, the basic hardware at the heart of refrigeration. The perfecting of the single screw idea, leading to the development of the Hallscrew compressor, has been the outstanding achievement of Hall-Thermotank Products Ltd (later renamed APV Hall Products Ltd), the manufacturing partner in the modern configuration of the Hall enterprise.

The importance of the single screw revolution can best be explained by looking at the progress of the reciprocating machine which had dominated refrigeration practice for so many decades. The first reciprocating compressors running at 50–60 rpm were very large and heavy pieces of machinery. As knowledge of valve behaviour and bearings and other factors improved, those speeds were increased to 500–600 rpm and it became possible to effect substantial savings in the weight and size of the machines. These machines were, however, called high speed only because of their relative superiority in that respect to the old much slower machines, but they were still massive and

Facing page: The Hallscrew compressor, and the Design Council's 1983 Award in recognition of this major contribution to refrigeration technology

Design Council Award
1983

Presented to

APV Hall Products Limited

on 9 May 1983
to mark the selection of the ·

HallScrew

designed by
L. C. Constant CEng MIMechE FInstR
and design team

The Award was presented by
HRH The Duke of Edinburgh KG KT

Sir William Barlow, Chairman

Keith Grant, Director

The Design Council, 28 Haymarket, London SW1Y 4SU

cumbersome and constituted large capital items in refrigeration plant. It was not until the Veebloc type of compressor arrived, in which cylinders and pistons could be arranged in a 'V' and 'W' formation, that highly compact machines were obtained running at much greater speeds. The introduction of this type of machine was a step in the desired direction. Over a period of twenty years speeds were increased to 1750 rpm, accompanied by substantial advances in valve design, materials and oscillating mechanisms. Apart from small Veebloc machines which can attain higher speeds, this type of machine must be regarded as the last of the reciprocating types used for gas compression. In order to achieve a more compact design a radical change was needed, away from the reciprocating compressor with its out-of-balance characteristics and towards a design based on a different dynamic principle.

By the late 1960s the new movement had started. Refrigeration engineers were envisaging a compressor with a rotary instead of a reciprocating action, employing a screw instead of a piston, and eliminating the valves which are the most sensitive parts of a reciprocating compressor. In 1966 a twin-screw compressor had come on to the market; this was already being manufactured in many countries under licence from the Swedish patent holders, and J. & E. Hall entered into a sales agreement with Howden, the UK licensee. The Hall-Thermotank subsidiary company in New Zealand, Ellis Hardie Syminton, had been ahead of them in using this compressor which they found well-suited to the needs of the big meat-freezing factories in New Zealand.

The twin-screw machine did not supersede the reciprocating types, but offered users a choice of compressor in the middle ranges of horse-power. The Veeblocs supplied most refrigeration requirements up to about 200 hp using ammonia, which was the traditional refrigerant for most process work and cold stores. For heavy duty the centrifugal type was used, providing a horse-power range of 400 upwards. There was thus a gap in general practice between the largest reciprocating machines and the smallest centrifugal machines; the twin-screw filled this gap. It had disadvantages, being noisy and requiring large ancillary oil equipment, but it was reliable, reasonably efficient and comparatively free from vibration. Its main merit, however, lay in its technical originality, foreshadowing so far as the company was concerned an eventual innovation with far-reaching possibilities, the single-screw compressor. The difference between the twin-screw and the single-screw represents a breakthrough of the greatest technological significance and brings a new dimension to refrigeration practice.

In 1973 it came to the notice of Halls that a Frenchman, Bernard Zimmern, had taken out patents on a single-screw compressor suitable for air compression, and subsequently licensed its use in France, the USA and Japan. It had not been widely used in refrigeration, but had properties which offered advantages over other rotary compressors for refrigeration purposes. A major feature was that the method of gas compression reduced the bearing loads almost to zero, which meant that the machine would be extremely reliable under the most adverse conditions. In fact, it seemed likely that with further development the oil might be removed completely from the machine, where the refrigerant in the system could be used both for cooling and sealing purposes. After considerable engineering and financial evaluation Halls signed a licence agreement with Zimmern to develop their own range of single-screw rotary compressors for refrigeration and air-conditioning. It is interesting to note how history had come full circle. French invention had played a decisive part at the beginning and end of the refrigeration century, with Giffard's cold-air compressor at the start and Zimmern's single-screw at the culmination.

After six years of research and development under the leadership of APV Hall Products' director of engineering, Len Constant, followed by two years of field trials with pre-production models, the Hallscrew compressor was ready to be introduced to the user industries. One of the models was displayed at the Heating, Ventilation and Air Conditioning Exhibition in 1976, where it aroused great interest. At the 1978 Exhibition the Hallscrew was officially launched and offered for sale in four sizes covering a nominal range of 200 to 700 hp. In that year the first Hallscrew machines were installed for land use, supplied by Assmann & Stockder GmbH to Hacker Pschorr Braeu AG of Munich. By the latter part of 1979 Hallscrew had been installed in the UK and countries throughout the world, including Australia, New Zealand, France and the USA in addition to Germany.

The Hallscrew project had been a triumph for Halls in even more than the technical sense. The company had undertaken to finance, research and engineer the development on its sole initiative at a time when trading was depressed, money for research hard to come by and profit had to defer to optimism for the outcome. The Group's top management shared this optimism and tolerated the inevitable sacrifices. Events in the years up to 1985 have vindicated the attitude and the effort. History will see the change from the reciprocating to the rotary engine as an achievement comparable in magnitude with the advance from steam engine to the electric motor; not simply a great technical improvement but a new conception affecting fundamental values. The exceptional qualities of the Hallscrew were recognized in 1983 by a Design Council Award (see page 207).

The immediately apparent difference between the Hallscrew and its predecessors is in size, weight and construction, its size and weight being about one-fifth of those of a Veebloc machine of comparable capacity. In structure the difference is even more impressive, since the Hallscrew has only three major moving parts – the cast-iron helical grooved rotor and the two non-metallic star-shaped rotors which mesh with it to compress the gas. The casing is in one piece and therefore allows easy inspection. The comparatively uncomplicated construction simplifies operation and maintenance. Perhaps the most promising feature of all is the virtual elimination of the need for oil. Implicit in these features are profound changes in current refrigeration practice and mainly incalculable prospects for the future.

To begin with the Hallscrew construction, one of the outstanding innovations has been the single-piece casing which means that without removing the compressor from the plant in which it is installed one can check completely the condition of the machine. This is done by removing the two side covers from the compressor, which enables all the internal motion to be viewed, clearances checked and a visual inspection of all parts carried out. In consequence, Lloyds and other surveying authorities can check the condition of the machine in one or two hours, whereas hitherto such a survey could have taken several days. The saving in turn-round time for ships at sea or down-time on an important and expensive process line needs no emphasis. If any part of the compressor needs to be changed, this too can be accomplished without removing the compressor from the plant. Lloyds have been sufficiently impressed with this facility to have issued the following statement (9 February 1983):

> We are pleased to inform you that in view of satisfactory service experience with refrigeration compressors of the HallScrew type in marine refrigerated cargo installations classed with this Society, the requirements for periodical surveys are now being brought into line with those for other types of screw compressor, i.e. dismantling for Special Survey at intervals of 25,000 running hours or six years, whichever is the sooner.

Simplication in construction, operation and maintenance is accompanied by the virtual elimination of oil. The reciprocating compressor is lavish in its oil requirement, and excessive oil impedes efficient working. With little or no oil except for lubrication, higher speeds become possible because of the reduction of viscous drag between rotor and casing. The gap between rotor and casing being quite small, when this is filled with oil there can be resistance to rotation at higher speeds. However, where liquid refrigerant with its much lower viscosity is used instead of oil, higher speeds are obtained without that disability. Packages can thus be supplied which do not require the expensive oil support system of oil separator, oil reservoir, oil filters, oil pump and all the associated pipes and valves. Now that oil injection free operation has been proven, new ranges of package can be supplied to air-conditioning and water-processing industries, fully tested in the factory and in many cases requiring from the customer nothing more complicated or costly at the installation stage than the connection of the electrical and service pipes.

A further development now under way is in the sphere of terotechnology – the identification of a problem in the early stages before it becomes a major factor. The Hallscrew lends itself to the application of this technique because, as has already been emphasized, the machine does not demand periodical maintenance work. It can be equipped instead with transducers and 'health' monitoring pick-ups for vibration and noise, which allow readings to be taken while the machine is running and so to determine the quality of its condition and performance. The company has – to borrow a term from the aircraft industry – a number of 'black boxes' which it applies to units in the field, but it aims with the help of electronics to reduce the size of the black box so that it can become either a permanent feature in the customer's control circuit or a health monitoring service available on a regular basis.

Electronic developments open up vast possibilities and the micro-chip is a much greater advance on electronics than electronics was on simple electricity. Bearing in mind the amount of information that can be stored on an integrated circuit board six inches square and an eighth of an inch thick, it is not difficult to appreciate what a wealth of fact can now become accessible to the control engineer about any package or installation. The power required to operate these units is so small that the transmission cables can be kept down to fuse-wire proportions, with consequent considerable saving in cost. The following is a typical example of what the microprocessor control unit can provide. Readings taken of the plant performance are fed into the microprocessor's memory, so that if the compressor breaks down for any reason information on events preceding the failure can be studied and the cause quickly identified. For instance, in the case of a typical oil failure one would be able to deduce that the oil flow had been gradually dropping, that the pressure drop across the filter had been increasing possibly because of dirt in the filter, that the oil temperature had been rising because of the reduced oil flow and that the temperature in various parts of the compressor had been gradually increasing as a result of the partial blockage in the filter, culminating in a failure maybe of a bearing or other part of the machine.

In commercial and industrial practice the refrigeration user is always fearful that he might have a plant failure which will stop his process line, destroy products in cold store or cause other inconvenience. Reliability is therefore of paramount importance and in this respect the Hallscrew has an advantage over the reciprocating machines in its comparative freedom from such problems as valve breakage and bearing wear. This is understandable when one considers that the typical reciprocating compressor has 1200 to the Hallscrew's 250 parts. The gas joints are also much fewer, so the possibility of gas leakage is reduced in the Hallscrew machine.

Further developments in refrigeration are not easy to foresee far ahead, since it is the need that calls forth the application, but the compressor as the central item of hardware does present possibilities which are being explored. For instance, the low bearing loads on the Hallscrew and the oil-free character of the machine mean that it could be applied where bearing loads or high temperature would inhibit the use of conventional machines. A likely development will be its use on industrial gases, and a start has been made under experimental conditions on applying it for compressing steam. Another possibility is to use the machine as an expander, in which case it could serve as a prime mover for generating power or driving other equipment. The producers are however wary of diverging too far from the main purposes of their machine. It is doubtful whether further reductions in the size of the Hallscrew would be useful. The drive motor is now many times larger than the compressor, and other units such as the heat exchangers are also large by comparison. A future development might be a reduction in the size of the motor by having high-speed units to match the potential of the Hallscrew. An additional advantage would be the ability to vary the speed of the motor and thereby the compressor, which would permit the removal of the capacity control which is normally fitted to the compressor. These developments are already in prospect.

Amid the details of current performance and of possibilities ahead, two fundamental facts about the Hallscrew compressor stand out. First, the Hallscrew became necessary because the prevailing compressors had, like the dinosaurs, reached the limit of their evolution. The continued progress and applicability of refrigeration engineering depended urgently on the success of the change. Second, the new concepts implicit in the Hallscrew conform to the spirit and the most insistent demands of our time. What those demands are and how they have been served have been shown throughout in this chapter. The paradox is that human beings demand ever more sophisticated benefits from an environment offering diminishing resources which are more difficult to exploit. The means must therefore more than compensate for the resistances: man must use ingenuity and technology for the better management of his environment. Refrigeration in all its aspects has demonstrated how this has been achieved, for it is in the broadest sense an economic process, the procurement of better value with reduced complication and cost, by means of a judicious simplification in the tools and methods employed and a clearer awareness of the need to conserve energy, to avoid spoliation, to enrich life for a community that is world-wide. Never before has the world environment been subjected to such intensive yet intelligent control. That is what the continuing industrial revolution has attained in this bicentenary year of one of the contributory enterprises.

CHAPTER 14
Double Century

By 1976 the Hall-Thermotank business seemed set on a level course with its 200th birthday less than a decade ahead. Structural weaknesses had been corrected, technological progress accelerated and profitability restored. All this had been achieved in spite of adverse economic conditions and world-wide and exceptionally high inflation at home. However, there is often a price to pay for success, and Hall-Thermotank's penalty was a kind of vulnerability which the business had experienced before in the J. & E. Hall days. As in 1959, this desirable enterprise was attracting covetous attention from empire-building conglomerates and speculators outside. Moreover the situation was rendered delicate by the fact that P. & O. was again anxious to unload its shareholding; this time the holding was only one-third, but it was big enough to make Hall-Thermotank a target for takeover if P. & O. were to act precipitately. Some of the hopeful takers were unacceptable to the Board, not least to the Chairman Sir Iain Stewart, second only to P. & O. in the size of his shareholding and, with D.K. Fraser – by then Deputy Chairman as well as Chief Executive – responsible for the restructuring that had restored the Group's fortunes. Once again, P. & O. were unlikely to be ruthless in cutting their commitments, but rumours flying around the City were causing concern to the Hall-Thermotank Board.

Sir Iain had tried to cool the atmosphere with the following statement in his 1974 Report:

> Some comment has been made in the press about P. & O.'s $33\frac{1}{3}$ per cent holding of the issued Ordinary share capital in Hall-Thermotank Ltd. They have been long term shareholders and regard this holding as a portfolio investment, but have now indicated that, although not actively looking for a buyer, they would be prepared to sell at a price which reflected the true value and potential of Hall-Thermotank Ltd. With P. & O.'s strong position, as reflected in their recent announcement of results for the year ended 30th September 1974, there is no urgency in the matter. Nevertheless, your Board is considering alternative courses that will not only provide a satisfactory price to the P. & O. Company, but may also assist in making available resources that will permit a further major expansion of the Group.

Speculation was not halted and in fact, the price of the Ordinary shares rose substantially in anticipation of an imminent event. The Board therefore thought it advisable to make an announcement (on 25 September 1975) to the Stock Exchange on the lines of the previous statement, adding that discussions were continuing with interested parties but that none had yet culminated in an offer. It was obvious to the directors that the Group would have to seek a satisfactory affiliation with a kindred type of business. They needed a partner who would want to further their expansion instead of exploiting the take-over for a quick capital gain. Thanks to Lord Inchcape, P. & O. Chairman, they were given time to look around and found the desired conditions in the APV Group of Companies. APV was no stranger to Hall-Thermotank, since they had done some business together and Fraser knew members of the APV Board. APV was not a collector of miscellaneous businesses, but consistent in its policy of acquisition and operating in many fields related or complementary to Hall-Thermotank's interests. The merger was as logical as had been that of Thermotank and Hall.

APV was founded in 1910 as The Aluminium Plant and Vessel Company Limited by Dr Richard Seligman, who held the first British patent for welding aluminium. Under his direction and that of his son, later Sir Peter, the business outgrew its exclusive concern with aluminium and at the same time the limitations of its name. By carefully chosen acquisitions of engineering companies specializing in the fabrication of corrosion-resistant metals, APV became a leading supplier in the UK and overseas of processing plant for the food, beverage and chemical industries. Hall-Thermotank was their largest acquisition, adding over 50 per cent to turnover* and increasing the number of companies controlled from the APV headquarters in Crawley to sixty-two, located in twenty-six countries. Before the negotiations with APV had started, Hall-Thermotank had already agreed to sell Searle Manufacturing Company Ltd to Prestcold Ltd. Searle had been consistently profitable, but had reached the limit of its possible progress in Hall-Thermotank's hands, whereas Prestcold was strongly entrenched in the heat exchanger market and better able to resist the competition from overseas. Both companies had much to gain from the deal, which brought Hall-Thermotank £3,846,000 in cash and thus provided the financial strength to meet APV on equal terms. The Prestcold deal excluded Searle's distribution under licence of certain refrigeration equipment manufactured abroad, which was transferred to a new Hall-Thermotank subsidiary Cemak Engineering Ltd (later known as APV Cemak Ltd). The formation of Cemak was consistent with the policy of leaving Hall-Thermotank Products and Halltherm Materials Centre free to supply the Group's competitors. It enabled Hall-Thermotank to enlarge its potential market for refrigeration and air-conditioning plant without losing customers for its own products.

On 22 October 1976 the directors of APV Holdings Ltd and of Hall-Thermotank Ltd agreed upon the terms of the merger. This was conditional upon Hall-Thermotank

*APV and Hall-Thermotank accounts for 1975 show sales, excluding tax, as £98,100,000 and £52,827,000 respectively

increasing its authorized share capital to £8 million, which was effected on 15 November 1976 by way of a one-for-one scrip issue. APV offered one Ordinary share of 50p and £2.75 nominal of $10\frac{3}{4}$ per cent Convertible Unsecured Loan Stock 1997–2002 for every twelve Hall-Thermotank Ordinary shares of 25p each (equivalent to six Ordinary shares prior to the capitalization issue), and one $5\frac{1}{4}$ per cent Cumulative Preference share of £1 for each Hall-Thermotank 7 per cent Cumulative Preference share of £1. That is, APV paid for Hall-Thermotank 2,151,000 Ordinary shares, 1,320,000 $5\frac{1}{4}$ per cent Preference shares and £5,915,250 $10\frac{3}{4}$ per cent Loan Stock. Six months after the merger the former Hall-Thermotank shareholders found that what they had gained by the exchange of shares with APV was equivalent to an increase of 75 per cent in the value of their shareholding. The City obviously approved.

The deal was accompanied by an exchange of directors between Hall-Thermotank and APV. Sir Iain Stewart joined the APV Board as a non-executive director and relinquished the chairmanship of Hall-Thermotank to D.K. Fraser, who was elected in addition a managing director of APV Holdings Ltd. Sir Peter Seligman retired as APV Chairman, to be succeeded by H.P.N. Benson, and both joined the Hall-Thermotank Board. Peter Benson had been the main driving force in bringing Hall-Thermotank into APV and by the time he retired in 1982, after twenty-five years' service with APV, he had seen the merger consolidated within a rationally reorganized parent group.

In 1981 normal changes were already under way on the main APV Board in preparation for Benson's retirement. He then handed over his function as chief executive to Peter B. Hamilton, and Sir Ronald McIntosh – who was to succeed him as Chairman the following year – joined the Board as Deputy Chairman. Peter Hamilton was also Chairman of Hall-Thermotank Ltd, in succession to D.K. Fraser.

The link between the Hall-Thermotank and APV Groups was an inspired move to the advantage of both participants. It brought to APV a specialized business, having a turnover comparable in size with their own, employing between 5000 and 6000 people world-wide and making a profit before tax of £3–4 million. Within the package APV had acquired one of the oldest engineering businesses in Britain, with a world-famous name for its pioneering of industrial refrigeration and its continuing leadership in that field after a century of practice. At the time of the merger the Container Terminal at Tilbury had been enlarged, electronics had transformed the control and perfection of foodstuffs in transport and in store, and the revolutionary Hallscrew compressor had come triumphantly through its field trials. For Hall-Thermotank the merger provided an ideal environment and a compatible partner, comparatively young, toughened by setbacks in a long struggle for survival but now fast-growing and prospering in business spheres complementary to those in which Halls had been active for generations. Some of the APV companies were among the leading suppliers of processing, distributive and storage plant for use in industries which were already big users of refrigeration: dairying, brewing, food, chemical, petrochemical and plastics production. Some of their members had long been Hall-Thermotank customers, but the APV connection opened up new business possibilities at home and in a vast range of markets abroad.

Halls in harness with APV represented the union of heat and cold under one command. It is not popularly realized that heat and cold are in the technical sense two sides of the same coin. After all, cold is produced artificially by the removal of heat and the heat pump is in effect a refrigeration plant in reverse.

The real beginnings of the modern APV group may be said to date from the early 1920s when Richard Seligman launched his plate heat exchanger. The evolved business is still largely concerned with heat transfer and the handling of heat-sensitive materials, and much of the equipment produced is used in processes such as pasteurization, sterilization, concentration and drying, in a range of industries comparable with those served by the refrigeration engineer and with similar emphasis on food and beverages. Companies in the APV group produce and provide plant units or complete automated processing systems for the production, treatment or storage of the great essentials of life such as milk, cheese and bread; food accessories such as ice-cream, salad dressing, instant coffee; convenience foods and luxuries, potato powder, meat products, biscuits, confectionery; and liquids from beer, wine and fruit juices to pure water. Beyond foods and beverages is a list of industries which, like those in the Hall-Thermotank book, covers almost every industrial activity, including oil, gas, and nuclear as well as the traditional sources of fuel and power; chemical products and pharmaceuticals, penicillin and other sources of medical treatment; cement, glass, paint and other construction materials and finishes, steel and fine alloys; alcohol recovery, effluent treatment, plant cleaning and sterilizing equipment and systems; mining, agriculture and all branches of metal work. Like Hall-Thermotank, APV have been increasingly involved with energy saving and environmental protection, and these provide new opportunities for cooperation on industrially and socially valuable projects.

Within that extensive spread of industrial activity the two parties to the business merger saw opportunities for a close and profitable marriage of their talents in the domestic market and overseas. Both groups were strongly represented in other countries. Some of APV's subsidiaries were in territories where Hall-Thermotank was already firmly established, such as Australia, New Zealand and South Africa; and in others – Brazil, Japan, Spain and the USA – where business for Hall-Thermotank could develop. There was less overlapping and therefore less need for drastic reorganization than there had been when Hall and Thermotank merged. Overseas as well as at home, the marketing strengths of the two companies were in this event complementary and the growth prospects promising.

In the four or five years following the merger, a formula had to be found for integrating Halls into the larger team. APV had acquired a number of companies by purchase, many of them long established and expert in relevant spheres of manufacture and processing, but Hall was no ordinary acquisition; its relative size and the nature of its speciality put it in a different class. What it had to offer was an extension of the group's

216

MR ARCHIE MACDOUGALL
Divisional Chief Executive of the Hall Thermotank and Africa Division

217

activities into important sectors of industry which it had not previously penetrated, necessitating structural adjustments in the parent organization.

The parent company, renamed APV Holdings PLC to conform with the requirements of the 1980 Companies Act, accordingly grouped its subsidiaries into five divisions with a divisional chief executive to be responsible for each. The broad purpose was to enable the parent company to be more closely involved with its subsidiaries without disturbing their autonomy. At the same time a Group Executive was formed under the chairmanship of the Group Chief Executive Peter B. Hamilton to handle general group matters, especially policies and strategies. When Peter B. Hamilton resigned from APV Holdings PLC in mid-1984 he was succeeded as Chief Executive by Fred W. Smith who had held senior executive positions with the APV Group and was, at that time, Chief Executive of the Americas Division.

Archie MacDougall had been appointed Divisional Chief Executive of the Group's Hall Thermotank and Africa Division, and additionally in 1983 had been made a director of APV Holdings PLC. He was chairman of each individual company in his division, but the overseas companies, where possible, had non-executive chairmen who were resident locally.

The name Hall-Thermotank was retained in the Divisional title, but 'Thermotank' was dropped from individual company names and 'APV' substituted. Initially, the renamed constituent companies were: in the UK, APV Hall International Ltd, APV Hall Products Ltd, APV Cemak Ltd, APV Halltherm Ltd (formerly Halltherm Materials Ltd) and – an addition to the Division – APV Parafreeze Ltd; overseas, APV Hall (SA) Ltd, APV Searle Bush Ltd, APV Hall Equatorial Ltd, APV Hall Zambia Ltd, and Assmann & Stockder GmbH. Later, two other companies were added: Jackstone Froster Ltd, Grimsby and APV Processing (Pty) Ltd, South Africa; as from 1 January 1984 APV Kestner (SA) (Pty) Ltd, with its subsidiary APV Kestner Engineering (Pty) Ltd also became a member of this Division. The Hall name was too important to obscure in the realignment, and Thermotank too retained its due prestige in the attribution of particular products and systems. Thus traditional practice would be served by referring to Thermotank Marine Systems, Thermotank Punkah Louvres, J. & E. Hall compressors, Thermotank cooling towers and so on. The total plan may appear to have been complex, but the outcome was essentially a simplification. A scheme had been cleverly devised to yield a more closely knit overall structure, while at the same time achieving a workable devolution.

Under the changed titles the two largest Hall-Thermotank companies retained their established identities: APV Hall Products as product manufacturers and suppliers, and APV Hall International as contractors and service engineers. They did, however, move closer physically at their base in Dartford. Investment in new manufacturing facilities during the 1970s and subsequent modernization of premises at the Hythe Street site enabled APV Hall International to vacate its office block in Home Gardens and take over part of the office accommodation alongside the factory complex. Thus by 1982

Board of Directors of APV Hall Products Ltd. *Seated* A. MacDougall, G.R. Connor, T.E.G. Humphrey, J. Nixon, P.A. Rudman, T.K. Barber. *Standing* A.H. Moor, L.C. Constant. *Between them*, K.F. Howell, Company Secretary

Board of Directors of APV Hall International Ltd. *Left to right standing* A.H.A. Cartwright, B.A. Phillimore, R. Perrin, H.M. Hunter. *Left to right seated* T.D. Ireland, P.W. Ball, A. MacDougall, D.H. Boothman

219

the two Dartford-based companies had returned to the site traditionally occupied by J. & E. Hall and their successors for nearly two hundred years.

The move reflected the latest changes in the status and fortunes of the business. It was more compact in structure and strengthened by the new association, but was still Halls of Dartford with all the prestige that the name had acquired in the preceding centuries. As a symbol of survival value Halls were outstanding in those troubled times. Britain in the 1980s was suffering more than most of its peers among the nations from an economic recession that was world-wide. Companies with famous names and long and honourable trading records had died – many because they could not keep up with changing trends, others because they were in declining industries. Halls had escaped both calamities and could look forward hopefully beyond their bicentenary. In April 1984 – appropriately in the 199th year of the business – they had the satisfaction of receiving recognition for technological achievement by the grant to APV Hall Products Ltd of the Queen's Award to Industry for the development of the Hallscrew single screw refrigeration compressor.

Though forecasting is less reliable than ever in these unstable times, perhaps a few general assumptions are permissible. The demands of the food industries will continue to dominate. We live in a hungry world where, according to circumstances, refrigeration supplies an established utility or life-saver for whole populations. Competition among the suppliers will intensify, but fighting competition successfully is a feature of survival. Applications in other industrial spheres can be expected to claim a larger proportion of the effort and Halls' latest achievements have pointed the likely directions. As we have seen, new challenges for the ingenuity of refrigeration and air-conditioning engineers can arise anywhere in the infinite variety of manufacture, processing and amenity. Urgent problems such as energy-saving and environment protection are still insufficiently appreciated, and await more vigorous attention from technology world-wide. The toughness of the international market and the pressures of political, economic and social events will concentrate the provision of ideas and aids in fewer and more high-powered hands. Halls of Dartford aim to hold a strong position among those few.

Sources and Acknowledgements

The search for early records of a long-lived business starts in the dusty corners where one may hope that fragmentary relics still linger. Halls of Dartford are rare even among bicentenarians in having occupied continuously a site in the same area as the piece of ground where the founder set up his original workshop. A few surviving documents (letter headings, labels, leaflets, sketches) have yielded revealing glimpses of the old pre-refrigeration ironworks and its jobbing engineering output. The ensuing generations have provided a massive and ever expanding volume of reference material in the form of catalogues, illustrated brochures, advertising leaflets, house journals (*Hallford Magazine, Group Gazette*), news items and Press features, company reports, chairmen's statements and Board minutes, technical writings and speeches by senior members of the company.

In addition to this hoard of company reference material, I have consulted more books and documents than can be conveniently listed here on the Industrial Revolution, the general background to the Hall double century, the company's home town of Dartford, the century of refrigeration stretching from Hesketh's original initiative to the Hallscrew compressor and numerous historical byways en route. Pride of place must be accorded to Everard Hesketh's little book *J. & E. Hall Ltd*, published in 1935 by the University Press, Glasgow, an industrial record of more than parochial value and especially important for the light it throws on the beginnings of refrigeration in the UK. The following list is a selection of historical works that I have found particularly useful:

Ashton, T.S. *The Industrial Revolution 1760–1830*. This is a classic in its field. (Oxford Paperbacks, 1968).

Briggs, Asa *Where We Came In: The Industrial Revolution Reconsidered* (BBC Publications 1957). A brief, concise and authoritative statement.

George, M. Dorothy *England in Transition*. (Routledge, 1931).

Gretton, R.H. *A Modern History of the English People 1880–1922*. (Martin Secker, 1930).

Halévy, Elie *A History of the English People in 1815*. (Pelican Books, 1937–1940).

Marshall, Dorothy *Industrial England 1776–1851*. (Routledge and Kegan Paul, 1973).

Plumb, J.H. *England in the Eighteenth Century*.

Thomson, David *England in the Nineteenth Century*.

England in the Twentieth Century. Three volumes in the excellent Pelican History of England series.

Trevelyan, G.M. *History of England*. (2nd edition, July 1937, Longmans Green)
  English Social History. (Longmans Green 1944)
Woodward, E.L. *History of England*. (Methuen 1947)
The Falkland Campaign: The Lessons (H.M.S.O. December 1982).

I must also acknowledge my indebtedness to two works outside the general historical category: a thesis by Helen Weeks, 50 Years of Social Welfare at J. & E. Hall Ltd. 1910–1960 (unpublished): and *From Little Acorns*, by G.A. Dummett: History of The APV Company Limited (Hutchinson Benham 1981).

Anyone seeking information on Dartford must be grateful to two assiduous local historians for their compilations of miscellaneous facts and anecdotes:

Dunkin, J. *The History and Antiquities of Dartford* (1844).
Keyes, S.K. *Dartford Historical Notes* (1933).
  Dartford Further Historical Notes (1938).

For additional and more up-to-date information, I have consulted guide-books and topographical works too numerous to itemize.

My main sources for details of the early applications of Hall refrigeration have come from within the company and include:

Hesketh, Everard The Application of Cold-Air Machines to Use on Board Ship. A paper read at the Naval and Submarine Engineering Exhibition April, 1882.
  Carbonic Anhydrite Refrigerating Machines. A paper read before the British Association and reprinted from *Engineering* 1 November 1895.
Ward, H.J. Refrigeration on Shipboard (Excerpt Minutes of Proceedings of the Meetings of the Institution of Mechanical Engineers February 1929).
Farmer, J.D. Recent Developments in Marine Refrigeration. A paper read before the Institute of Marine Engineers. 7 April 1936.
  Various Types of Refrigeration Machinery for Ships. A paper read before the North-East Coast Institution of Engineers and Shipbuilders, 28 February 1947.
Gordon, Lord Dudley. Recent Developments in Refrigeration (the 29th Thomas Hawksley Lecture, delivered at the Institution of Mechanical Engineers, 6 November 1942).
Russell Roberts, E.G. Marine Refrigeration. Published by The Institute of Marine Engineers 1939.

For recent major developments in refrigeration I have found the following works helpful:

ICI: *Refrigeration Service Engineers' Handbook* October 1967.
Clarke, R.J., Hodge, J.M., Hundy, G.F., and Zimmern, B. A. New Generation of Screw Compressors for Refrigeration. A paper presented before the Institute of Refrigeration on 1 April 1976.
Trott, A.R. *Refrigeration and Air Conditioning* (McGraw-Hill 1981)

I also owe much of my enlightenment on technical matters to the company's training material.

So much for the printed record. In the story of a living organization, however, some of the most illuminating detail is derived from personal interviews with existing and retired members at all levels and in all departments. It is difficult for reasons of space to name them all and could appear invidious to select a few. I shall therefore have to be content with a general expression of gratitude for the time and effort so willingly expended by so many people in contributing to the interest and accuracy of this history. Finally, I wish to thank the Dartford Public Library and its staff for so generously placing their files on J. & E. Hall and books on local history at the disposal of the company and its historian, and for providing facilities for study of the material.

Index